Legendary Sessions

THE ROLLING STONES
Beggars Banquet

Legendary Sessions

THE ROLLING STONES
Beggars Banquet

Alan Clayson

Foreword by Paul Du Noyer

FLAME TREE
PUBLISHING

Publisher and Creative Director: Nick Wells
Commissioning Editor: Polly Willis
Editor: Julia Rolf
Consultant Editors: Rob Bowman and Paul Du Noyer
Project Editor: Cat Emslie
Picture Research: Gemma Walters
Art Director: Mike Spender
Layout Design: Lucy Robins
Digital Design and Production: Chris Herbert

Special thanks to: Claire Walker, Toria Lyle and Chelsea Edwards

09 11 10 08

1 3 5 7 9 10 8 6 4 2

This edition first published in 2008 by
FLAME TREE PUBLISHING
Crabtree Hall, Crabtree Lane
Fulham, London SW6 6TY
United Kingdom

www.flametreepublishing.com

Flame Tree Publishing is part of the Foundry Creative Media Co. Ltd

ISBN 978-1-84451-296-6

A CIP record for this book is available from the British Library upon request.

Printed in China

To Donna Cichocki

'This was a very special album. It was fun to make, and it got more and more exciting as each track built up – and I did realize that we were getting the essence of the Stones down on tape.'
Keith Richards

List of Illustrations

CONTENTS

FOREWORD

Ignore the scrawled-upon toilet wall that was the Rolling Stones' first choice for the cover of *Beggars Banquet*. Forget the blandly elegant invitation card that the record company wanted instead. No, the real image of this album is its inner sleeve photograph, taken at a Hampstead house on 7 June 1968. Amid the detritus of some unspeakable feast, sprawled in five assorted poses of depravity, our decadent rock'n'roll princelings embody the true promise of *Beggars Banquet*. This was music conjured up from somewhere fabulous and dark, somewhere beautiful and evil. It was not about peace or love or even the good old 12-bar blues. It was the first sign of a new era in the Stones' story – the curtain-raiser to the most mythically charged, musically splendid period of their whole career.

When *Beggars Banquet* appeared in late 1968 the Summer of Love was long gone. In fact the Rolling Stones had never looked plausible as hippy prophets of flower power anyway. Now the world was up in arms from Paris to Vietnam, from Prague to Palestine. New Jagger-Richards songs, like 'Street Fighting Man' and 'Sympathy For The Devil', caught the mood with chilling, intuitive precision. And other numbers, like 'Parachute Woman' and 'Stray Cat Blues', were simply as low-down and sleazy as anything anyone had ever recorded. Turmoil was everywhere in 1968, whether in global affairs or the Rolling Stones' private lives. Their drug busts vied in the headlines with political assassinations. Their sexual entanglements had reached new heights of sheer, mind-boggling weirdness.

Now that they had split from their shadowy mentor Andrew Loog Oldham, the Stones suddenly had to stand on their own ten feet. But they had a gifted new producer, Jimmy Miller, on hand to assist. With his help the Rolling Stones rebounded from a shaky dalliance with psychedelia to unearth the toughest roots in music. Soul, blues and country styles were explored with style, humour and intelligence. For the Stones it wasn't merely a case of going 'back to basics' – in the *Beggars Banquet* sessions they mined rich seams of scholarship that powered their music to entirely new levels. If poor Brian Jones was floating further from them by the day, off to some ill-fated, twilight place, the rest of the band was finding its true height and purpose. They were hitting the stride that would carry them on to masterpieces like *Let It Bleed* and *Exile On Main Street*.

So, there is scholarship and sleaze in *Beggars Banquet*, against a backdrop of wars, sexual intrigue and impending tragedy. We're fortunate that such a landmark album was captured on film, as well. The director Jean-Luc Godard was at Olympic Studios in South West London to document the recording process. (One night his lights over-heated and nearly burned down the building; the album's master tapes were rescued by Miller and Bill Wyman.) Godard's eventual movie, *Sympathy For The Devil*, was a Maoist rant-cum-fantasy that many found unwatchable. But, for the patient Stones-watcher it's nearly as revealing as the Beatles' own fly-on-the-wall effort, *Let It Be*.

Where the Fab Four's movie was ultimately about decay, the Stones' film was about creation. A new methodology was being invented before our eyes. In the course of *Beggars Banquet* the Stones learned what lay beyond the great pop group they had been before. They discovered in themselves an organic and self-renewing rock'n'roll band – one with the power to re-define the possibilities of rock itself. Such was the splendid feast prepared by our five decadent princelings. So let's join them. And now, the Banquet awaits....

Paul Du Noyer, 2007

PROLOGUE: METAMORPHOSIS

'I don't think rock'n'roll should be analysed or even thought about deeply.' Keith Richards[1]

Exile On Main Street, the Rolling Stones' only non-compilation double album, has become the yardstick by which all output by the group tends to be judged. Alongside *Pet Sounds* by the Beach Boys and *Sgt. Pepper's Lonely Hearts Club Band,* it is always near the top of these 'Hundred Greatest Albums' polls that rear up periodically in the media. Yet, despite critics bequeathing unto it a flashback grandeur, it was issued in 1972 to so-so reviews, and not even the Stones themselves regard it as the classic that today's younger pop journalists have been brought up to think it is. Mick Jagger, for example, felt that *'Beggars Banquet* and *Let It Bleed* were better records.' Writing purely objectively, that was true enough – and I would also include *Aftermath, Between The Buttons* and *Their Satanic Majesties Request, Beggars Banquet's* three predecessors, on the list too. Significantly, all five consist entirely of originals by Jagger and Keith Richards.

Of them all, *Beggars Banquet* surfaces as second to *Exile On Main Street* whenever the tidy-minded pop chronicler, hunched in front of a word-processor, has to name the Greatest Stones Album Ever Released. Well, I wouldn't necessarily agree – but, as it is with many pop records, this judgement has less to do with its musical content than memories of the emotional circumstances under which my teenage self first thrust *Beggars Banquet* on to the monophonic Dansette record player in my bedroom. Earlier that day in February 1969, I had behaved as if most of a fortnight's wages for a Saturday supermarket job was nothing to me when, to impress some hippy chick, I bought the album without any haggling from a market stall along Petticoat Lane in London's East End.

My veneer of cool and, beneath it, the sinking in of the enormity of my uncharacteristic extravagance was transparent to the girl – mainly because I was self-conscious in heart-breakingly short hair and ill-fitting flower-power trousers that had parted me from the best part of a pound a few months earlier, after a marked-down batch of them reached the high street clothes shop of my dreary country town in Hampshire, where the distance to Swinging London was measurable in years as much as miles.

Late that afternoon, I was hurtling back to it. As the waste-piped backs of suburban terraces gave way to meadows and woodland in the encroaching twilight, I kept taking my new purchase – the first Stones LP for which I had actually paid hard cash as opposed to, well, 'acquiring' it – out of my tie-dye shoulder bag, and staring at it as you would at a very

Mick Jagger hunched by his microphone, with Keith Richards in the background, during the filming of Jean Luc Godard's film *Sympathy For The Devil* in 1968.

recent and still-livid wound, my stomach knotting with the thought that the knockdown twenty-five shillings could have been better spent – perhaps on something I had actually heard and enjoyed.

Why did I never learn? It had been the same when a Boy Scout patrol leader I admired had said the Dave Clark Five were his favourite group, and thus they became mine too. For the next three or so years, I acquired every disc the Five ever released in Britain, and took the mildest disparagement of them as a mortal insult; to paraphrase US statesman John Jordan Crittenden, I hoped to find the Dave Clark Five in the right; however, I stood by them, right or wrong.

Beggars Banquet did not incite similar passion, in that I didn't set about trying to get hold of everything – past, present and future – that the Stones, collectively and individually, had ever released. Nevertheless, that summer, I rampaged through 'Sympathy For The Devil', *Beggars Banquet*'s opening track, to my own acoustic guitar accompaniment in church when the youth club was permitted by a with-it curate to take over Evensong one Sunday. It was pretty awful but, nonetheless, indicative of the degree to which I'd absorbed an LP now with a scuffed sleeve, and scratched and hissing with surface noise.

Having invested that amount of cash, I'd intended to spin it until it was dust: sometimes concentrating on, say, only the guitars or the drumming, then only the lyrics, making myriad private observations that drew me from either mirror-freaking or lying full-length on the bed, hands under head, to the Dansette in order to lift the needle back to something I'd just noticed about a keyboard phrase during a fade-out or a particular vocal intonation on a second chorus. I'd been determined to get my money's worth.

After a while, *Beggars Banquet* gave way to newer sounds, and I didn't listen to it again for years. By then, although the way it had come into my possession, and the resulting weeks, maybe months, of automatic replay resonated still, I had got it into a wider perspective, and had become better able to understand the social, cultural, economic, environmental and further undercurrents that polarize and prejudice what is known generally about the context of its making and the period when it was in – and on – the air. By 1974 – one of pop's slowest moments when there was nothing especially hysterical or outrageous going on – I was reading more about music than actually listening to it.

Partly, this was down to the development since the late 1960s of a too analytical if book-learningly respectable form of pop journalism that intellectualizes the unintellectual, turns metaphorical perfume back into a rotten egg, and was to tell you what Ian MacDonald thought about the three-minutes-fifteen-seconds of 'Street Fighting Man' ('as powerful and ambivalent as Lennon's "Revolution" ... a subversive variant on Martha & the Vandellas' "Dancing In The Street"'[2]) and what Lester Bangs might have thought he meant.

Why should I be any different by not dismantling the not-quite-three-quarters-of-an-hour of *Beggars Banquet* and putting it back together again? Yet I wouldn't have embarked on this project if I hadn't come to disassociate the album from personal perspective and appreciate it as simple vibrations hanging in the air – or if I hadn't felt that such an investigation was a worthwhile historical exercise after a preliminary re-plumbing of the depths of associated oceans of press archives, as well as the many discographies, biographies, day-by-day chronologies and further explorations in print and website – from the broadest outline to the most meticulous detail – of every nook and cranny of the Rolling Stones' career. Then I sub-divided the consequent and voluminous notes into files with labels like 'Influences', 'People', 'Session', 'Times', 'Business' and 'Aftermath' (albeit with outlines dissolving and contents merging between all of them).

In doing so, I tried to avoid the more familiar quotes and anecdotes. As well as often obscure secondary sources, this account has been drawn too from conversations and formal interviews over the past two decades with friends and acquaintances of the Stones such as Pat Andrews, Marsha Hunt, Phil May, Dick Taylor and other intimates that may prefer not to be mentioned.

I am grateful too for the reminiscences, clear insight and intelligent argument of Don Craine, Keith Grant-Evans, Jonathan Meades, Jim McCarty, the late David Sanderson and the late Art Wood.

Please put your hands together for editor Julia Rolf, commissioning editor Polly Willis, project editor Cat Emslie and the rest of the team at Flame Tree.

Whether they were aware of providing assistance or not, let's have a round of applause for these musicians: Frank Allen, Roger Barnes, Alan Barwise, Peter Barton, Arthur Brown, Mike Cooper, Pete Cox, Paul Critchfield, the late Lonnie Donegan, Chris Dreja, 'Wreckless' Eric Goulden, John Harries, Brian Hinton, Alan Holmes, Robb Johnston, Garry Jones, Graham Larkbey, Andy Lavery, the late Carlo Little, Tom McGuiness, Jacqui McShee, Andy Pegg, Brian Poole, Reg Presley, John Renbourn, Paul Samwell-Smith, Jim Simpson, Mike and Anja Stax, John Steel, the late Lord David Sutch, John Townsend, Paul Tucker and Fran Wood.

Give it up too for the BBC Music Library, the National Sound Archives, Colindale Newspaper Library and Barry's Auto Repairs.

Thanks are also due in varying degrees to Stuart and Kathryn Booth, Robert Cross (of Bemish Business Machines), Kevin Delaney, Ian Drummond, Tim Fagan, Katy Foster-Moore, Richard Hattrell, Paul Hearne, Michael Heatley, the late Susan Hill, Trevor Hobley, Dave Humphries, Rob Johnstone, Allan Jones, Mick and Sarah Jones, Martin Lewis, Iris and Giselle Little, Steve Maggs, Elisabeth McCrae, Russell Newmark, Mike Ober, Mike Robinson, Mark and Stuart Stokes, Anna Taylor, John Tobler, Michael Towers, Warren Walters, Gina Way and Ted Woodings as well as Inese, Jack and Harry Clayson for whom I was absent in spirit for much of the writing of this book.

Alan Clayson, January 2007

NOTES

1. *The Rolling Stones In Their Own Words* eds. D. Dalton and M. Farren (Omnibus, 1980)

2. *Revolution In The Head* by I. MacDonald (Pimlico, 1995)

Chapter 1
JIGSAW PUZZLE: INFLUENCES

'On one hand, I was playing all that folk stuff on the guitar. The other half of me was listening to all that rock'n'roll, Chuck Berry, and saying yeah, yeah.' Keith Richards [1]

The 'classic' Rolling Stones line-up had found each other by early 1963. Sharing small stages in and around London with vocalist Mick Jagger, guitarist Keith Richards, pianist Ian Stewart and general factotum Brian Jones – an amalgamation of players from two rehearsal groups – were drummer Charlie Watts and, on bass, Bill Wyman, who replaced Dick Taylor. With singer Phil May, Taylor was next to lead the Pretty Things, fleetingly on terms of fluctuating equality with the Stones as belligerently unkempt degenerates, detested by adults.

The Young Ones: the Rolling Stones pose in London in 1964. From left to right: Mick Jagger, Keith Richards, Charlie Watts, Brian Jones and Bill Wyman.

As such, the Stones cut appropriately malign figures on the front photograph of their eponymous debut LP. However, anyone awaiting seething musical insolence was disappointed, because its content was as weighty with rhythm-and-blues (R&B) standards as each of the maiden albums yet to come by the Animals, the Yardbirds, the Kinks, the Downliners Sect, Them, the Pretty Things, Dave Berry and the Spencer Davis Group, and on the first two Beatles LPs put together. Indeed, the likes of 'I'm A King Bee', '(Get Your Kicks On) Route 66' and 'Walking The Dog', a recent US smash by Rufus Thomas – not to mention 'Money' and 'Poison Ivy', both on the Stones' first EP – were the common property of countless beat groups across the country, although the general intention was to make them sound different from any other outfit's version. In this, the Stones succeeded as exemplified by 'Money', in which they substituted harmonica for the usual piano or lead guitar.

The Stones' first LP was, therefore, more a proficient culmination of everything that had gone before than the start of something new. Most pivotal to this result had been seasons from early spring to late summer 1963 at both Ken Colyer's Studio 51 in central London on Sunday evenings and the Craw Daddy, a club that convened every Sunday afternoon in the function room of a Richmond pub. A kind of committed gaiety from increasingly more uproarious crowds had lent an inspirational framework to performances that covered an almost entirely black US waterfront from pre-war country blues to the latest from Chuck Berry, still a chart contender. In between lay works by Elmore James, Muddy Waters, Jimmy Reed, Rufus Thomas and Bo Diddley plus irresistible concessions to rock'n'roll and what was becoming known as 'soul'. The envelope was stretched further to embrace the Coasters, a black vocal group with a 'fool' bass singer and gimmick hit records like 'Searchin'', 'Yakety Yak', 'Charlie Brown' and 'Poison Ivy'.

Elsewhere, the Stones' choices were quite erudite. Perhaps they would be reluctant to acknowledge it, but all members had fundamentally scholarly natures that dictated researching and analysing the music they enjoyed and delving down to its nitty-gritty. Jones, for example, had acquired Paul Oliver's *Blues Fell This Morning*[2], then a standard history, as soon as it was published by Cassell in 1960, and had worked his way through as much of its bibliography that could be ordered from the public library in his native Cheltenham, fanning out to titles about, say, plantation field hollers or the African roots of blues.

Meanwhile over in Dartford, Kent, Jagger was engaged in similar exploration, having put himself on the mailing lists of US record labels that traded chiefly in black music, among them Chess, Imperial, Vee-Jay, Excello, Aladdin and Atlantic, which, while aided financially by the likes of mainstream white Bobby Darin and imported one-hit-wonder Acker Bilk, preferred to specialize in blues, the blues end of jazz, R&B and, after the 1960s slipped out of neutral, soul. Even when British firms began issuing R&B singles such as James Brown's 'Think' (on Parlophone in 1961) and, via Pye International's R&B series, material in all vinyl formats by Bo Diddley, Howlin' Wolf, Muddy Waters and other executants of the sacred sounds, letters were sent by Mick entreating them to release more.

While 'Poison Ivy' on Atlantic had penetrated the UK Top Twenty in 1959 (via a Decca subsidiary), 'You Can Make It If You Try' by Vee-Jay's Gene Allison had leaked to Britain that same year and thence to the deletion rack, though it had crossed over from what used to be known as the 'race' or 'sepia' list in *Billboard*, the US music business periodical, to spend a solitary week in the mainstream Top Forty. Likewise, 1957's 'Susie Q' by rockabilly entertainer Dale Hawkins – who recorded for Checker, a subdivision of Chess – was reworked in less robust fashion by the Stones, mainly by adding an awry lead guitar part. Though 'Susie Q' was by a white artist, it passed muster because it gave credence to one critic's summary of rockabilly as 'the blues with acne'[3] – for, no matter how far away from it they were to stray, the Stones would always come back to the blues.

All roots and branches had been represented in the repertoire of Blues Incorporated, formed in London in late 1961 as, arguably, the first British outfit who played the stuff to the exclusion of everything else. Both Watts and Jagger had been semi-permanent members of Blues Incorporated – not so much a group as a loose 'collective' – yet the most conspicuous manifestation by then of the British blues movement, which is usually dated from Mississippi songster Big Bill Broonzy's London concert debut, with his then-novel twelve-string guitar, in September 1951. Born when Queen Victoria was still alive, the influential Broonzy passed away in 1958, leaving younger men to define what are now clichés of the idiom.

Still cult celebrities then, Broonzy and later visitors to Europe – among them Sonny Boy Williamson II, Muddy Waters, Victoria Spivey, Otis Rush and John Lee Hooker – were to obtain a sharper profile via bohemian scorn for the hit parade toot-tooting of traditional jazz (trad) even if many famous pop musicians were either inspired by the form or gained their first toehold in show business by falling meekly into line in a semi-professional trad band, and donning matching stage costumes in the manner of Acker Bilk and his Paramount Jazz Band, for ever on BBC Television's opportunist *Trad Tavern* series. Musically, too, it often seemed that every trad band was the same: banjos, a confusion of front line horns and 'dads' who imagined that a hoarse monotone was all you needed to sing like Louis Armstrong.

From Chris Barber's New Orleans Jazz Band – whose Top Ten entry with 'Petit Fleur' had kicked off the trad craze – two sacked sidemen, mouth-organist Cyril Davies and guitarist Alexis Korner, became the mainstays of Blues Incorporated, finding a home for the ensemble in a downstairs room between a jeweller's and the ABC teashop on Ealing Broadway. From its inaugural evening on St Patrick's Day 1962, what became known most commonly as 'the Ealing club' was patronized immediately by blues zealots from other West London suburbs as well as Surrey, Middlesex, Kent and beyond. At later meetings, customers would learn of other blues strongholds such as the Craw Daddy and L'Auberge – both in Richmond – Twickenham's Eel Pie Island hotel ballroom, Studio 51 and Blues Incorporated's weekly nights at the Marquee, the National Jazz Federation's principal London venue.

As a hangover from trad, Blues Incorporated was primarily an instrumental unit with a core personnel consisting mostly of hoary old troupers, but was flexible enough to accommodate younger participants from the throng of art students and weekend dropouts who queued to thrash guitars and holler the blues. These amateurs were responsible for many well-intentioned musical assassinations but among the frayed jeans, CND badges and beatnik beards in the audience were future Kinks, Yardbirds, Manfred Mann, Rolling Stones and Pretty Things – all poised to breach the Top Twenty within three years without unduly compromising their hirsute images, and by sticking to their erudite guns artistically.

Nevertheless, both financially and stylistically, it wasn't an easy road to travel back in 1962. Cyril Davies was to leave Blues Incorporated after making clear his preference for a narrower interpretation of the music rather than Alexis Korner's 'everything from Louis Jordan to Martha & the Vandellas'[4] – and, with a scholarship at the Central School of Art beckoning, Dick Taylor had baulked when the Stones had suggested going professional. Yet mixed feelings at their unforeseen clamber into the Top Thirty the following year caused Dick to contemplate that the rewards of being a Stone might now extend beyond beer money and a laugh.

The Stones' commitment to this 'starvation music' had had them performing for as little as a round of drinks after an opening recital as an intermission act at the Marquee on 12 July 1962, where they had walked an uncomfortable line between reassuring 'Ealing club' crowd pleasers and the R&B that crossed the frontiers of pop, principally that of Bo Diddley and Chuck Berry.

After they had been signed to Decca, which vied with EMI as the kingdom's foremost record company, the group was to pay respects to Diddley via the selection of his 'Mona' for their debut album, a 'Mona'[5] drenched in reverberation, but still riven with the relentless shave-and-a-haircut-two-bits rhythm patented by Bo – the influence of which would be discernible years later on *Beggars Banquet* within the subtle cross-rhythms that underlined 'Sympathy For The Devil'.

Of all the Grand Old Men of R&B and classic rock, however, the first and foremost for the Stones, particularly Keith Richards, was, and always would be, Chuck Berry. Today, Richards, well into his sixties, is reputed to spin a ritual Berry disc in the dressing room just prior to venturing onstage – though his latter-day Stones have been less inclined to insert Berry numbers into the set since Keith's organization of an all-star backing combo for *Hail! Hail! Rock 'n' Roll* (1987), a film centred on Berry, whose alternate grouchiness and bored indolence had marred its preparation. 'I couldn't warm to him,' grimaced an exasperated Richards, 'he's got a big chip on his shoulder and, now and again, it's knocked off, and he's a fascinating, sweet guy, but suddenly he checks himself like he's given away too much, having too much fun, and the armour goes back on.'[6]

The experience faded, and Keith was able to separate the music from the personal weaknesses of its creator. Besides, there remained memories of the struggle back in 1962 when it wasn't much of an exaggeration to say that Chuck Berry songs – and those associated with him – filled a good third of a typical Stones set. Something of a group signature tune – as exemplified by its inclusion amongst up-to-the-minute *Beggars Banquet* items in the group's *Rock And Roll Circus* extravaganza in 1968 – was '(Get Your Kicks On) Route 66', the most famous composition by US film actor and jazz pianist Bobby Troup, which had been appropriated by Berry. It was a close second, along with 'Hoochie Coochie Man', to 'I Got My Mojo Working' as the British R&B movement's anthem. Furthermore, that

Chuck had also revived 'Down The Road Apiece' had been reason enough for the Stones to attempt it in similar rocked-up manner.

Actual Berry compositions that were to be interpreted by the Stones on disc were 'Carol', 'You Can't Catch Me', 'Talkin' 'Bout You' – the last Berry opus they would issue on vinyl until 1970 – 'Little Queenie', 'Let It Rock' and, of course, 'Come On', their accelerated cover of a 1963 Berry B-side as a debut single, gingered up with the wail of Brian's harmonica, and the corniest of key changes heralding the final verse.

As his name emerges so often in any account of the Stones' career, it may be constructive to outline the remarkable Berry's background in some detail. Born and raised in St Louis, the adolescent Charles Edward Berry was refused entry to the very theatre where *Hail! Hail! Rock 'n' Roll* would be filmed in a more enlightened age – because any admixture of negro blood was deemed sufficient to restrict its owner to 'colored' places of entertainment. Yet Berry's first mainstream pop breakthrough, 1955's 'Maybelline', would owe as much to white country-and-western (C&W) as black R&B. It would also predate 'Heartbreak Hotel', Elvis Presley's first million-seller.

Almost ten years older than Elvis, Berry had absorbed the most disparate ingredients in the musical melting pot of the Americas: calypso, vaudeville, Latin, C&W, showbiz evergreens, and every shade of jazz, particularly when it was transported to the borders of pop via, say, the orchestral euphoria of Count Basie, Ted Daffan and his Texans' Western swing ('hillbilly jazz'), the vocal daredevilry of Anita O'Day and Frank Sinatra, the humour of Louis Armstrong and the jump blues of Louis Jordan.

At twenty-six, Berry had turned professional as front man of his own Chuck Berry Combo, playing local venues with occasional side-trips further afield to Chicago, where blues grandee Muddy Waters was so sincerely loud in his praise that Chuck was signed to the Windy City's now-legendary Chess label in 1955 (as was Bo Diddley).

After 'Maybelline' peaked at Number Five in the Hot 100, 'Roll Over Beethoven' climbed almost as high. With melodies and R&B chord patterns serving as support structures for lyrics celebrating the pleasures available to US teenage consumers, another fat commercial year generated further smashes in 'School Days', 'Rock And Roll Music', 'Sweet Little Sixteen' and 'Johnny B Goode', the number that would be most synonymous with him.

These set-works would remain the cornerstone of Berry's stage act, first experienced by the world beyond the States when he appeared in *Jazz On A Summer's Day* (1960), a US film documentary about a turn-of-the-decade outdoor festival. With his crotch-level red guitar and trademark duck-walk, Chuck offended jazz pedants, but captured the imaginations of European teenagers. Certainly, the young Keith Richards was soon turning to Berry's Chess LPs as frequently as a vicar to the Bible. In an age when an LP cost three weeks' paper round wages, such a youth listened to 1958's *One Dozen Berries* or an imported *Chuck Berry Is On Top* (1959) endlessly, savouring the tactile sensation of handling the cover, and finding no printed detail too trivial.

From absorbing Berry and, to a smaller extent, further US icons, Keith dug deeper. 'Chuck was at Chess,' he noticed, 'and so was Muddy Waters, so you go through the roster of Chess. Then I looked at the names of the musicians on Chuck Berry records, and the ones for Bo Diddley, Muddy Waters ... same cats.'[7]

Richards and the other Rolling Stones-in-waiting were to discover too that explicit precedents to Berry – and rock'n'roll in general – could be heard in particular records. As well as any number of gutbucket Mississippi and Chicago blues offerings, examples included Hank Williams's 'Move It On Over', 'Boogie Woogie Bugle Boy' by the Andrews Sisters and, more obviously, Roy Brown's 'Good Rockin' Tonight' from 1947.

Brown was black, but 'Good Rockin' Tonight' lent itself to a quasi-C&W arrangement when revived by Elvis Presley. Besides, with its blend of cowpoke pessimism and Victorian broadness of gesture, what else is country music if not white man's blues? The incorporation of blues into the stylistic *oeuvres* of C&W giants such as Jimmie Rodgers, Hank Williams and Johnny Cash – who all dealt in 'hard' country, as opposed to Jim Reeves-Slim Whitman 'sweetcorn' – was exemplified by vocals couched in rural black imagery and phrasing, an unusual preoccupation with rhythm, and a commitment to the spirit of their songs – and it was when contents of black and white music merged that Presley was able to advance beyond local popularity as the principal rock'n'roll specialist on Sun, the record label founded in Memphis, Tennessee, 'the home of the blues'.

As a boy, Keith Richards had discovered Hank Williams and his backing Drifting Cowboys via a 1952 ten-inch LP (*Hank Williams Sings*), which contained an overhaul of 'Prodigal Son', a 1928 opus by the Reverend Robert Wilkins, a medicine show huckster who yapped his spiel about snake-bite tonics and cure-all elixirs throughout the Deep South between the wars. The Stones' tailor-made revival on *Beggars Banquet*, however, leaned more heavily on the rustic sounds of the Appalachian highlands where early English settlers had stabilized a conservative repertoire, which, with minimal melodic variations, was the formal opposite of jazz.

'You should never underestimate the importance of country in rock'n'roll,' Keith would pontificate[8] – and there would be at least a nod to C&W on most Stones albums. In the context of this discussion, it rears up most conspicuously on *Beggars Banquet*'s 'Dear Doctor', albeit impregnated with that element of jocularity telegraphed by such of the 'Something Happened To Me Yesterday' finale of *Between The Buttons* (1967) and *Their Satanic Majesties Request*'s (1967) 'On With The Show' and, more covertly, a vignette of 'We Wish You A Merry Christmas' at the close of the first side. On that same album, there is what amounts to an appealingly arranged countrified melody amid the psychedelics of '2000 Man'. The instrumentation on 'Factory Girl' also draws elements from country traditions.

Yet, while he was acknowledging C&W musical repercussions, Keith was aware too that Hank Williams in particular was also among the prototypes of the rock'n'roll anti-hero. As his fame had spread, so had Williams's notoriety as a drinker, before he graduated from Southern Comfort to amphetamines and worse. The short-lived magic of narcotics eased the agony of a distorted spine. Becoming an erratic performer, he walked a self-destructive line between shambles and dazed inspiration. If provoked by excessive ingestion of alcohol and drugs, the all-embracing 'natural causes' brought down the curtain on Williams on New Year's Day, 1953. To Jerry Rivers, one of his backing Drifting Cowboys, 'the news was shocking, but not unbelievable.'[9]

Arkansas-born Johnny Cash was also a stimulant-addled booker's risk – until the love of a good woman enabled him to confront and master his inner chaos. He assumed Hank Williams's mantle as one of C&W's greatest figures. Both Brian Jones and Keith Richards had come to like Cash's music (and there would be an element of it in both the Stones sets at the Craw Daddy and, the comedy falsetto in the final verse apart, 'Dear Doctor') – but they were also to share his (and Hank Williams's) self-destructive tendencies.

More a role model for Mick Jagger was Oregon's Johnnie Ray, 'The Prince Of Wails', whose melodramatic onstage exhibitionism was derived from R&B. A pivotal onstage moment during a Ray performance was when he lurched into his 'cover' in 1954 of 'Such A Night'. Such a whitewashing of an R&B favourite (originally by Clyde McPhatter & the Drifters) for the mainstream pop charts was anticipated and even welcomed by black recording acts of the early 1950s, as it brought their music, if not their performances of it, to a parallel dimension of teenage consumers with money to burn.

In the early 1950s, some unadulterated R&B had crept into *Billboard*'s pop Hot 100, notably in Fats Domino's ambulatory lope and Berry's sly lyricism. Though Elvis Presley's first release – a jumped-up treatment of

'That's All Right' by black songster Arthur 'Big Boy' Crudup – sprang, like 'Maybelline', from a country as well as a blues environment, some radio presenters were reluctant to schedule such a racially integrated disc. Presley's 'That's All Right' rose high in the US C&W chart (and would still be selling in 2005 when its re-promotion was a UK Number One). Further smashes with similar material guaranteed that Elvis was both loathed and adored throughout the southern states. In the same way that it would the Rolling Stones and the Sex Pistols, adult blood had run cold at Presley and the many other 'rockabilly' artistes who flowered in his wake. Yet, in a nonplus of repellent fascination, many teenagers were just as aghast as their parents – because rearing up before them was everything that their upbringing had taught them to both despise and fear.

Culturally window-shopping, Mick Jagger, then a grammar school pupil, spared – perhaps surprisingly – little time for Presley, much preferring the more unhinged Little Richard, whose effeminate behaviour had led his father to disown him. In billowing drapes and precarious pompadour, Richard's bombastic vocal delivery swooped from roar to shriek in 'Tutti Frutti', 'Keep A Knockin'', 'Good Golly Miss Molly' and all the rest of his exercises in sexual doggerel sanitized to joyful gibberish and, therefore, palatable to a white public – while he punished a grand piano with parts of his anatomy other than his hands.

Entranced, Mick and Keith placed a given British single by Richard or Presley on record players in their respective Dartford bedrooms, and arranged themselves in front of wardrobe mirrors. From opening line to final twelve-bar run-down, they sang soundlessly and pretended to slash chords or hammer ivories, and pick air solos with negligent ease. They flicked back their quiffs – soon to be trimmed at mother's behest – and mouthed the lyrics to thousands of ecstatic females that only they could see. Yet, when not embroiled in this time-honoured rite of thwarted eroticism, Mick discovered that 'Good Golly Miss Molly' and 'Hound Dog' could be filtered through his own lithe, full-throated – and quite serviceable – breaking voice.

Jagger's bawled 'No-no-no!' at the close of 1965's 'The Last Time' and the 'What's my name!' coda from 'Sympathy For The Devil' could have been lifted by time machine from a Little Richard concert finale in the 1950s, and Mick had sounded a little like Presley on 'I Want To Be Loved', B-side of 'Come On' – though he was his own man eighteen months later on 'Down Home Girl' (on the second LP), co-written by Jerry Lieber – who, with Mike Stoller, had provisioned Elvis as well as The Coasters and The Drifters with chart fodder. This citified perspective on country blues might have been made-to-measure for Presley, but the blueprint was by Alvin Robinson, whose version flopped. At Hollywood's RCA Studios, it was improved upon by the Stones with help from Jack Nitzsche, Phil Spector's arranger – and maker of (mostly instrumental) discs under his own name. This urban-tinged county/blues sound that the Stones explored early on in their recording career is hinted at in some of their later work, such as *Beggars Banquet*.

That the Stones had been aware of Alvin Robinson – and Gene Allison – as obscure now as they were then, is affirmation of the degree to which they were still exploring the more remote branches of the stylistic flow charts that fanned out from prominent pop artists they admired. If no longer teenagers, Jagger, Richards and Jones in particular were not so far removed from obsessed supporters of a football team, taking a blues fixation to the extent that they did not care if others mocked them for it.

In the privacy of their own homes, the Rolling Stones' high command became schoolboy fans again, gloating over their growing collections of vinyl treasures, finding much to study, notice and compare in liner notes, composer credits and so forth. They scoured the weekly music press, especially *Melody Maker*, which covered jazz and blues as well as pop, and risked daylight visits to Dobell's, a specialist shop in central London's Charing Cross Road, that stocked recordings of black Americana at import prices.

On instant replay for weeks at Brian's flat in Belgravia was *Folk Blues Of John Lee Hooker* (1959), issued in Britain in the days when he could not afford it and had no opportunity to steal it. With a less lackadaisical regard for business than poor Arthur Crudup, an older contemporary, Hooker's career had taken off in the late 1940s with 'I'm In The Mood' and 'Boogie Chillen', huge sellers in the US 'sepia' tabulation without figuring at all in the parallel dimensions of 'popular' and 'C&W'. His biographical credentials as a bluesman were impeccable; an upbringing in Clarksdale, in rural Mississippi, was followed by a youth spent in Memphis. Next came migration north, purchase of an electric guitar and 'discovery' by a record company talent scout during a club residency in Black Bottom, a Detroit suburb.

After his initial brace of hits, Hooker made his US television debut in 1949 as further smashes such as 'Driftin'', 'Hobo Blues' and a remake of 'I'm In The Mood' established him as a major blues exponent. During his British tours in the early 1960s, he was often backed – as Sonny Boy Williamson II was – by one of myriad native R&B outfits whose imaginations he had captured. Among these were the Groundhogs – and the Spencer Davis Group, whose 1963 single, Hooker's leering 'Dimples', was vanquished when the original was released, slipping into the British Top Thirty. The same fate befell Tommy Bruce & the Bruisers' leeringly creditable attempt at Hooker's 'Boom Boom'.

Perhaps for this very reason, the Stones did not touch John Lee's portfolio, though 'Boom Boom', 'I'm Mad Again' and similar examples of his gutbucket hollering and eccentric rhythmic shifts were resurrected too by the Animals, Them, the Yardbirds – who took over from the Stones at the Craw Daddy – and many other groups. Nevertheless, at seventy-two Hooker was to open a satellite-linked Stones concert in New Jersey in 1989, and Keith Richards felt honoured to be asked to play on a Hooker album, *Mr. Lucky* (1991), co-produced by Keith's sometime friend, Ry Cooder.

Just as a hypnotic boogie undercurrent was the stylistic trademark linking Hooker's early sides with 'Parachute Woman' on *Beggars Banquet* as well as *Mr. Lucky*, so a bottleneck approach was the common thread between Elmore James – whose version of the classic 'Rollin' And Tumblin'' was to be a blues 'standard' – and his mentor, pre-war bluesman Robert Johnson. For years, Brian Jones had been a student of James's identifying application of rural 'bottleneck' (or 'slide') technique to electric guitar, discovering that Elmore neither played in an orthodox fashion nor used standard tuning. With no one to instruct him or even a worthwhile manual available, Brian gathered what he could from discs and by trial-and-error, after winding his instrument with heavy-gauge strings as James did. Even before meeting Jagger and Richards, Jones's bottlenecking had become distinctive through a ringing clarity and an exactness of phrasing that was all the more rewarding for its studied restraint – as demonstrated on his contribution to *Beggars Banquet*'s second track, 'No Expectations'.

Traceable to Hawaiian music as well as early blues, and not dissimilar to the pedal-operated steel guitar in C&W, slide guitar is difficult to play creatively and well, as it involves exploring the possibilities of *glissandi* rather than 'clean' notes, via the careen of strings tuned to an open – usually major – chord, and a fretboard stroked with a 'slide', generally a glass or metal tube placed on the finger. Because it is necessary to heighten the bridge, the frets become only an approximate visual guide as to where to find a given note. This means that an ear able to differentiate between pitch variables of at least quarter-tones is essential to accurate bottleneck playing.

'He used to play me Robert Johnson and Elmore James records,' reminisced Pat Andrews, Brian's first 'serious' girlfriend, 'and explain how they got their sounds. He believed they used actual bottle necks to get the slide effect – so he broke a bottle neck off and tried it. He got the sound, but it was a bit dangerous. One day, we went round to a number of garages, and Brian found a bit of pipe cut to fit his finger.' In parenthesis, Lowell George, one of the most renowned exponents in the 1970s – who first attempted bottleneck after hearing Brian – began with the casing of a spark plug.

Though Elmore James also struck a later chord with Keith Richards, he was something of an acquired taste for most white blues guitarists, who were more inclined to relate to another major post-war blues voice, Aaron 'T-Bone' Walker, whose terse guitar passagework was echoed by Albert King. In turn, Albert's influence was felt by Alvin Lee, Stan Webb and, more acutely, Eric Clapton – notably in Cream's revival of 'Born Under A Bad Sign' in 1968 – and other 'guitar heroes' who had paid heed during the first 1960s wave of British blues. When a Yardbird and then as one of John Mayall's Bluesbreakers, Clapton was one of these guitarists who tended to step forward into the spotlight to react with clenched teeth to underlying chord patterns rather than the more obvious aesthetics of a number. His eyes would fix on the neck of his instrument as if stupefied by his own dexterity.

If King left his mark on Richards' solo and valedictory contributions to 'Sympathy For The Devil', and bottleneck was to the fore on 'No Expectations' and 'Parachute Woman', there was none of that Clapton-esque flash on *Beggars Banquet* where, as on the Stones' previous records, lead and rhythm guitars were inclined to merge in interlocking harmony. In this respect, there can be a comparison to the decorative acoustic virtuosity of Bert Jansch and John Renbourn, flatmates who, together and apart, had emerged as swiftly as reliable attractions on the UK folk circuit as the Stones had at Craw Daddy-type venues.

Renbourn was one of a number of later famous guitarists with roots in English art schools. At Kingston College, where South London collides with genteel Surrey, he had been as knowledgeable as Jones, Richards and Jagger about the folk and blues bedrock that lay beneath skiffle's chewing gum-flavoured topsoil. 'The R&B craze had replaced skiffle, and the best band was considered to be Alexis Korner's Blues Incorporated,' recollected John, 'I played in an Art School R&B band for a while, Hog Snort Rupert's Famous Porkestra, using a borrowed electric guitar. I found that some of the band's riffs sounded interesting played fingerstyle on an acoustic.'

Further stalwarts of the British folk club circuit known to Brian, Mick and Keith were Mick Softley, Jon Mark (accompanying guitarist to Marianne Faithfull, soon to be Jagger's girlfriend), Wizz Jones and a certain Ralph May from Richards and Jagger's part of Kent, who, having adopted the stage surname 'McTell' in genuflection to a Mississippi bluesman, had taken to the road like dustbowl balladeer Woody Guthrie, 'armed only with a guitar and a pocketful of dreams'[10]. McTell, Jones, Mark and Softley were, like Renbourn, 'all in awe of Davy Graham'. While his singing didn't match his playing, expatriate Scotsman Davy had made 1962's *The Guitar Player*, an LP of insidious impact for its finger-picked reconciliation of jazz, folk, blues with an occasional breath of the Orient, and baroque too.

Brisk sales of Jansch and Renbourn's *Bert And John* (1966) were in part a manifestation of the respect accorded to them as 'musicians' musicians'. 'They both had huge followings of the kind of guitar enthusiast who'd sit in the front row, watching their fingers,' observed Jacqui McShee, later *chanteuse* with Pentangle, formed by the two in 1966.

'Eric Clapton was often there,' added Wizz Jones, 'when Bert and John played at the Olive Tree in Croydon'[11]. Among other onlookers were Brian Jones, Keith Richards and George Harrison, taking particular note of the Eastern influences that were more than a trace element of Renbourn's style — betraying evidence itself of hard listening to both the eclectic Davy Graham and, to a smaller degree, John Mayer's Indo-Jazz Fusions and the 'trance jazz' of guitarist Gabor Szabo, which contained titles such as 'Search For Nirvana', 'Krishna' and 'Ravi'.

Keith Richards showed less interest in this aspect of Renbourn than the overall subtlety and elegance of acoustic guitar — as shown not only on 'Prodigal Son' and 'Factory Girl', but far earlier in the vibrant manner in which he drove 'Not Fade Away', the Stones' third UK chart strike, and his finger-picking on Marianne Faithfull's wan second single, 'Blowin' In The Wind'. She was to recall an occasion when Richards and Jones's tinkering together on acoustic instruments resulted in the creation of a Stones hit, 1967's 'Ruby Tuesday': 'It began from a bluesy Elizabethan fragment Brian was fiddling with. It was nothing more than a wispy tune, but it caught Keith's attention. Brian said it was a hybrid of Thomas Dowland's "Air On The Late Lord Essex" [*sic*] and a Skip James blues.'[12]

From the beginning, the concept of Jones and Richards cementing each other's runs with subordinate chords hadn't been a consideration as, over Dick Taylor's and then Bill Wyman's low throb, the two learned to anticipate and attend to each other's idiosyncracies and clichés. Moreover, in common with George Harrison, the Dave Clark Five's Lenny Davidson, Tony Hicks of the Hollies and other guitarists in more openly pop outfits, their ensemble playing was constructed to integrate with melodic and lyrical intent. Depending on your point of view, this was either bland left

Hard at work: Brian Jones (left) and Keith Richards playing their guitars in late 1963.

attractively unfussy against those in most of 1964's sudden crop of R&B groups. This may explain why, 'Sympathy For The Devil' notwithstanding, the likes of T-Bone Walker and Albert King, though revered, made less impact than might be imagined on both *Beggars Banquet* and the 1960s Stones' guitarists in general. Another was B.B. King, perhaps the most respected of all present-day black blues executants for his clean note-bending and jazz-tinged fretboard style. In broad terms, he had lived much the same life as, if not the younger Albert King, then John Lee Hooker and T-Bone Walker – as had Howlin' Wolf, possessor of the most bestial voice in pop.

Wolf surfaced from a Mississippi Delta boyhood to migrate in 1948 to Arkansas where he became a full-time musician, backed by one of the first electric blues bands in the Deep South. He was spotted by Ike Turner, then a freelance talent scout for the West Coast record company for whom Wolf first recorded. More crucial, however, were the tracks he taped at Sun studio in Memphis a few years before Elvis Presley's recording career began there. These were then purchased by Chess after Wolf moved to Illinois in 1952.

Though the metropolis left an indelible mark on his style, Wolf would never renege on his rural roots as he entered the most commercially fruitful chapter of his career. Composed principally by himself, many of the singles he released up to 1964 would surface as set works for white artists as varied as the Yardbirds, the Rolling Stones, the Doors, Ten Years After, Manfred Mann, Led Zeppelin, Canned Heat, Cream and Electric Flag.

After visiting England in the early 1960s as part of an American Folk-Blues Festival package, the burly Wolf was feted by middle-class rebels for a stage act of sweaty intensity and earthy *braggadocio*. A re-issue of his eight-year-old 'Smokestack Lightning' standard even made the UK Top Fifty in 1964. Before the year was out, he would top the chart by proxy with an unrevised arrangement of his 'Little Red Rooster' by the Rolling Stones, penned for Wolf by Willie Dixon, the omnipresent double-bass player at Chess. Wolf hovered too over Jagger's vocal delivery of 'Parachute Woman' and the overall lyrical mood of this and 'Stray Cat Blues', one of *Beggars Banquet*'s highlights, chiefly in its more overt eroticism. Moreover, when the Stones had been scheduled to appear on the US television pop series *Shindig* to plug the 'Little Red Rooster' follow-up ('The Last Time'), they insisted that Wolf should be the guest star and, during his spot, sat in a devout semi-circle at his feet.

Through Brian, Keith and Mick's implicated persistence too, the Stones had become pragmatically captivated by the grippingly personal styles of post-war country bluesmen such as Snooks Eaglin, Lightnin' Hopkins, Bukka White, Tommy McClennan, Skip James and Peetie Wheatstraw, toast of Louisville's red-light quarter, who named himself at various times 'the Devil's Son-in-Law' and 'the High Sheriff of Hell'. Collectively, however, the group was more obsessively fond of Robert Johnson who, unlike Wheatstraw, was tormented rather than apparently aided by an inferno of devils, phantoms and monsters. The most piquant of his rural exorcisms in this vein – 'Hellhound On My Trail' and the Faustian 'Me And The Devil Blues' – were each taped on 20 June 1937.

Virtually all of Johnson's output was recorded during an eight-month period, shortly before his death apparently by poison at the age of twenty-four. Nonetheless, thanks in part to revivals of his songs by bands such as Cream and the Rolling Stones, critical awareness and reassessment of Johnson has resulted in some noted pop pundits – including Charles Shaar Murray – regarding him as possibly the greatest musician ever to walk the planet.

Robert Plant of Led Zeppelin was to undertake a pilgrimage to Mississippi in an attempt to trace a surviving acquaintance of the Great Man. He was driven to knocking on doors almost at random. 'I've never been so ridiculous in my life,' guffawed Robert, 'When I was at school, I had a paper round to earn money, and I bought the original first Robert Johnson album with the gatefold sleeve and a picture of a sharecropper's shack on the front. When I heard "Preaching Blues" and "Last Fair Deal Gone Down", I was probably a year or two behind Keith Richards and Mick Jagger, but I went, "This is it!"'[13]

'The Brits took it much more seriously,' grinned Ahmet Ertegun, founder in 1948 of Atlantic[14]. 'American blues meant one thing to a group of black guys from Long Beach,' added Eric Burdon of the Animals, a former Newcastle art student who had ritually inked the word 'BLUES' in his own blood across the cover of an exercise book into which lyrics of the same had been copied, 'and quite another to people like me, Eric Clapton, Jimmy Page and Keith Richards.'[15]

It had been a genre that none of them had been able to touch at first. Their purpose once was just to receive the messages as they came without replying. Blues appeared to be peculiar then to black American experience, and much of it was purchasable in the Stones' London only after wending across the ocean to outlets like Dobell's and, in suburban Streatham, Carey's Swing Shop.

Yet record sessions would evolve into endeavours by some listeners to reproduce what was in the grooves. At some point during the consequent fun and games, they might mull over suitable names for a hypothetical group to perform these numbers. When Keith, Mick, Dick Taylor and other youthful devotees from their area of Kent were thus occupied, someone suggested jokingly 'Little Boy Blue & the Blue Boys'. For want of something better, they labelled with this name a tape they sent to the venerable Alexis Korner in 1962.

More a blues appreciation society than anything else, the lads re-christened themselves the Rolling Stones after a Muddy Waters A-side, 'Rollin' Stone Blues', on joining forces a few weeks later with Brian Jones and Ian Stewart. Neither of these two disliked rock'n'roll on principle. Besides, Ian and Brian argued – as much to themselves as anyone else – what was so wrong in pleasing the crowd – as long as much more detectably purer blues remained in strong evidence too?

The Stones did both when scrimmaging around the unsalubrious, low-ceilinged and dimly-lit clubs that began littering British towns during the Merseybeat craze, and when the group was becoming world famous. Among those genre preferences that made it on to disc were two associated with Muddy Waters: a speeded-up 'I Just Wanna Make Love To You' – penned for him by Willie Dixon – and downbeat 'I Can't Be Satisfied', the work of Waters himself and featuring what Jones was to cite as 'one of the best guitar solos I've ever managed.'[16] Certainly, it confirmed Alexis Korner's opinion that Brian was one of the finest British bottleneck players he had ever heard.

The antithesis of Muddy's full-throated ferocity, Chicago-via-Louisiana contemporary Jimmy Reed's relaxed, slurred singing left a more pronounced mark on the teenage Jagger, who would quote Reed titles and lyrics as if they were proverbs. A Stones scoring of Slim Harpo's 'I'm A King Bee' on the first LP stood as tall – though, while he was not trying consciously to copy this particular blues giant, Jagger had absorbed by osmosis too much of Harpo's laconic style to escape being an imitator – at least on this track. Yet he coped well with the insidiously feverish lechery of 'I'm A King Bee' over an appropriate backing epitomized by a suggestive, lowdown riff from Keith.

In the early 1960s, crazy, far-out music such as this – and acts like the Stones – was hardly the stuff of the British ballroom circuit, where it was incumbent upon groups to exude a happy, inoffensive onstage atmosphere to defuse potential unrest as well as play the hit parade assortment that dancers knew. In any of its sub-categories, blues could not be disguised as plain and simple pop, and remained, to all intents and purposes, the exclusive property of a knotted-brow fringe that patronized venues like the Ealing club. It was a comparatively unknown quantity even in the USA, lurking in the shadows at most in mainstream pop. Furthermore, if releases by artists such as Hooker, Reed, Waters and Wolf continued to sell by the ton in Uncle Sam's 'race' market, they didn't irritate even the lowest reaches of the US music trade periodical *Billboard*'s pop Hot 100. Into the bargain, blues was not particularly popular amongst citified young blacks either, being music that their migrant parents still liked.

Back in the rural Deep South, Buddy Knox, one of a wave of C&W artists who made hay with rock'n'roll in the 1950s, could not recall hearing a single disc by a black singer until he visited New York – though, through radio static, others his age might have tuned in by accident to muffled bursts of what white segregationalists heard as 'the screaming idiotic words and savage music'[17] of faraway Shreveport's R&B station KWKH where 'Stan The Man And His No-Name Record Jive' span the Midnighters' 'Sexy Ways', 'Sixty Minute Man' by the Dominoes and 'Too Many Drivers' by Smiley Lewis – all about sex and all banned from white radio. 'If you don't want to serve negroes in your place of business,' ran one racist handbill, 'then do not have negro records on your juke-box.'[17] For Britons insensible of ingrained racial tension, such discs – when they got round to hearing them – were 'something new and exciting,' deduced Ahmet Ertegun, 'In a sense, they were appreciating something the Americans did not value.'[14]

'As far as white people were concerned, especially suburban kids,' continued Mick Jagger, 'it was interesting because it was underclass music that they'd had no experience of or, in fact, that didn't exist by the time they had got to it anyway, almost. It was disappearing. That culture was on its way out.'[18]

Seeing what was coming, Duffy Power, once an also-ran pretender to Billy Fury's or Cliff Richard's crown as an English 'answer' to Elvis, was to release in 1964 'I Don't Care', a virtual rewrite of 'Hoochie Coochie Man' just as 'I'm The Face' by the High Numbers (soon to become more renowned as the Who) was Slim Harpo's 'Got Love If You Want It' grafted to Mod-speak lyrics. Attention to *Muddy Waters At Newport* (1960) had resulted in sound readings of 'Hoochie Coochie Man' by Dave Berry, Manfred Mann and Long John Baldry. Then there was to be the Pretty Things' riveting dash through Bo Diddley's 'Road Runner', and the Primitives – who had their long hair cut on a TV chat show[19] – with their passable go in 1964 at Sonny Boy Williamson's 'Help Me' with the original as a helpful demo.

However, lending credence to trad-jazz trumpeter Kenny Ball's jaded opinion that British R&B was just 'rock and roll with a mouth-organ' were legion executions of items that might have gone down a storm onstage, but sounded thuggish on vinyl in their blunt lyrics and stylized chord cycles. Outfits with names like the Howling Wolves, the T-Bones, the Boll Weevils, the King Bees and the Smokestacks would try to emulate the Jimmy Reed, Slim Harpo and Howlin' Wolf items from the juke joints and speakeasies of black America, but the outcome – especially vocal – was, more often than not, nothing like.

Yet 1964–65 was a fierce time for R&B. After the Stones had set the ball rolling, the Animals, the Kinks, the Pretty Things, the Yardbirds, Them and others among the fresh harvest of R&B hitmakers were becoming national pop celebrities, almost despite themselves.

Formed by Dick Taylor and singer Phil May, students from the same north-west Kent art college as Keith Richards, the Things had been, with the Stones, part of London's 'little white R&B movement', Led Zeppelin's John Paul Jones would sneer, 'more punk than R&B'[14]. Yet, if he hadn't been a conspicuous fan – unlike Van Morrison, Sex Pistols svengali-in-waiting Malcolm McLaren and Charlie Harper (of The UK Subs) – Jones had followed the group with interest from its genesis. So, more anxiously, did the Stones, especially when the Things were causing them so many nervous backwards glances that, through co-manager Andrew Loog Oldham, they found it necessary to issue a directive that the rival outfit was not to be re-booked on ITV's *Ready Steady Go!* upon pain of the Stones boycotting this most atmospheric of all Swinging Sixties television pop shows.

The Things' long-haired and reprobate image had held instant allure for record company talent scouts looking for an act to combat the chartbusting Stones in mid-1964 – and it was they rather than the Stones who were to emerge as patron saints of other 'hairy monsters' like Them, the Downliners Sect and lesser lights such as the Fairies, the Primitives and the Manish Boys (whose David Bowie would revive the Things' first two 45s on 1973's *Pin Ups* album). The Stones saw even the Beatles as a smaller threat and it was reported in the late 1970s that Jagger had owned up to copying Phil May's onstage gyrations.

According to Screaming Lord Sutch, the Things 'had everything it took to overtake the Stones. They were years ahead of their time image-wise – the Sex Pistols of their day. The Stones just about walked the line; the Pretty Things went way over it.' Projected as wilder, fouler and more peculiar than the Stones, the Things flashed into respectable homes via *Top of the Pops* cameras. While the most liberal parents fought for control of their features, the effect was most keenly felt by their short-back-and-sides sons, guiltily transfixed by the Things' androgyny, offset only by Dick Taylor's cultivated beard.

They and the Stones were anti-Beatles. After their four-song segment in 1963's *Royal Variety Show* had rendered the Fab Four harmless and swung the weather-vane of adult toleration, if not approval, in their direction, a Beatle, see, could not be imagined passing wind, urinating, committing a felony or being truly obnoxious any more than a sexless cartoon figure or teddy bear. By contrast, it was hard fact that three Stones were fined in 1965 for pissing against a wall, and a Fairy served time for causing death by dangerous driving. A Pretty Things road manager was prosecuted after some unpleasantness with a shotgun after an engagement in Swindon, and, remembers Phil May, 'in Stockport one night, some screaming bird tore my shirt during the first set, and Viv Prince, our drummer, put down his sticks to rip her blouse and bra off, and sock her in the mouth.'

Such outrages increased turnout at bookings, but always the Things expected their celebrity to end. Fontana, their record company, did too, and rush-released an eponymous (and big-selling) LP, padded with the latest hit, some derivative originals, and the expected Diddley, Berry and Jimmy Reed retreads. No longer an overnight sensation, fading interest was confirmed when the Things bid a final farewell to the UK singles Top Fifty with a cover of a Kinks LP track, 'House In The Country'. As cultural representatives of Britain overseas, a 1965 tour of New Zealand was overridden with resounding outcry from the old and square that the Things were on a par with the Horsemen of the Apocalypse, spreading plague and destruction wherever they passed. Epitomized by a reputedly drunken Prince being escorted from a grounded Kiwi aircraft after an altercation with its staff, it was comparable to the chaotic fortnight in the USA that was to finish The Sex Pistols in 1978.

The highlight of the Rolling Stones' first US tour – that occupied them for most of June 1964 – had not been public, as they seized the chance to record much of their second LP in the building where Chicago blues lived as pungently and as pragmatically as it did in the down-and-out State Street busker lilting an unaccompanied and never-ending 'I'm A King Bee'. Inside the Chess studios, the Stones were putty in the hands of the same house team that had forged the definitive works of Muddy, Wolf, Chuck and Bo. Indeed, the venerated Waters chanced to be present when the Stones were working on 'I Can't Be Satisfied'.

Muddy and those of his Chess familiars who also looked in learnt that the group was well acquainted with a form of R&B more modern than theirs. Along with 'classical', 'soul' is the most abused expression in pop. Steve Winwood, front man of the Spencer Davis Group, had become wary of praise for his soul singing because 'no matter how you try, you can never sing it like a coloured person. That's their life they are singing about.'[20] Yet Atlantic soul shouter Wilson Pickett's 1965 hit 'In The Midnight Hour' describes a situation not exclusive to his black experience. Both the late Wilson and white Londoner Chris Farlowe – who covered the song, and was billed as 'the Greatest Blues Singer in the World Today'[21] – sound equally thrilled about the prospect of a tryst beneath the stars. How then do you make a judgement like Winwood's? The argument about Caucasian incapacity to 'sing the blues like a coloured person' loses ground through Farlowe's version of T-Bone Walker's 'Stormy Monday Blues' which, released under the guise of 'Little Joe Cook', tricked most into believing Farlowe was an obscure black blues singer.

What, therefore, is soul? Is it the West Indian next door with his crooned small eternity of 'Stand By Me' as he creosotes the tool shed – or is it the hammy ritualism that most of the Stax and Tamla Motown revues demonstrated in the mid-1960s? Perhaps it is Mick Jagger's slightly strained vocal on the Stones' cover of Marvin Gaye's 'Can I Get A Witness' on their first LP, resulting from a dash to the high street to purchase the sheet music.

While the States was still unmindful of the Rolling Stones, 'Can I Get A Witness' was a sound choice – because no one could assume then that the group was going to be more than a strictly British – or, at most, European – phenomenon, like Cliff Richard or Billy Fury. With their deepest roots in US culture, it might be taking coals to Newcastle. Therefore, while the States was seemingly off-limits, it made sense to retread recent US-only hits by US artists that either yet meant nothing in the UK or whose chart climbs there were not foregone conclusions. As far as everyone from the director of the Light Programme to a bee-hived dolly-bird shuffling about in the gloom beyond the footlights in a Darlington palais was concerned, the Stones' version of 'Can I Get A Witness' was the *only* version. The same was almost true of 'Hitch Hike', Marvin Gaye's debut 45, which had been proffered as an alternative to the Twist, along with the Fly, the Locomotion, the ungainly Turkey Trot, the Madison, the back-breaking Limbo, the Mickey's Monkey *et cetera*.

Gaye was a principal act of Tamla Motown, a promising black label centred in Detroit, that had manoeuvred its first fistful of signings into the

Hot 100 at the beginning of the decade, and was now vying with Atlantic as the sub-continent's foremost soul label. By 1964, Martha & the Vandellas were as much of a major asset to the company as Marvin Gaye, so much so that, as well as all but topping the US list, their 'Dancing In The Street' *magnum opus* lasted the best part of two autumn months in the lower reaches of the British Top Fifty, largely on the back of a UK breakthrough by sister Motown artists the Supremes, the first black act to top the realm's singles charts in almost four years.

While the Kinks chanced a cover of 'Dancing In The Street', the Stones, if tempted, shied away from it – though it was to filter in an oblique way into 'Street Fighting Man', an anthem of social revolution on a par with 'Sympathy For The Devil' as *Beggars Banquet*'s key track. In there too was a more veiled hint of Gaye's 'Hitch Hike', which had still been in vogue when the Stones decided to record it in 1965 – with a guitar solo that lived a separate life from the rest of the number.

However, it was Jagger's talent for vacuuming the characteristics of a given vocalist without descending to caricature that lent character to 'Mercy Mercy', originally a US hit for Don Covay on Atlantic in 1964. Covay, one of Jagger's favourite soul artists, had been in a 1950s vocal group, the Rainbows, with Marvin Gaye and had borrowed much from Little Richard when, like Gaye, he struck out on his own. He was to wait until 1974 for his only UK chart entry, 'It's Better To Have (And Don't Need)'. Conversely, the late Sam Cooke, another *protégé* of Little Richard, had been an established, if sporadic, hitmaker in Britain between 1958 and 1962. Yet it was one of his latter-day misses, 1964's 'Good Times', that was the vehicle of the Stones' homage to him on their 1965 album *Out of Our Heads*, though their reading was not considered potent enough for the group to work it into the stage act.

Not many within the British domain of teenagers with more money than sense knew about Sam Cooke's 'Good Times'. However, the Stones' attempt at 'Under The Boardwalk' by the Drifters, a group then in the throes of a run of UK chartbusters, was a calculated risk, albeit as an album track and an Australia-only hit 45. Yet, rather than trying to pre-empt the Drifters and other internationally famous US soul names like the Supremes, the Stones usually gave themselves a more sporting chance by injecting their blues repertoire with a massive shot of items by less globally known North Americans, such as Marvin Gaye and Solomon Burke, a former gospel singer from Philadelphia, who was as much of a flagship act for Atlantic as Gaye was for Motown.

Burke's 'Everybody Needs Somebody To Love' would open *The Rolling Stones Vol. 2* (1965). It had not even been a particularly big hit for Solomon on his native turf, but it became to him what 'Rock Around The Clock' was to Bill Haley via the endorsement of a group that was now arguably, if briefly, ahead of the Beatles in North America – to the degree that the Merseysiders were sniping at the Stones in the press, whilst reputedly sending an underling out mid-session to purchase the Stones' latest LP.

Delivered in the studio by Jagger in the secular but 'testifying' manner that was to connect stylistically with both the play-out section of 'Sympathy For The Devil' and turn-of-the-millennium rap, the quality of 'Everybody Needs Somebody To Love' on the boards depended much upon the mood of the hour, but it was a stage fixture for a long while – and was to rear up again as late as 2004 when selected for *Live Licks*, a double CD memento of a record-breaking world tour. Furthermore, this actually featured none other than seventy-eight-year-old Burke – now reduced to singing seated – sharing vocals with Mick.

Prior to *Beggars Banquet*, The Stones had liked Burke's output enough to record two more of his Hot 100 inroads, both of them placatory ballads that were the antithesis of 'Everybody Needs Somebody To Love'. Eclipsing an arrangement by co-writer Wilson Pickett, 'If You Need Me' was one of the most played tracks on *12 X 5* (1964), the Stones' second US album – while, though consuming needle time on *Out Of Our Heads*, 'Cry

To Me' was also to be the Pretty Things' final British Top Twenty entry. Yet, before paths diverged – the Stones suffering world-wide acclaim and supertax while the Things began decades of struggle that would have destroyed a lesser outfit – there had been an uproarious *esprit de corps* moment on 7 March 1965 when, following a stopped show at the Palace Theatre in Manchester, Keith and Mick taxied across the city to leap onstage with the Things, who chanced to be playing the Manchester Cavern the same evening. Amongst numbers on which Jagger duetted with Phil May was 'Cry To Me'.

It was not dissimilar to the fractionally more uplifting 'Time Is On My Side' by Irma Thomas, the arrangement of which the Stones copied while lending it an individuality that hinged on Jagger's emotion-charged spoken passage. At the same funereal pace, Thomas's follow-up, 'Ruler Of My Heart', was adapted immediately by Georgia's Otis Redding as 'Pain In My Heart' – upon which the Stones swooped with the promptness of vultures, as they did upon three further items recorded by Redding: 1965's 'I've Been Loving You Too Long', his first major Hot 100 hit; 'My Girl' and 'That's How Strong My Love Is', a Redding B-side that had been in the shops mere weeks when the Stones covered it, utilizing the same slow build-up, but minus Redding's accompanying horns.[22] 'That's How Strong My Love Is' was included on *Out Of Our Heads*, a stop-gap album created over several months in different studios in Britain and the States. It contained a preponderance of non-originals and many were covers of the soul records then permeating the dance floors of the London clubs frequented by the figureheads of the Swinging Sixties.

The Stones – particularly Mick Jagger, Brian Jones and Keith Richards – were often sighted holding court, whiskey and Coke in hand, with only their near-equals contradicting them at the Cromwellian, Blaises, the cloistered Scotch of St James a stone's throw from Buckingham Palace, the supercool Speakeasy, the Bag O' Nails off Carnaby Street, the Ad Lib near Leicester Square, the Pickwick or wherever else was currently 'in'. Before saturation plugging on Britain's new pirate radio stations eased them either into the charts' lower rungs or on to record decks in provincial clubland, the group had thus long been *au fait* with songs such as, say, 'Harlem Shuffle' by Bob & Earl, Chuck Jackson's 'Any Day Now' and Edwin Starr's 'Headline News'.

Both house discotheques and increasingly more splendid domestic record players would pulsate to Betty Everett, Don Covay, Kim Weston and Dobie Gray, as well as more illustrious entrants in the *Billboard* soul lists such as James Brown, Marvin Gaye, Wilson Pickett, the Miracles and (Little) Stevie Wonder, and old-timers such as the Drifters, the Coasters, Chris Kenner, Chubby Checker and the Chiffons. It was hip to say you preferred the originals of such UK covers as the Hollies' 'Just One Look' (Doris Troy), the Spencer Davis Group's 'I Can't Stand It' (The Soul Sisters), Dean Ford and the Gaylords' 'The Name Game' (Shirley Ellis) and the Dave Clark Five and Nashville Teens' 'I Like It Like That' (Chris Kenner).

British beat-group interpretations of soul music did not always go down well in the music press either, and the Stones were not exempt from this on the evidence of the mainly tepid critical reaction after copies of *Out Of Our Heads* washed up round reviewers' typewriters. The most vitriolic assessment was 'samey and boring' by *Disc and Music Echo*, even though, unlike, say, Dean Ford and his boys, the Stones were advantaged by trans-Atlantic travel and interrelated human goldmines such as a yapping New York disc-jockey with the *nom de turntable* Murray the K. The brashest – and possibly the most powerful – of them all, he had had the unmitigated audacity to style himself 'the sixth Rolling Stone' (and, before that, 'the fifth Beatle') – though it was Murray who turned the Stones on to many of the soul tracks they purloined, such as the more obscure 'Oh Baby (We Got A Good Thing Goin')' by Barbara Lynn Ozen, included on *Out Of Our Heads*. The group transformed the slow original into something more danceable, with Brian and Keith's guitars holding their own behind a slightly embittered lead vocal.

Out Of Our Heads was unfinished and its US predecessor *12 X 5* just a week in the shops when the group found themselves among many other weavers of the rich tapestry of mid-1960s pop at Santa Monica Auditorium in late October 1964, participating in the huge Teen-Age Music International (TAMI) show – entitled *Gather No Moss* when screened at the cinema. Allegedly, Mick smoked the entire contents of an apprehensive packet of cigarettes as the group's allotted time approached. His behaviour was not only due to the event being filmed for posterity. It was because he was consigned to be preceded by James Brown, who would be totally justified in the 1970s in bruiting himself as 'the Godfather of Soul'. Watching Brown hurl a hand-mic into the air, swivel round, do the splits, jump upright and catch the mic again in the space of two effortless seconds would have cowed any callow beat-group singer, chart-riding and frantic, waiting in the wings and pondering how long his entrance could be delayed to allow the Brown-enflamed crowd to cool down.

'You had to be the biggest dreamer in the world to think you could export our stuff to America,' agreed a similarly pessimistic Keith Richards[8]. Yet typifying the underlying affability of pop's most optimistic period, James deigned to join the assembled TAMI cast for a finale centred on the Stones, and was to be most courteous when Jagger and Richards were conducted into his backstage presence at the Harlem Apollo which was to Brown as the Craw Daddy had been to his callers. 'They were standing there like scared teenagers,' remembered Ronnie Spector of the Ronettes, 'They introduced themselves. He shook their hands, and that's all there was to it. I don't think James even knew who these weird English guys were, but Mick and Keith were practically shaking.'[23] Later, Brown would insist that he brought Jagger on to the stage and introduced him to the Apollo's black audience; that the Stones 'got over real good'[24] at the Santa Monica spectacular, and that he thought of them as 'brothers'.

Likewise, protest singer-in-transition Bob Dylan hung out with Brian Jones and was pleased to hear that Mick preferred the 'House Of The

Rising Sun' on the first Dylan LP to the Animals' million-selling version. Though it meant sweating a bit over words, the Stones absorbed 'protest' to a more sophisticated and less all-purpose end than other, more opportunistic artists such as Barry McGuire. This was instanced most notably on *Beggars Banquet* in 'Jigsaw Puzzle', 'Street Fighting Man', 'Salt Of The Earth' and 'Sympathy For The Devil'.

Finally, it's only fair to mention that, while Ray Davies, the Kink Komposer, had listened hard to Dylan and those in his direct debt too, he was in the process of forging a new, intrinsically English form of pop music based on a literate, watchful lyricism. The first manifestation of this was 'Well-Respected Man', premiered on *Ready Steady Go!* in 1965, and was to climax commercially with a 1966 Number One in 'Sunny Afternoon' – though the following year's 'Waterloo Sunset' and 1970's 'Lola' each came within an ace of duplicating this feat. If it was beyond the Stones to admit it, they may not have envisaged 'Jigsaw Puzzle', 'Factory Girl' and 'Salt Of The Earth' as viable pop songs without Davies's pioneering accomplishments.

When Keith Richards took the first verse of 'Salt Of The Earth', his reedy, wobbly delivery was, intentionally or not, reminiscent of Davies. It was a back-handed compliment of a kind too that the mesmerically ugly-sounding Dylan, believed Jagger, was 'good but too fashionable to stay as popular as he is'[25]. There had been cause for concern about the Stones' popularity, the most perceptible sign of danger being the failure of *Out Of Our Heads* to top the British LP chart, spending less than half the time in the Top Twenty that *The Rolling Stones* (1964) had. A change of basic tactics was in order, namely a more prolific and higher standard of self-penned numbers to match growing technological confidence.

Dylan was a major source of inspiration. 'Bob showed us all a new approach,' averred Keith Richards, 'new ways of writing songs. He came from a folk tradition, which had much looser possibilities, and he showed you that rock'n'roll didn't have to be quite so restricted by that verse-chorus-verse formula. We all pushed each other in those days.'[8] Like anybody who appreciated lyrical poetry, Richards understood that Dylan was jolting pop's under-used brain into reluctant action. Keith, however, was not then much of a wordsmith himself, preferring to focus on melody, riffs and chord structures. 'It's sound I'm after, not so much a piece of music,' he enlarged, 'Getting ideas for songs is a totally unconscious process.'[26] The Stones' entourage had learned to leave him alone and field all outside interference whenever, as Marianne Faithfull observed, he would 'take the germ of a song and nag at it, all the while keeping himself to himself. He played the guitar constantly. I never saw him without it.'[12]

Under self-imposed economic pressure to compose, Richards did not have the time to be in as thickly with Bob Dylan – who Keith, in perverse mood, was to refer to as 'the prophet of profit'[27] – as Brian Jones became. A foreseeable bond had soon tightened between the blond Stone, who had left Cheltenham Grammar School under the darkest possible cloud, and one who, in 1959 too, had wantonly abandoned his studies at the state university in Minneapolis to take his chances in Greenwich Village, New York's vibrant beatnik district, where the civil rights movement was fusing with folk song to be labelled 'protest'.

As well as downhome intonation, untutored phrasing and eccentric breath control, Dylan had a way peculiar to himself with a mouth-organ and was a fair acoustic guitarist. There had been no complaints either from Jones or the other Stones about the intrinsic content of his first albums, which collectively embraced semi-traditional material as well as impromptu 'talking blues' and more earnest Dylan originals such as 'Blowin' In The Wind', 'Masters Of War', 'A Pawn In Their Game' and similar comments on topical and socio-political matters.

Though they had hailed him at 1963's Newport Folk Festival, many Dylan enthusiasts had been disturbed by the lyrics of 'My Back Pages' and other items on *Another Side Of Bob Dylan* (1964), which seemed to reject earlier profundities as forced and naive, and included a higher percentage

Bob Dylan poses with his obligatory cigarette in hand at a press conference in London in 1963.

of personal statements. He was thought to have 'sold out' altogether on the transitional *Bringing It All Back Home* (1965) with its opening 'Subterranean Homesick Blues', for instance, sung against a rock-group backing and lifting salient points from Chuck Berry's 'Too Much Monkey Business'.

Discernible too was Dylan's captivation with British beat groups and their US imitators who had reciprocated by dipping into his songbook. Off-the-cuff examples are the Animals with 'Baby Let Me Follow You Down' (re-titled 'Baby Let Me Take You Home') and 'House Of The Rising Sun' (another adaptation on Dylan's debut LP), Them ('It's All Over Now Baby Blue') and, most spectacularly, the Byrds, on whose million-selling 'Mr. Tambourine Man' the Pretty Things had had first refusal. Dylan was courted for unreleased compositions such as 'If You Gotta Go, Go Now', a British Number One in 1965 for Manfred Mann (who, Dylan opined, were the most effective interpreters of his songs). The hunt was also up for a British Dylan; the job going initially to a denizen of the folk clubs named Donovan who, with harmonica harness and nasal inflection, began on *Ready Steady Go!* as a more beatific edition of the master.[28]

Dylan was also applauded, crucially, by John Lennon, whose newer songs – especially 'I'm A Loser' from 1964's *Beatles For Sale* – betrayed an absorption of Dylan through constant replay of his albums. The Beatles and the Stones, with respective wives and girlfriends, all attended Dylan's Royal Albert Hall concert, the London stop on his troubled 'electric' visit to Britain in 1966, during which his photograph was taken every time he negotiated the circular door of the Savoy Hotel. 'It was awe-inspiring to see girls screaming and trying to climb into his limo,' remembered 1970s recording artist Dana Gillespie, only a sixteen-year-old fan herself at the time, 'Every night the Stones and Beatles would come to the Savoy to play him their latest recordings. Everyone was in awe of Dylan, and he was the one person the Stones and Beatles had great admiration for. When he held court in one of those hotel rooms, everyone sat and listened.'[29]

Somehow, Dana wormed her way into the charmed circle, as did Donovan and Alan Price, late of the Animals. Furthermore, Dylan was captured on film busking the latest chartbusters by Dave Berry and, sardonically, Herman's Hermits – with whom the Stones had been involved in a dispute over billing prior to a US concert the previous year. 'We think their music is wet and watery,' confided Jagger to a scribbling newshound shortly afterwards[30] – but he would be nowhere as dismissive of the Troggs from the sleepy Hampshire market town of Andover, even after Reg Presley, their lead vocalist, was touted fleetingly as his rustic rival, and their immortal and gloriously dim stop-start thrash 'Wild Thing' all but hurled 'Paint It Black', the Stones' latest, from its perch at Number One in Britain in May 1966.

Jagger was sufficiently gripped by 'Wild Thing' to pop his head round the door to offer advice during the taping of another Troggs chartbuster, but Reg Presley pre-empted – to a degree – the production criteria of *Beggars Banquet*. He also articulated the view of a mid-1960s majority not in complete agreement with the likes of the Stones as the watershed year of 1967 loomed: 'Pop lately has got bogged down with cleverness. We have reverted to an elementary lyric and three elementary chords. "Wild Thing" was like a breath of fresh air to ordinary listeners. Pop music should be progressive, but it shouldn't wander too far ahead of the public.'[31]

Yet, among the reasons that the Beatles downed tools as a working band in 1966 was that their music was becoming harder to perform in concert using conventional beat group instrumentation – though some sections could be approximated by using John Lennon's skills on the Vox Continental electric organ that now travelled alongside the guitars and drums. While the backwards-running coda of the 1966 B-side, 'Rain', was yet to come, for 'Yesterday' from *Help!* (1965), Paul McCartney would sing to solely his own guitar strumming, as there was little to be gained in taking to the road with the string quartet hired for the recording. Money was no object. It was just that the fans had bought tickets for a tribal gathering rather than a musical recital. Had it too been flung into the screams, 'You've Got To Hide Your Love Away', garnished with flutes on the same LP, would have been akin to feeding a pig strawberries.

The flute was a sound more peculiar to West Midlands pop than any other area, employed as it was by the Moody Blues and the Falling Leaves. When Second City pop came belatedly of age, *circa* 1967, Traffic and Tea-And-Symphony would feature flautists too, and after the Hellions had renamed themselves Deep Feeling in 1966, their drummer, John Palmer (later of Family) had transferred to flute – and vibraphone, also yet to be of more-than-negligible significance in a pop context – likewise, the amplified squeeze-box employed by the Amazons, a Birmingham girl group.

In an infinitely higher commercial league than the Amazons – who appeared never to have got as far as making a record – orchestral string instruments fairy-dusted various Jagger-Richards songs for both the Stones and other artists such as Marianne Faithfull, Twice As Much and Chris Farlowe – as well as caressing the Troggs' soft underbelly in 'Any Way That You Want Me' and 'Love Is All Around'. With the opposite effect in mind, horn sections assumed parts that could have been allocated to lead guitar on Manfred Mann's chart-topping 'Pretty Flamingo', The Hollies' 'What Went Wrong', the Pretty Things' 'Death Of A Socialite', the Beatles' 'Got To Get You Into My Life', the Stones' trumpeting 'Have You Seen Your Mother Baby Standing In The Shadow', and The Dave Clark Five's 1967 revival of 'You Got What It Takes'.

On other records by beat groups, more intriguing effects were now being heard, some of them courtesy of talented multi-instrumentalists like Brian Jones, Steve Winwood, Manfred Mann's Mike Vickers, Denis Payton from the Dave Clark Five, Alan Blakely of the Tremeloes – and Graham Bond at ease playing sax and organ simultaneously on *Ready Steady Go!*. Open-minded about new instruments, he was patiently demonstrating, on the same edition, the mellotron – an electro-mechanical keyboard activating tapes of instrument sounds – for compere Cathy McGowan.

Brian Jones was lauded for his weaving of quainter instrumentation into the fabric of 1966's *Aftermath*, such as the marimba on 'Under My Thumb' and 'Out Of Time', dulcimer and harpsichord on Tudor-flavoured 'Lady Jane', and, in unison, dulcimer, bottleneck and twelve-string guitar tuned to a lower octave on 'Mother's Little Helper'. Never again would he work so fully according to his considerable capacities – although, looking on, Keith would notice that 'Brian gradually gave up all interest in the guitar. He just wouldn't touch it – so it was down to me to lay down all the guitar tracks while he would be leaping about on the dulcimer or the marimba.'[32]

The following January, there would be more marimba on 'Yesterday's Papers' as well as flute on 'All Sold Out', the unearthly wails of a theramin on 'Please Go Home', harmonium on 'Who's Been Sleeping Here', trombone on 'Something Happened To Me Yesterday', dulcimer again on 'Backstreet Girl' – to which the talented Brian's Amazonian piano-accordion would also bring a mordant Jacques Brel-esque 'Belgitude'. These tracks appeared on the UK LP *Between The Buttons*, which fell between *Aftermath* (1966) and December 1967's psychedelic *Their Satanic Majesties Request* – on which Brian would be one of the first British pop musicians to investigate the bleeps and flurries of one of these newfangled monophonic Moog synthesizers, which previously could only be hired from US dealers.

As antique a keyboard instrument as the Moog wasn't, Brian's 'Lady Jane' harpsichord had been employed previously either as a gimmick (e.g. Jerry Lee Lewis's 1964 reading of 'Rockin' Pneumonia And The Boogie-Woogie Flu') or to convey an overtly olde-tyme flavour – as on Jimmie Rodgers' 'English Country Garden', a Top Ten hit in 1962. The Yardbirds had succeeded in pushing it further into pop prominence on 1965's 'For Your Love', which came within an ace of topping the charts on both sides of the Atlantic. The Who were to feature bass player John Entwistle's French horn on 'Disguises' and 'I'm A Boy', while the autoharp of

Pinkerton's (Assorted) Colours (and New York's Lovin' Spoonful) had been pre-empted by the Downliners Sect, whose Don Craine had been stroking one on the boards since 1961.

Instances of more out-of-the-ordinary experimentation were the Small Faces filling their bladders when trying to tune a tumbler to A, and peeping a soccer referee's whistle on 'Understanding', one of their B-sides. A potpourri of polyrhythmic percussion supplemented Mick Wilson's drumming on Dave Dee, Dozy, Beaky, Mick and Tich's 'Save Me' as a balalaika did the guitars on 'Okay' – and a bullwhip noise (an empty beer-bottle zoomed down a fretboard as two bits of plywood were smacked together) would punctuate their 'Legend Of Xanadu'. Meanwhile, the hum of a faulty organ would mark 'There's Always Work', a John Mayall instrumental.

As the age of Aquarius crept closer, the most memorable sound that mingled with those of the common-or-garden guitars-bass-drums was that of the sitar, an instrument formerly associated by those who knew what it was with John Renbourn, John Mayer's Indo-Jazz Fusions, Gabor Szabo and, especially, Ravi Shankar, a classical sitarist who, in 1965, recorded an album that his record company released as *Portrait Of Genius* during his seventh world tour as one of India's leading cultural ambassadors until his profile was sharpened by the interest of the Beatles. There would follow, as Ravi himself put it, 'a sitar explosion. All of a sudden, I become [*sic*] superstar'[11].

The deepest breath of the Orient exhaled by the Stones would be courtesy of who else but Brian Jones's masterful sitar *obligato* running through their third British Number One, 'Paint It Black'. Mick Jagger's production of Chris Farlowe's 1967 version of the jazz standard 'Moanin'' had sitar where a busking saxophone might have been – and it would surface again on 'Street Fighting Man', along with the tabla that knocked the C&W bluegrass instrumentation out of true on 'Factory Girl'.

As well as experimenting with previously unlikely instruments, groups were beginning to explore new lyrical avenues. Bob Dylan told Keith Richards to his face that 'I could have written "Satisfaction", but you couldn't have written "Desolation Row".'[33] If nothing else, the latter, approaching the quarter-hour mark as the finale of 1965's *Highway 61 Revisited*, 'released everyone from that whole three minute thing,' noted Keith, 'not to mention making it unnecessary to use sentiments based around "I Want To Hold Your Hand".'[33]

By 1965, Dylan had long stopped going on about war being wrong, fairer shares for all and so on, and was singing about myriad less wistful topics, his rapid-fire literariness revealing greater possibilities beyond boy-meets-girl. Words dominated over melody as he negotiated open verbal surrealism via incongruous connections (e.g. 'Einstein disguised as Robin Hood' in 'Desolation Row' or 'Ma Rainey and Beethoven once unwrapped a bed-roll' in 'Tombstone Blues') and streams of consciousness with sometimes little more than a repeated series of notes to carry it. When the underground periodical *Oz* was launched in Britain, one 1968 edition would feature a mind-boggling word-for-word analysis of Dylan's twelve-minute 'Desolation Row' by an obsessive who, in order to prove one pet theory, had placed an ad in an *Oz*-like outlet in New York for a Dylan urine sample. You would have had some search to find a corresponding Jagger-ologist, but, as the wordsmith in the partnership with Keith then, he concurred with Phil May, his opposite number in the Pretty Things, that 'we couldn't sing about chain-gangs because we'd never been on one. We were trying to get our language on to record, using R&B as a framework and later finding a new direction'.

The previous spring, 'The Last Time', the first Jagger-Richards A-side for the Stones, had been in essence a modest affair with basic boy-girl rhyming couplets – and a chorus borrowed from 'This May Be The Last Time', a traditional song first popularized after a specialist fashion in 1953 by the Five Blind Boys of Mississippi, a black gospel ensemble whose recorded works were purchasable in Dobell's, still patronized by Mick and Keith when they could spare the time. Nonetheless, Keith and Mick have been more inclined to cite the 1962 version by the Staple Singers, another gospel outfit, as the inspirational source.

The Things – or, to be precise, Dick Taylor and Phil May – were still finding their feet as composers when Mick and Keith were congratulating themselves on the huge personal triumph that was 'The Last Time'. Within a year, however, any artistic borrowing by the Stones' songwriting duo on disc only put eyebrows on what were already strong songs that dwelt frequently on unexpected subjects. 'Mother's Little Helper' was an enduring scrutiny of the habit-forming tablets which hasten a frantic housewife's 'busy dying day', while 'Under My Thumb', charged with sexual arrogance and also on *Aftermath*, still appeared in the Stones' concert sets decades later.

There would be much to praise too about Jagger's libretto to *Between The Buttons*. The *NME* noted 'shades of Dylan' pervading 'Who's Been Sleeping Here'[34], and the discerning Frank Zappa thought that the entire album was 'an important piece of social comment at the time'[35]. Yet he may have been astounded by a recording methodology that also appeared slap-dash to the Beach Boys' presiding genius, Brian Wilson, present at the session for 'My Obsession': 'There seemed to be a hell of a party in progress. Tables overflowed with booze, drugs and food. Girls were everywhere.'[36]

While Dylan-esque wordiness was also a prominent component of 'Satisfaction', any infuriating familiarity that it may have had to 'Dancing In The Street', the litigational Chuck Berry's 'Thirty Days' or the Standells' 'Dirty Water' was not as apparent to the other Stones as it was, purportedly, to Keith when the Stones had assembled in May 1965 to tape a so-so 'Satisfaction' at Chess. 'A week later, we recorded it again in Los Angeles,' recalled Keith, 'This time, everything went right.'[37]

It was reported later that Brian Jones hadn't been present on the final session for this key aural artefact of the Swinging Sixties. Certainly, he wasn't on 'My Obsession' and at least two more *Between The Buttons* tracks. Disenfranchised as a composer for the Stones by the near-monopoly of Jagger and Richards, he was channelling much of his creative energy into being the best-looking member of the group. Once, he had adhered to Mod conformity, ordering made-to-measure suits with a discreet correctness to be worn with either a roll-necked nylon pullover or a shirt and tie. By the middle of 1966, however, elegance no longer meant invisibility for Jones. Turning his back on Carnaby Street, no longer an epicentre of menswear for such Mods that still existed anyway, he scoured Portobello Road and Chelsea Antique Market, and made himself resplendent in olde-tyme lace ruffles, frock coats, costume jewellery pinning bandana-like cravats, and trousers that, prior to dyeing, looked as if they had once hung round the legs of an Edwardian sailor. He also took to wearing floppy, wide-brimmed hats that were a little bit *femme*. By contrast, there would be later experiments with dundreary whiskers and, briefly, a beard. He was thus ahead of fashion and even the very boutiques he visited, notably one soon to be renamed I Was Lord Kitchener's Valet – which thrived on a craze later in 1966 for Victorian military uniforms – and the likes of Hung On You, Granny Takes A Trip and like establishments that sprang up in London and the bigger cities, peddling art nouveau variants on old-tyme garb, and imported Oriental exotica.

Jones was also as narcissistic as any Regency dandy, treating his appearance as a work of theatrical art, made afresh before he faced each day. To what degree may be discerned in remarks made by Bobbie Korner, wife of Alexis, after she saw Brian 'in that period of dressing up in eighteenth-century clothes. We went to a concert, and Brian came into a box above us, and I looked at him and thought, "My God, he's gone. That isn't someone dressing up, it's someone who has disappeared."'[38] The impact, however, was to spread over the decades. Just as the widest river can be traced to many converging trickles, so a source of glam-rock, New Romantic, Gothic and beyond must lie with Brian Jones.

An emotional disaster area, Brian was staying his personal and vocational phantoms too through a drug more sinister than either the amphetamines that wired him up for the show or the marijuana 'spliff' to unwind tense coils within afterwards. With Keith Richards, he first tried lysergic acid diethylamide 25 – LSD – in December 1965.

Satirical comedy duo Peter Cook and Dudley Moore had maximized their small-screen popularity by taking pot-shots at the Top Fifty, most recently with the spoof 'LS Bumble Bee', a single that was indicative of a general knowledge, if not use, of LSD, which had been part of the anything-goes spirit of Swinging London for about a year before it was outlawed for recreational purposes in 1966. It had already launched Brian Jones and Keith Richards on a psychic – or 'psychedelic' – voyage that was to carry them further from beat music than any consumer of 'Come On' could have foreseen.

By comparison, Mick Jagger – as befitted the son of a physical fitness instructor – had had little to do with narcotics of any description. He had hesitated before sampling marijuana for the first time, allegedly, in a cigarette rolled by Paul McCartney at the Beatle's house in St John's Wood. Nevertheless, once Jagger got round to LSD too, he was loud in its defence as a means to self-discovery: 'You see everything aglow. You see yourself beautiful and ugly, and other people as if for the first time. You should take it in the country, surrounded by all those flowers. You'd have no bad effects. It's only people who hate themselves that suffer.'[40]

The Pretty Things too knew 'acid' well on the evidence of song titles like 'Trippin'' and just plain 'LSD'. Dick Taylor remembered that 'The guys above my flat in Fulham were students who organized these lock-out nights – "raves" you'd call them now – at the Marquee when acid was legal. Personally, I was extremely wary of it.'

'I had a good time on LSD,' countered Phil May, 'but other people had problems. In Germany, our lighting guy did the lights for the act that went on before us, thinking it was us.'

Known in the Middle Ages as 'St Anthony's Fire', LSD's paranormal sensations and surreal perceptions vary from person to person, from trip to trip. One psyche might boggle with nonsensical frenzy. For another, it could be akin to an extreme religious reverie or the start of a fantastic voyage to untold heights of creativity. Too often for Brian Jones, he would surface from a quagmire of horror. 'Brian never recovered from his first trip,' thought Marianne Faithfull, 'Acid and pills only worsened his condition and compounded his paranoia into a full-blown persecution mania – but he embraced his horrors as if on acid he was able finally to confront his afflictions in a palpable form.'[12]

Marianne and others of Brian's friends began hearing less about his attempts at composing verse-chorus pop. His music had always been stronger than his songs – if they existed – in any case. In an electronic den at his Chelsea studio flat, he was more inclined to potter about with pieces of intellectual rather than aesthetic intent. Scant of lyric or concise melody, these had less to do with '(I Can't Get No) Satisfaction' than the pioneering tonalities of Varese, Stockhausen and Cage, now as likely as anything from the Top Forty to blast from the car stereo of the self-improving rock musician. While spending 'an extremely pleasant evening' *chez* Jones that autumn, Keith Altham of the *NME* found his host 'enthusiastic, but embarrassed by his efforts. One tape was astoundingly effective with a weird, psalm-like chant going on in the background like an electrified Black Mass. Some further electronic experimentation sounded like the Who after a few drinks.'[41]

Expressions such as 'cross-fade', 'white noise', 'tape loop' and 'square wave' pocked conversations with Dave Thomson, a film student Brian had met at Glasgow's Odeon Theatre during the Stones' last UK tour. They were collaborating on a screenplay for an 'experimental' film that was no more 'about' anything than any you might see in installations at final exhibitions for Fine Art degrees at your local university. It is not known whether the Jones-Thomson liaison was either vaguely, if mostly head-scratchingly, entertaining or an antidote to pleasure on the principle that the more arduous the effort needed to appreciate it, the more 'artistic' it is. There are doubts about whether the film was even started, as Brian's butterfly concentration alighted on another project. What is more, he stuck with the new venture long enough to bring it to fruition.

After actor Anita Pallenberg, his current paramour, had landed a leading role in a German film, *Mord Und Totschlag* (US title: 'Degree Of Murder'), late in 1966, Brian – motivated perhaps by jealous imaginings – had materialized whenever possible on set in Munich, watching her act on a monitor screen, and monopolizing her attention during the lengthy intervals as cumbersome movie-cameras were repositioned. His omnipresence entered discussions by the film's backers, aware of both its budget and the publicity value of a Rolling Stone's involvement. Recently, work of this kind had fallen into George Harrison's lap too – for an oddity of a cinema film called *Wonderwall* (1968). His incidental music was the saving grace of a movie graphically condemned as 'a right load of codswallop'[42] – but, regardless of its quality, the words 'George Harrison' in the credits guaranteed it attention.

With this kind of consideration in mind, Volker Schlondorff, the twenty-seven-year-old director of *Mord Und Totschlag* (1967), was elected to sound out Jones about composing the soundtrack. If flattered, Brian confessed that he had no idea how to go about it, but rather than turning away from the task, he decided to muddle on with it, learning what he could *in situ* and unwittingly dismissing many ingrained preconceptions and introducing new ones. As if it was the most natural thing in the world, he was 'spotting' each sequence with a stop-watch, and flying back to London to routine it in his new Chelsea apartment – along upmarket Courtfield Road – before repairing to a professional studio – Olympic Sound in South West London – to supervise the taping of music that was impressive in its own right, regardless of imagined visuals. Within its tight strictures, it was to testify to the presence of more intrinsic virtues than had been expected of one in an industry where sales figures are arbiters of success.

With a Deutschmark sign over every note, Brian himself attended to sitar, organ, dulcimer, banjo, harmonica and autoharp, but he also called the shots to a small ensemble hand-picked by himself and longtime Stones studio engineer Glyn Johns, among them guitarist Jimmy Page, now a Yardbird, session pianist and ex-Screaming Lord Sutch Savage Nicky Hopkins, who would make his own unique contribution to *Beggars Banquet,* and vocalist Peter Gosling of Moon's Train, a group co-produced by Bill Wyman. Their blithe dedication to the job in hand was refreshing, and they enjoyed being under Brian's surprisingly straightforward baton as, rather than sinking morbidly surreal teeth into *Mord Und Totschlag* and exploring an abstract unknown that needed to be explained rather than scored, he delved into C&W, blues, soul and what might be described as 'country-and-eastern' – though the lightweight main title theme was reprised in wracked, menacing fashion in keeping with the illicit burial of a corpse on the construction site of an autobahn. Elsewhere, a serene if subdued ghostliness vied with severe dissonance, but little was designed to divert attention from the action – which was precisely what Volker Schlondorff required: 'It wasn't just that his music was special. It was that the score was so spontaneous and vital. Only Brian could have done it. He had a tremendous feeling for the lyrical parts, and knew perfectly the recording and mixing techniques to achieve the best sound.'[43]

To Brian's chagrin, *Mord Und Totschlag* wouldn't be subtitled or dubbed and put on circulation in Britain. Neither was its soundtrack to be issued on vinyl. Therefore, while quite free with his views on the Vietnam war, persecution of homosexuals, the new Abortion Act, drugs and religion, he did not touch on *Mord Und Totschlag* – and neither did Keith Altham mention it – when they met again in a Kensington pub not long after the New Year of 1967 got under way.

Keith Richards was hovering on the edge of this interview, as he had when Altham had visited Brian's apartment in October. It might not have been connected, but he had been round Brian a lot since the advent of Anita.

When recovering from the profound upset of Keith stealing Anita from him a few months later, Brian's rise from half-death became perceivable when he was spotted with John Lennon absorbing a Fourteen Hour Technicolor Dream at Alexandra Palace where the effects of LSD were emulated via the contrast of flickering strobes and ectoplasmic *son et lumière* projections on the cavernous walls as bands played on and on and on. One after another, they 'did their thing' on platforms erected at either end of the exhibition centre. As well as old pals like Alexis Korner, the Pretty Things and Graham Bond – some garbed in expedient kaftans, beads and like flower-power tat – the extravaganza featured the very top drawer of British psychedelic pop – the Pink Floyd, Tomorrow, the Move, the Soft Machine and the Crazy World of Arthur Brown. Jones was most impressed by the Move, whose singer, Carl Wayne, charged on stage with an axe to hack up effigies of notable world figures before turning his attention to imploding televisions. 'They are really an extension of the Stones' idea of smashing conventions,' he had remarked to Keith Altham, 'Destroying TV sets *et cetera* is all part of dissatisfaction with convention.'[39]

While Brian dug the Move, of all the new acts at large in London in 1967, he was particularly captivated by the Jimi Hendrix Experience, a trio built round a psychedelic Wild Man of Borneo, who was frightening every guitarist in the audience with the scope and vision of his playing – with drummer Mitch Mitchell and, on bass, Noel Redding keeping nimble pace. Dick Taylor remembered 'chatting to Jimi in some crowded dressing room as he tinkered on his Stratocaster – and I kept losing the thread of the conversation because he was just as amazing musically on an unamplified electric guitar as he was with one plugged into a 200 watt stack.'

Jeff Beck was to confess that he 'just hadn't the guts to come out and do it so flamboyantly'[44], and every other lead guitarist across the UK pop spectrum – Taylor, Dave Davies, Pete Townshend, Eric Clapton among them – was stunned by the newcomer's display of eclecticism and

Brian Jones swaps the stage for audience participation at the Monterey Pop Festival in 1967.

unpredictability in compatible amounts. Of no less import was an opinion given by a stranger who sidled up to Paul McCartney at an Experience bash and, pointing towards Hendrix, muttered, 'You ought to get a bloke like that in your band, mate.'

Townshend, Clapton and Brian Jones reportedly went to every Jimi Hendrix Experience engagement in the capital prior to the trio's first assault on North America. So forceful was the publicity build-up that the Experience headlined over a bill covering a spectrum from Ravi Shankar to the Who to local-boys-made-good, the Grateful Dead, during the International Pop Music Festival in Monterey, some miles down the coast from the flower-power city of San Francisco, now as vital a pop Mecca as Liverpool had been.

'Things weren't coming in half-measures,' ruminated Noel Redding, 'I was flying first class to New York, seated next to Brian Jones, who had taken me under his wing.'[45] With Eric Burdon, another passenger en route to Monterey, Jones underwent an LSD trip of such length and piquancy that, grinned Burdon, 'by the time we'd got to our hotel, Brian and I were about ten feet off the ground. After checking in, we managed to make it to the elevator – but neither of us made it out. We rode up and down for hours, laughing hysterically at each passenger who was unlucky enough to come through the doors and ride with us.'[15]

With the party on the internal flight was Christa Paffgren, known to the pop world as 'Nico', who, following a part in 1966's *Chelsea Girls*, Andy Warhol's most enduring movie, had been prominent in his mixed-media 'Exploding Plastic Inevitable' troupe as an adjunct to the Velvet Underground. This group's perspectives on seedy-flash New York life had taken tangible form as literary-musical wit on a sensational debut LP that appealed to Brian Jones – as well as Keith and Mick – for its unprecedented coverage of drug addiction, sexual taboos and mental instability. Jagger later claimed that some of the material on *Beggars Banquet*, in particular 'Stray Cat Blues', had been influenced by this.

If the Velvet Underground hadn't yet pressed their hardest on how far they could go, Jimi Hendrix's act was as staggering as it would ever be when, introduced at Monterey by Brian as 'the most exciting performer I've ever heard', he streamlined all the outrages that were old hat back in London: jack-knifing into the air, practising fresh air cunnilingus, gnawing his guitar strings, collapsing to his knees and, during the 'Wild Thing' finale, sacrificing his instrument in a pitiless *woomph* of lighter fuel.

Jimi was to find that moment during his first few weeks in England, and was present when the group was finishing 'Ruby Tuesday'. It and Hendrix's 'Hey Joe' – and the latest by the Move, Cream and the Who – would be nestling uneasily in the Top Twenty among slushy ballads peddled by the likes of Engelbert Humperdinck, Petula Clark and Des O' Connor, thus demonstrating that the opposite of a prevailing trend is always represented to some extent – but what *was* the prevailing trend? Paradoxically, the watershed year of 1967 was as much a boom year for schmaltz as psychedelia.

It also cradled a shift in the parameters of pop with regard to albums – to which, as trade figures were to signify, record labels would be committing more of their time and money. The long-player had hitherto been regarded, more often than not, as a testament to market pragmatism rather than quality – usually, a throwaway patchwork of tracks, a hit 45 and its B-side. The new attitude had been heralded when groups that carried any weight began operating ambiguously with relatively avant-garde fancies on LPs and, under pressure, trying for the singles charts with the most trite or mainstream tracks – as did the Pretty Things with 'Private Sorrow' from *SF Sorrow* (1968), unquestionably the first 'rock opera' (if, technically, a song-cycle). 'What we were after,' elucidated Phil May, 'was an album that was one piece. That's why it had a story – the only way we could give it continuity.'

Britain at large remained deaf to *SF Sorrow*, and its US release was delayed for nearly two years, prompting unfair accusations of plagiarism and jumping on the rock opera bandwagon. Pete Townshend was supposed to have had *SF Sorrow* on instant replay for nearly a week before getting to grips with *Tommy*. Moreover, it was not *SF Sorrow*, but the Beatles' more expensive and syncretic *Sgt. Pepper's Lonely Hearts Club Band* (1967) that set the precedent for record companies underwriting further such *magnum opi*; Pye, say, with the *Arthur* (1969) rock opera from the Kinks, Track with the Who's *Tommy* (1969), Immediate with *Ogden's Nut Gone Flake* (1968) by the Small Faces, and Decca entering the arena with John Mayall's *Bare Wires* (1968) – and the Rolling Stones' *Their Satanic Majesties Request*.

Aswarm with often jarring vignettes of music, *Satanic Majesties* hinted that its principal composers were under the influence of the mind-boggling drug that was causing some of its celebrity advocates to seem a bit gaga in interviews. Marianne Faithfull and George Harrison, for instance, were two who would talk openly about their LSD escapades, acknowledging no difference between the 'straight' press and 'underground' organs like the fortnightly *International Times*. George would mention the 'magic eyes'[46] in the beads of his necklace or the grasshopper that only he could see jumping out of a speaker cabinet. Sofa-ed on a television chat-show, Marianne shot her mouth off about acid being more important than Christianity.

'It was a very druggy period,' frowned Charlie Watts, 'though not for me. I was never into drugs much at that time.'[47] He had known all about marijuana since his days as an art student, but LSD was on another narcotic plateau. He was 'terrified of the stuff. The psychedelic thing really messed a lot of people up, but it made people really talk to each other too.' In retrospect, he seemed to mourn not trying it just once for a possible glimpse, however chemically induced, at the eternal: 'maybe I'd have been a better person if I'd gone through all that'[48]. Or maybe not. Bill Wyman didn't touch LSD either – though the venture to the interior that was 'In Another Land' – original title: 'Acid In The Grass' – one of but two compositions penned solely by Bill that would ever appear on a Stones disc, may be seen – erroneously – as contradicting this.

'In Another Land' was to be track three, side one of the Stones' most nakedly psychedelic LP, started during the summer weeks prior to the best-known drugs trial in pop, the result of police invading Keith Richards' country house near Chichester in February 1967 and uncovering enough 'substances' to secure jail sentences for its owner and a visiting Mick Jagger, albeit followed by dismissal on appeal within a week. Brian Jones would be awaiting trial in October for similar offences. 'It gave the Stones this image of being like a real bunch of dope fiends,' Jagger would snigger twenty years later[49].

Another relevant sign of the times was Mick Jagger thumbing through hardbacks of mystical, religious and fashionably aerie-faerie nature – *Autobiography Of A Yogi, The Golden Bough,* Tolkien et al. via the account that everybody who was anybody had at the Indica bookshop off Piccadilly. His clear expositions in private conversation, if not interviews, of karma, the transmigration of souls and the world of illusion was evidence of more than cursory poring over these tomes – and it was no surprise that his name cropped up in an item of news that dominated front pages in the sillier newspapers during 1967's August Bank Holiday. At a university faculty in the seaside resort of Bangor, the Beatles and their immediate entourage were to undergo a ten-day induction course in transcendental meditation under the tutorage of an Indian guru, the Maharishi Mahesh Yogi. It was scheduled to last nearly a fortnight. While packing, the Fab Four telephoned others who might want to go.

So it was that Jagger and Marianne Faithfull would be cramming into the same compartment as the Beatles and this Maharishi character on what had been dubbed the 'Mystical Express' from Euston to North Wales. Not sure whether the Maharishi was a charlatan or seer, Jagger, waylaid by a bellowed question from the crush of fans and media at the station, had dismissed the outing straightaway as 'more like a circus than the beginning of an original event'[50]. In the event, the would-be meditators' stays were curtailed after two days by the sudden death of Beatles manager Brian Epstein in a Swinging London that was now a storm-centre of flower-power.

This was epitomized by *the* West End musical of the season, *Hair*, imported from New York and destined to run for eleven years. While the fundamental plot centred on a youth eligible for induction into the US army, it also delved into aspects of hippy culture: the tabloids making much of the nakedness which closed the first half, as well as the extremity of improvisation and audience participation. Fortunately, *Hair* was blessed with memorable songs that were to infiltrate eventually the realms of jazz and Las Vegas cabaret. More immediate, however, was a rash of cover versions such as 'Aquarius' by both Paul Jones and, in German, Spencer Davis. From the cast, Sonja Kristina, Paul Nicholas and Alex Harvey were all to crack the domestic charts, one way or another, and so – just – was Marsha Hunt, a singing actor with a shock of fuzzy black hair, who was to have a pronounced and lasting bearing on Mick Jagger's life.

Just as Marsha was to emerge as the character most illustrative of *Hair* – as demonstrated by the full-colour double-page head-and-shoulders portrait of her in *Disc* one October week – so Jagger was to be the central figure on *Satanic Majesties trompe l'oeil* front cover as well as chief advocate of the musical content. Inasmuch as the Stones' 'We Love You'/ 'Dandelion', a riposte to the outcome of the drugs busts, was a 'concept' single – with a segment of the former serving as coda for the latter – the LP issued in December was, theoretically, a continuous 'work' like *SF Sorrow*, with little or no spaces between tracks, containing segues; a reprise of the opening song, leitmotifs, interlocking themes and the vague sustaining of a recurring mood that was far more reaching than simply stringing together a bunch of songs about, for example, hot-rod cars (as the Beach Boys had in 1963). With retrospective honesty, nevertheless, Keith Richards thought that 'basically, *Satanic Majesties* was a load of crap. It was really almost done semi-comatose, sort of "Do we really have to make an album?"'[8]

How could he criticize an item of merchandise that, like the latest from the Beatles, was assured of a gold disc before its conception, let alone its release. The Stones and Beatles were a mutual admiration society most of the time, and so it had not been surprising that Lennon and McCartney had been pleased to lend their voices on 'Sing This All Together', an admittedly desperate attempt at a ditty as catchy as the Beatles' flower-power singalong 'All You Need Is Love', on which Jagger and Richards were heard. Elsewhere, church organ and a funereal bell – *dungggggg* – began 'The Lantern', some tired business that, completed at the beginning of August, seemed to pre-empt what the Maharishi would be prosing about at Bangor four weeks later. However, the lyrics of *Satanic Majesties* 'Gomper' reveal Jagger's then-current digestion of tomes from the arty Indica shop. Brian Jones too had started to devour much the same literature. Such books looked well on the shelves in his flat, a veritable witches' coven of decadent illuminati, rock princelings and hip nobility. As one Jagger-Richards A-side followed another, if Jones couldn't be the most dominant Stone, he was going to be, as well as the most beautiful-looking one, the most mystical. Mention of him as he was then still brings out stories of what visitors claim they saw and heard. One was that Brian needed but the slightest excuse to play them a tape of his *Mord Und Totschlag* music.

Yet, though everyone agreed that Brian had acquitted himself admirably and innovatively as a provider of music for foreign celluloid, Brian's income still depended on the daytime mundanities of Rolling Stones record sales, especially after the group gave unknowingly its last stage appearance for over two years at a *New Musical Express* poll-winners concert on 17 April 1967. Moreover, for all Mick and Keith's *Satanic Majesties* explorations in song, and Brian's *Mord Und Totschlag* cleverness, they remained bluesmen at heart, a preference that was to align with the decade's second wave of mass interest in electric blues as interpreted – frequently in the most ham-fisted fashion – by white British and US groups.

Always hovering in the background of blues music, phantasmagoria had been infiltrating Richards' – and Jagger's – musical vocabulary since they first listened to Robert Johnson's 'Hellhound On My Trail' and 'Me And The Devil Blues', plus like ditties from the spectrum of black music, whether Peetie Wheatstraw or rock'n'roll clown Screamin' Jay Hawkins, who directed his road crew to drop handfuls of rubber bands from the gallery and stage-whisper 'Worms!' during an act which began with his sulphurous and pedantic emergence from a coffin, bathed in eerie fluorescence. Garbed in, perhaps, turban, zebra-striped formal attire and pink cloak, Hawkins would produce props like a cigarette-puffing skull mounted on a stick and an array of powdery potions, and his singing would flit fitfully from warbling mock-operatics, half-spoken recitative, insane falsetto shrieks, low grumbles and the raucous, blood-chilling dementia of someone in the throes of a fit. A handful of those watching would remember a shy chap from Cleveland, Ohio with a warm baritone not unlike that of Nat 'King' Cole, just as folk who had gone to the Ealing club would an LSE student's restrained blues interpretations that preceded the vocal extremities that followed.

After thankless years of one-nighters and flop records, Hawkins had struck US 'sepia' chart gold with 1958's 'I Put A Spell On You'. With the best of intentions, he had bustled into the studio with a light, romantic ballad. The session was not going particularly well, and some liquor was purchased to loosen up proceedings. Several takes later, the song had mutated into the manic, goggle-eyed exorcism of a man so drunk that he was recording flat on his back. Refining his cartoon scariness, Hawkins reworked the formula with the likes of 'The Whammy', 'Feast Of The Mau-Mau' and 'Little Demon' on disc, and, if none made the same impact as 'I Put A Spell On You', he became a treasure of classic rock, though the subtleties that suited the intimacy of theatre or club were wasted on a mob impatient for the main attraction when he opened for the Stones for two nights at Madison Square Garden in November 1981.

Hawkins was a master of his art, but not its only practitioner. The earliest British example was Screaming Lord Sutch, a familiar of the

Stones since before the Craw Daddy/Studio 51 era. The most famous British pop star who never had a hit, Such was the leader of the Savages, whose original drummer was Carlo Little, who also served the Cyril Davies All-Stars, and was the most prominent of Charlie Watts's predecessors with the Stones. David Sutch's apparent suicide in 1999 put a full-stop to what was, in its own terms, a triumphant professional career as an entertainer (and political leader). However, in the context of this discussion, he is important not only for his precedents of outrage – exemplified by pre-Rolling Stones long hair – but also for his nurturing of the talents of individuals that loom large in the Stones' legend, notably Little and Hopkins.

Borrowing most insidiously from Sutch, the Crazy World of Arthur Brown captured the Stones' imagination – Jagger's in particular – as *Beggars Banquet* crept closer. Brown's group came into being circa 1967 when philosophy graduate and cosmic ham Arthur teamed up with organist Vincent Crane and a drummer with the technicolour name of Drachen Theaker. The toast of London's psychedelic dungeons, the act was as good as it would get when the Crazy World 'went public' on gaining a recording contract. Robed and sporting a helmet spouting flames (originally a candlestick attached to a sieve), Brown had the vocal arsenal of a Screamin' Jay Hawkins at his behest as he cavorted and stared psychotically while Crane bucked and lunged at the keyboards, and Theaker was overly busy at his kit. The group kowtowed to prevailing trends on their first single with the droll 'Give Him A Flower' but its A-side, 'Devil's Grip', was a truer reflection of the Brown dialectic with its lyrical update of 'The Whammy'. After this created a stir, The Crazy World of Arthur Brown went for the jugular with 'Fire' – how Arthur as 'god of hellfire' will 'destroy all you've done' – a *tour de force* that was their only hit, before a troubled US tour finished with the resignations of Theaker and Crane, and with Arthur and Vincent as joint composers of 'Fire' being sued for plagiarism by another songwriting pair. Yet, the abiding memory of Brown in all his glory as the self-proclaimed 'God of

Hellfire' left its mark on both Mick Jagger's vocal style and a *Beggars Banquet*-associated promo film for which the Stones slapped on warpaint.

At least a twig on the 'family tree' of further influences of this kidney was Dr John the Night Tripper, whose voodoo circus traversed North America and beyond with reverberant zombie wails, sibilant lead vocals, throbbing murk and choreographed Creole psychedelia, jittery with timbales and wordless choral passages. Then Dr John would vanish back to the Louisiana swamps — and his alter-ego Mac Rebennack to studio employment in Los Angeles. That his image was not entirely contrived became evident when, on meeting New Orleans-born Rebennack socially, many would be charmed by his linguistic gymnastics, a mixture of English, Cajun and rhyming mumbo-jumbo. On a 'Desert Island Discs'-type outing on BBC Radio One, Mick Jagger chose 'Gris-Gris Gumbo Ya Ya', a track from the Doctor's 1968 debut album, *Gris-Gris*; Marsha Hunt — with whom Jagger had an affair — was to harry the lower half of 1969's Top Fifty with a further *Gris-Gris* excerpt, 'Walk On Gilded Splinters', and Mick himself contributed vocals to another Dr John LP, *The Sun, The Moon And The Herbs*.

Of note too is 'The Supernatural', an instrumental from John Mayall's Bluesbreakers, showcasing the sustained, resonant fretboard shivers of Peter Green, and 1965's 'From The Bottom Of My Heart', the most exquisite record ever made by any incarnation of the Moody Blues from its ominous piano introduction to a wailing coda that would have served as incidental music for a Hammer House of Horror movie. Then there was Frank Zappa's Mothers of Invention — whose fans included Mick Jagger — closing their 1966 debut album, *Freak Out,* with twelve minutes of 'The Return Of The Son Of Monster Magnet', an 'unfinished ballet in two tableaux'.

The late 1960s fad for diabolism in rock picked up speed with yet-unsigned UK outfits like Black Sabbath with their inverted crosses and Satanic fetishist gear, and Black Widow, whose onstage 'sacrifice' of a naked woman during an audience participation number, 'Come To The Sabbat' ensured healthy attendances at their engagements as well as a public warning from noted white witch Alex Saunders about meddling with dark forces.

Perusing *Melody Maker* as a stockbroker would the *Financial Times*, Mick Jagger would remark, 'There's a big following for these hocus-pocus bands, so obviously the subject has a vast commercial potential.'[49] He seemed also to be supportive of less superficially spiritual changes afoot circa 1968. He appeared, for instance, on the cover of *The Process*, mouthpiece of the Church Of The Final Judgement, a magazine that, like *Oz*, was going the rounds of college and sixth form common rooms. However, Marianne Faithfull – who had articulated her perspective in an issue dedicated to 'Death' – regarded her now on-off boyfriend as 'far too sensible and normal ever to have become seriously involved in

Recording takes its toll: Mick Jagger and Keith Richards in 1967.

black magic.'[12] Either way, there is an underlying darkness to *Beggars Banquet*, most prominent in 'Sympathy for the Devil', that may draw on dabblings in black magic as well as the more sinister side of blues and rock'n'roll music.

Jagger and the Stones, however, had not quite shaken off being Nice Lads When You Get To Know Them – a tag foisted on every pop outrage from Johnnie Ray to Queens Of The Stone Age – and they were not so far above the adoration of schoolgirls to not have have recent photographs available on request for *Boyfriend*, *Rave!*, *Fabulous 208*, et al.

The latter gazette seemed to be reflecting teenage interest in rugged cowboy types like Doug McClure in *The Virginian* on BBC 1 as much as, say, pretty Peter Frampton of the Herd, the soon-to-cease *Rave!*'s 'Face Of '68'. In more serious-minded journals pitched at youth, there was a divide too – between vulgar 'pop', and 'rock', which only the finest minds could grasp, and which was being shepherded away from psychedelic contrivance by, among others, a certain Ingram Cecil Connor III, with whom Keith Richards was keeping company. He was the 'preppy' scion of a Florida orange-merchandising dynasty, albeit one blighted by his father's suicide, his mother's alcoholism and his sister's commitment to a mental institution. Moreover, though he won a scholarship to study theology at Harvard, Ingram did not graduate, preferring to take his chances as an all-round C&W musician, using the stage alias 'Gram Parsons'. His influence is discernible in the country feel that characterizes certain tracks on the Stones albums of the late 1960s and early 1970s.

In 1968, as a member of the Byrds, he was the prime mover behind their stylistic transition from the jingle-jangling 'acid-folk' of 'Mr. Tambourine Man' et al. to the yee-hah, boots-and-saddles exuberance of 1968's *Sweetheart Of The Rodeo*, an album pre-empted vaguely by *John Wesley Harding* (1968), Bob Dylan's plain-and-simple new morning, recorded in Nashville. As austere and understated, if not as lyrically direct, was *Music From Big Pink* (1968) by Dylan's backing Band – formerly the

Hawks. Named after their communal pink-painted house not far from Dylan's own rural retreat in upstate New York, this LP was a True West blend of electric folklore that had been nurtured over years in hick Canadian dance halls with Ronnie Hawkins.

More bona fide 'ethnic' music was in – and on – the air too in 1968. On Radio One, the late John Peel, for ever the station's most cutting-edge presenter, had moved from inserting twenty-minute Indian ragas between progressive fare on his *Night Ride* programme to bowing to frequent requests for 'that boot-slapping thing' (Zulu step-dancing), 'the Russian with the funny voice' (a singer from Azerbaijan, USSR) and further curiosities that he had picked from Broadcasting House's sound archives. A national pop station filling off-peak ether with nose-flutes, Romanian *cobzas* and further outlandish examples of what would later be termed 'world music' had been unthinkable three years earlier when Brian Jones's sitar had lacquered 'Paint It Black'.

The Womad festival that used to swell the population of Reading for summer weekends from 1982 until it was moved to Wiltshire in 2007, epitomized the continued impact of 'world music'. Although English remains the predominant language of pop, it's more feasible than ever before for both the US Hot 100 and what is left of the British charts to be infiltrated by acts from Iceland, France, Senegal, Spain, Japan, you name it – and among the first creaks of a door that would open wider on this treasury had been Brian Jones's musical safaris in Morocco in 1968. It had been during a week's holiday with Anita Pallenberg two years earlier that the rhythm of the sun-scorched life there had got under Jones's skin. When benighted in a settlement of the Joujouka, part of a nomadic tribe of the Rif foothills, he had become engrossed by ancient music played around the oil lamps and hookahs by the G'naou, an ensemble of hand-drummers and exponents of the high-pitched *rhaita* pan pipes – which, it was said, could only be blown by a true Joujouka. Sent into a sonic reverie by the experience, Brian understood then why the natives revered their music as a force of, and inseparable from, nature.

In spring 1968, Brian took less a vacation than a field trip – with regular Stones studio engineer Glyn Johns along for the technological donkey work – which produced a net result of some tapes of the G'naou for purposes that were non-specific – though Brian would speak of grafting on backing tracks by those New York session players most capable of dissolving outlines between jazz and rock. His most fruitful expedition took place in August when George Chkiantz, another Stones console technician, flew over at short notice to assist in the recording of highlights from the week-long Rites of Pan festival. 'When Brian was in the mountains, he was splendid,' said George, 'He was attentive, and a great, considerate host.'[16] He was also an honoured guest of the tribesfolk. Indeed, if not quite Spanish adventurer Francisco Pizarro amongst the Incas, the descent of a robed and golden-haired alien into their Joujouka midst left a legacy in 'Brahim Jones', a ditty sung still by children of the village. Translated, the third of its five lines runs:

'He recorded our music for the entire world to hear.'

Between five and ten hours of Joujouka material was taken back to London for editing down to album length. Thrusting aside the G'naou notion of adding Western accompaniment, 'it was decided to retain the original music,' explained Chkiantz, 'but also lend it a new dimension in the studio in order to make it an expression of the journey.'[16] Yet, though phasing and other studio effects were to pervade side one of 1970's posthumously-released *Brian Jones Presents The Pipes Of Pan At Joujouka*, 'The 4,000 Year Old Rock & Roll Band'[51] was heard *au naturel* on side two.

For those compelled to buy everything on which the Rolling Stones ever breathed, *The Pipes Of Pan At Joujouka* required effort. It was not remotely in the realms of pop, but some listened again – and again, and again – until it reached out and held them for ever.

NOTES

1. *Rolling Stone*, August 1971

2. *Blues Fell This Morning* by P. Oliver (Cassell, 1960)

3. *The History Of Rock*, vol. 1, no. 5 (Orbis, 1982)

4. *Beat Merchants* by A. Clayson (Blandford, 1995)

5. Entitled 'I Need You Baby' on some pressings.

6. *Q*, November 1992

7. *The Guardian*, 5 September 2003

8. *Keith Richards In His Own Words* eds. M. St Michael (Omnibus, 1994)

9. *Death Discs* by A. Clayson (Sanctuary, 1997)

10. *Streets Of London: The Official Biography Of Ralph McTell* by C. Hockenhull (Northdown, 1997)

11. *Experimental Pop* by B. Bergman and R. Horn (Blandford, 1985)

12. *Faithfull* by M. Faithfull and D. Dalton (Penguin, 1995)

13. *The Guardian*, 14 October 2005

14. *Jeff Beck: Crazy Fingers* by A. Carson (Carson, 1998)

15. *Don't Let Me Be Misunderstood* by E. Burdon and J. Marshall Craig (Thunder's Mouth, 2001)

16. *Record Collector*, July 1989

17. Pamphlet quoted in *The Story Of The Blues* by P. Oliver (Penguin, 1969)

18. *Best Of Guitar Player*, Rolling Stones special, December 1993

19. And were nothing to do with the late 1980s pop group of the same name.

20. *New Musical Express*, 12 February 1966

21. On posters for his appearance at Redhill Market Hall on 30 January 1964.

22. In reciprocation, Redding had the gall to overhaul their 'Satisfaction' as a single within weeks of it being the first of many US Number Ones for the group.

23. *Be My Baby* by R. Spector and V. Waldro (Pan, 1991)

24. *James Brown* by J. Brown and B. Tucker
    (Sidgwick & Jackson, 1987)

25. *Melody Maker,* 12 February 1966

26. *Daily Mail*, 19 July 1990

27. *Down The Highway* by H. Sounes (Doubleday, 2001)

28. Donovan was to marry Linda Lawrence, the mother of one
    of Brian Jones's children.

29. Dana Gillespie in interview with Spencer Leigh.

30. *Stone Alone* by B. Wyman and R. Coleman (Viking, 1990)

31. *Rock's Wild Things* by A. Clayson and J. Ryan
    (Helter Skelter, 2000)

32. *Rolling Stones '76* ed. M. Farren (Cumbergrove, 1976)

33. *The Rolling Stone Interviews Volume One* ed. J. Wenner
    (Straight Arrow, 1971)

34. *New Musical Express*, 14 January 1967

35. *Zigzag*, May 1973

36. *Wouldn't It Be Nice* by B. Wilson and T. Gold
    (Bloomsbury, 1991)

37. *New Musical Express*, 3 September 1965

38. *Alexis Korner* by H. Shapiro (Bloomsbury, 1996)

39. *New Musical Express*, 4 February 1967

40. *Self-Portrait With Friends: The Selected Diaries Of Cecil Beaton,
    1926–1974* ed. R. Buckle (Book Club, 1979)

41. *New Musical Express,* 21 October 1966

42. Elkin Allan in *Movies On Television* (Times Newspapers, 1973)

43. *Ugly Things*, No. 18, summer 2000

44. *The Yardbirds* by A. Clayson (Backbeat, 2002)

45. *The Guardian*, 30 August 1990

46. *Disc*, 19 August 1967

47. *Sunday Times*, 10 August 2003

48. *The Rolling Stones In Their Own Words* eds. D. Dalton and M. Farren (Omnibus, 1980)

49. *Rolling Stone,* 5 November 1987

50. *Mojo: The Psychedelic Beatles – Special Edition*, 2001

51. Sleeve notes to *Brian Jones Presents The Pipes Of Pan At Joujouka* (Rolling Stones Records COC 49100, 1971)

Chapter 2
PRODIGAL SONS: THE PEOPLE

In 1963, the plug had been pulled and Bill Wyman, the Rolling Stones' only true *workin' class 'ero*, had been sucked into a vortex of events, places and situations that had not even belonged to speculation when he was born William George Perks in 1936 in Penge, a depressed quarter of South East London. When Bill was two months away from sitting his GCE 'O' level exams, his father chose to withdraw him from grammar school, having found him a junior clerk position with a bookmaker in the West End. After Bill's required two years of National Service had been fulfilled, he became a storekeeper for an engineering firm in Streatham, shortly before he started married life in autumn 1959 with Diane Cory.

Around this time, Bill was playing in a band that became the Cliftons, a rock'n'roll outfit that lasted for two years punctuated by little peaks and troughs. By the end of 1962, the Cliftons were becoming embroiled in cash-flow problems, and talking more and more about the tailing off of engagements and the bad faith of certain promoters. Yet from this, the group's darkest – and final – hour, the slow pageant of sunrise was about to begin for their bass guitarist.

Shortly before Christmas, Tony Chapman, the Cliftons' drummer, called on Bill to tell him that a group in which he was moonlighting needed a bass player. Ideally, this person would be one who could reproduce lines like those on the tape of Jimmy Reed tracks that Tony threaded on to the machine he had brought with him. The following night, he and a couple of the other members were going to the Red Lion in Sutton to see Ricky Tyrrell and the Presidents, fronted by a singer who, in private life, was called Glyn Johns. Bill ought to come along too. As it happened, the Stones were represented in the bar only by Ian Stewart, the pianist, who invited Wyman to a rehearsal in the back room of a Chelsea pub two evenings later.

Keith Richards (foreground) and Bill Wyman working on their sound during a recording session in 1967.

Brushing non-existent specks from the suit he wore to work, Bill strode into the Wetherby Arms to be introduced to Mick Jagger, who seemed amiable enough, certainly more so than the two scruffy guitarists who all but ignored the newcomer. Bill thought Brian and Keith were posers; they thought he was a yob – or was it vice versa? The ice melted slightly when he lugged in both of his pristine, state-of-the-art amplifiers.

Even the spare one was more splendid than either of theirs, and Jones and Richards remained borderline civil throughout the subsequent music-making. For his part, while Bill liked Ian, he was not entirely convinced about Brian, Keith and Mick, but he still left his equipment at their nearby flat, so that he could travel independently to the next session by tube rather than endure a drive through the tail end of the rush hour. If conspicuously older than his new musical acquaintances, Bill did not impose unsolicited ideas upon the established stylistic determination. Peripheral to the Stones socially too, 'Bill didn't make waves,' noticed Phil May later, 'He accepted that he wasn't in the inner sanctum and was OK about it.'

After the Rolling Stones started going places, Wyman tended to side with Eric Easton, the more venerable of the group's two managers. Balding and nearing his forties, this former end-of-the-pier organist's cautious business acumen was more assuring to one who had borne more of the brunt of post-Depression austerity than the other Stones. The younger members of the band tended to have more in common with Eric's teenage sidekick, Andrew Loog Oldham, who, from once aspiring to pop stardom himself, now saw himself as the next Larry Parnes, the fast-talking 1950s pop svengali and inspired generator of correlated publicity.

At Oldham's directive, Wyman deducted seven years from his age. 'I knew how old he was,' smiled Stan Blackbourne, the group's accountant, 'He said you mustn't tell anybody. You could tell he was much older; it was his whole attitude.'[2] Then the only married Stone, he preferred not to take drugs; he was reliable as he was mature and, most of the time – as Phil May intimated – he was excluded from their private jokes and folklore at first. He was, however, at one with Jones, Jagger and, to a lesser degree, Richards in being perpetually on the lookout for illicit sex. Indeed, to many within the Stones' entourage, old Bill was something of a lothario on the road, especially after he changed his name officially by deed poll in March 1964, calling himself after a fellow conscript whom he befriended during his period of National Service: 'It completely altered my life. I felt confident. I was proud of the name.'[1]

That is not to say that Wyman didn't care about Diane, now mother of his infant son, Stephen – for all the confusion there had been since the Top Thirty breakthrough with 'Come On' in 1963 between Bill the husband and Bill the 'available' pop idol. However, even if mutterings about his extra-marital antics had not filtered through to Diane, a man so preoccupied with his job is apt to be an inattentive spouse, and one morning late in 1966, Bill had no apparent option but to set wheels in motion to end his marriage, pleading 'if I hadn't been a Stone, perhaps it would have been different, but my career was in the way, and I know in my heart that this was to blame. The Stones' success took me all over the world – and away from home. We found ourselves struggling to make the marriage work.'[3]

Within the group, Wyman's endeavours to lead as conventional a home life as was tenable for a mid-1960s pop star was a source of amusement. He took it well, and even bonded with the most wayward Stone of all, lending sympathetic ears to Brian Jones's grievances about the state of the Stones, particularly his tacit demotion since 1963 from de facto leader to a rank similar to Bill's, i.e. somewhere between the humblest equipment humper and the high command of Jagger, Richards and the management.

Before 1965 was out, strange news had flown up and down that Brian had approached vocalist Paul Jones of Manfred Mann, Eric Clapton of John Mayall's Bluesbreakers, ex-Shadows bass player Jet Harris and Viv Prince from the Pretty Things with a view to forming a new group. If the rumour had substance – or even if it hadn't, but Brian had started it – it was regarded as a registered protest rather than boat-burning. Nevertheless, none of the others thought to plead or remonstrate with pop's most prominent and malcontent supporting player, although Ian Stewart knocked on Brian's door with a reminder about the following week's Stones recording session at Olympic Sound.

If rhythm guitarist Brian Pendleton could be persuaded to transfer to bass, Brian was well-placed to have filled a vacancy that had occurred in the Pretty Things, even if Dick, Phil et al. tended not to have hits any more. It was whispered too that Jones and Bob Dylan had formed a desultory songwriting team, and that Bob had offered Brian the post of harmonica-player in the Hawks. On 6 November 1965, midway through a Stones US tour, Jones, Dylan and a retinue that included Al Kooper, organist on Bob's most recent single, 'Positively 4th Street', had spent an evening in New York, adrenalin pumping and talking shop constantly, in various night clubs prior to looking in at a studio where Wilson Pickett was recording possible follow-ups to 'In The Midnight Hour'. Later that same week, a power cut necessitated candles when Dylan and Robbie Robertson, the Hawks' guitarist, came to Brian's room at the Lincoln Square Motor Inn, a stone's throw from Central Park, to make music and discuss future get-togethers. Before he jetted home this time, Brian was also treated as an equal by the late Richard Fariña, a respected Irish-American 'protest' singer who presented him with a vintage dulcimer (a medieval stringed instrument, struck with hand-held hammers).

In Britain too, Jones was admired as both a multi-faceted musician and a 'regular guy'. Within minutes of returning from a long tour of another continent, he had answered the pounding of Steve Winwood plus the Spencer Davis Group's nominal leader and road crew. Emotionally insecure as he was, Brian over-valued the goodwill of the more revered of his peers – even those still struggling. Banishing sleep, he made them welcome in his way: 'Man, you should see the stuff we've got through,'[4] he boasted hours later, indicating the marijuana 'roaches' and empty bottles among the discarded album sleeves, half-eaten food, and used duty-free filter-tips littering the place.

'I remember Brian as being funny, sensitive, smart – with a slightly affected and fake upper-class intonation,' added Dave Davies, the Kinks' lead guitarist, 'a little pretentious, and very camp. I liked him a lot.'[5]

'Yes, but you don't know him,' Ian Stewart might have murmured darkly whenever he caught similarly kind remarks. 'Brian actually set out to be as stupid as he could be,' grimaced Stewart, 'and as soon as he got any real inkling of money and success, he just went mad.'[6]

Stewart's friendship with Jones, never strong at the best of times, had not been the same since, on the point of take-off in 1963, Ian had been told by Andrew Loog Oldham and Eric Easton that he was no longer to be a visible member of the group. The reason was, purely and simply, his rugged, lantern-jawed face on which craggy eyebrows jutted from a forehead topped by a slicked-back smarm of a haircut. There was no denying, Oldham explained with a show of kindness, that, as far as a teenage pop-picker might be concerned, Ian looked a bit, well, you know.... To nineteen-year-old Jim McCarty, then two months away from joining the Yardbirds, 'Ian always reminded me of "Hoss Cartwright" in *Bonanza*.' A comparison to the obese and dim-witted character in the 1960s TV cowboy series may have been uncharitable, but another of Andrew's considerations was 'I didn't know a really successful group with six people in it. The public can't count up to six.'[7] It was a cruel necessity, although Ian could carry on as an charter member of the organization, so Brian had promised him – as if Brian was still in a position to do so. Ian could be the chief road manager, if he liked.

Stewart seemed to come to terms with his banishment, his shaving mirror telling him why, but he was disgusted that none of the other Stones, especially Brian, the one he had known the longest, made little more than a perfunctory attempt to disagree with the management – as Ian himself had done when Jones had appeared quite willing to sacrifice Mick: 'Easton said to Brian, "I don't think Jagger is any good" – and so Brian said, "OK, we'll just get rid of him." I felt sure Brian would have done it. I said to him, "Don't be so bloody daft."'[8]

An understandable dark night of the ego passed, and Stewart decided to stay on. While he would always refer to the Stones as *us* rather than *them*, his widow was to insist that, 'Whatever Ian or anyone else said, he did care about being relegated. The bottom line for Andrew was that his face didn't fit. Andrew loved the pretty, thin, long-haired boys. Ian felt bitter about the savage way he was kicked aside.'[8]

'He was the glue that held us all together' was to be Keith Richards' assessment following Ian's sudden death in 1985, 'Very few people realize how important he was to the Stones.'[9]

As early as 1964, however, Stewart was to be subject of a *New Musical Express* article in which he assured himself as much as the readers that he was 'happy collecting the odd three farthings that come from the records. I don't want to be pointed out in the streets, and get torn to pieces.'[10] It was published a few months after a feature in *Melody Maker* about Pete Best, the drummer who had been dumped just as the wheels of the universe came together for the Beatles.

As things were to turn out, Brian, rather than Ian, was to be the Stones' Pete Best. That he was becoming increasingly less integrated into the main creative process by 1966 aggravated a sense of isolation and bolstered what was now a fixed idea that his sole purpose as a Stone was to gild Mick and Keith's patterns of chords and rhymes. Often, he added his musical icing just as the cake was baked, and spoke of it later without pride as he weighed up the easy money and unchallenging procurement of sexual gratification against being in what was, as far as he could see, mutating into as much of a hard-sell pop act as Herman's Hermits. Frank Zappa, now leader of the Mothers of Invention, would 'remember seeing Brian Jones very drunk at the Speakeasy one night, and telling him I liked *Between The Buttons*, and thought it superior to *Sgt. Pepper*, whereupon he belched discreetly and turned around.'[11]

Yet, by mid-1966, a prouder Brian was playing six different instruments during the course of any given concert – and, off duty, he seldom missed opportunities to jam, settling for piano rather than guitar, even if he relinquished it to Ian occasionally – as he did after hours in a

Richmond pub, with Dave Berry on vocals and one of his accompanying Cruisers on harmonica. If in less musical a mood, he sought tawdry compensation for real and imagined slights by Mick, Keith and Andrew by pulling birds on a satyric scale, and stressing his 'fear' of marriage in music press interviews with a wink that was almost visible in print. This was motivated too by resentment at Jagger's image as the group's principal sex symbol, and delight at the quicksilver prancer's irritation when Jones stoked up screams by just standing there.

On the quiet, certain fellow Stones were appalled by Brian's frequent callous conduct towards girls, but Bill Wyman wasn't one of them: 'Along with Charlie, Brian was my best friend in the Stones. He and I used to share the same hotel rooms. It was usually me and Brian that would go to the clubs to see the local groups and try to pick up the ladies. Mick and Keith would stay in the hotel, working on songs, while Charlie would usually go off to an art gallery or something.'[12]

Space restrictions and the laugh-a-minute ambience of the tour bus on the round-Britain 'scream circuit' circumscribed serious attempts at composition for any Stone – not just Keith and Mick – who fancied himself as a would-be beat-boom Gershwin. Flashes of inspiration could be revised and developed in hotel seclusion, and the result might be offered to the group's quality control. Like a travelling salesman with a foot in the door, Bill or Brian had to make a pitch with the most enticing wares. Clearing his throat, one of them would start chugging coy introductory chords; a deep breath and into the first line. When the song died, he would blink at his feet before glancing up with enquiring eyebrows. Sometimes, he would realize it was useless as soon as he opened his mouth. At other demonstrations, he could not comprehend his listeners' distracted indifference.

Such was the predicament of Bill Wyman and, especially, Brian Jones. Though fragments of a 1963 Jones item originally entitled either 'No One Knows' or 'I Want You To Know' were to surface in the bootleg market, it seemed to be beyond Brian to come up with one solitary acceptable composition of his own, let alone one, maybe two, per album as John Entwistle did for the Who, Dave Davies for the Kinks or George Harrison, junior partner in the Beatles. Indeed, Jagger was to admit to having never heard a Jones opus from start to finish. He and Richards were not very receptive to the work of other members of the group, 'so it was quite hard to know if Brian really wanted to do songs with us that he'd written,' sighed Mick, 'I think he did, but he found it rather hard to lay it down to us – and we didn't try to bring it out of him.'[13] Keith Richards' corroboration was blunter: 'As far as I know, Brian Jones never wrote a single finished song in his life. No doubt he spent hours, weeks, working on things, but his paranoia was so great he could never bring himself to present them to us.'[14]

Conversely, the more thick-skinned Bill Wyman had no such qualms, and was handsomely endowed with a capacity to try, try again in the face of either howls of affectionate derision or critical prejudices that brought forth the same hectoring arguments (like hook-lines from diabolical songs): 'We write for this band, not you. In any case, we don't need more than what we're playing already. If we did, we might wait for ever for you to come up with anything of the necessary standard.'

The number of compositions by Wyman alone that were recorded by the group could be counted on the fingers of one offensive gesture but, all told, that was quite an achievement. Speculating in production and artist management, he was able to offload some of his remaindered numbers on to the End, Bobbie Miller, Joey Paige, the Cheynes – whose drummer was none other than a teenage Mick Fleetwood – and other unprofitable acts. 'I didn't have Andrew Oldham behind me, like Mick and Keith did,' he shrugged, 'I was always left on my own to write and produce, so I had to learn the hard way. That meant I failed a lot, producing these unknown bands who remained unknown, most of them.'[15]

'It was Glyn Johns who got me involved with the End – because he'd produced a single with them,' explained Bill, 'We'd been talking for some time about putting a production company together. Everybody else was doing it – so he brought me in on that, and I just popped in at the end of a session. We formed Freeway Music, but Glyn soon dropped out – so I was lumbered with looking after them.'[16]

Mick Jagger with band manager Andrew Loog Oldham in New York City in 1965.

Before Andrew Loog Oldham and Eric Easton had even secured the Decca contract, Johns' console prowess had been applied to the Stones' sound at IBC, a central London studio that waived charging by the hour in exchange for first refusal on the rights to the items completed. No regimented clock-watcher, twenty-year-old Johns had heard and liked the Stones at the Craw Daddy and when they had supported his own group in the Sutton pub where Bill Wyman had first entered the Stones' orbit.

Glyn worked again with the Stones after their national breakthrough later in 1963, but only became a tangible part of the set-up in 1966 when he was at the desk for much of *Between The Buttons*. His association with them from the IBC session until then was principally as a catalyst for extra-mural projects such as Jagger and Richards' production work for Immediate, co-founded in 1965 by Andrew Oldham as Britain's first truly successful independent record company. 'I was greatly involved with most of the product on that label,' he recalled, 'It was my major client as an engineer.'[17]

Pressure of such work may explain why he surrendered the End, a group of similar parochial standing in north Surrey as Ricky Tyrrell and the Presidents, to Wyman – who was still striving on an ailing End's behalf even as *Beggars Banquet* shifted out of neutral, co-writing both sides of a 1968 single, 'Shades of Orange'/'Loving Sacred Loving'. That single, while attracting rave reviews didn't make the group rich, partly because Wyman wasn't as much the public face of the Stones as Mick Jagger, who, if simply a team player in the studio, had been singled out, however unwillingly, as not only the group's central figure, but a separate entity. 'Is It Mick And The Stones Now?' asked a *Melody Maker* headline[18], prompted perhaps by a televised '*Ready Steady Go!* Rave Mad Mod Ball' at Wembley's Empire Pool, when the five were introduced by master of ceremonies Jimmy Savile as 'Jagger M. and the Rolling Stones'. That wasn't all. 'The main personality of the group is, of course, Mick Jagger,' confirmed Albert Hand in a *Teenbeat Monthly* editorial, 'He has managed to get away from the "group image". Especially on TV shows by the sheer fact that the cameras are rarely off him!!!'[19]

The Number One individual group member in a tabulation in *Record Mirror* (a publication that did not trouble to hide its preference for the Stones over the Beatles), Mick had been present in spirit when the Manish Boys' singer renamed himself David Bowie – after the Wild West adventurer's idiosyncratic side-arm – because he had heard that 'jagger' in Old English meant 'knife'. Mick reared up again in the brooding intensity and pooched lips of vocalists in numerous also-ran R&B outfits who found it instructive to watch 1965's *NME* Poll-winners Concert on TV for their role model's 'faultless timing and knowing just where to put the emphasis in his phrasing'. The critic went on: 'The faster tempo of "Around And Around" saw Jagger going into his more violent movements, and he whirled around at one moment like a berserk windmill. Showing how important it is to give the audience something to watch as well as listen to, Mick's facial dramatics during "The Last Time" were an education.'[20]

More cerebrally, Mick had become as fluent and as individual a lyricist as Chuck Berry or Dylan. 'The Under-Assistant West Coast Promotion Man' – a dig at a desperately trendy and finger-clicking publicist – had B-sided the US pressing of the epoch-making 'Satisfaction', a broader social comment that might have been a dissection of the Warhol-like aesthetics of consumer culture or just Mick moaning about the vicissitudes of his travelling life. He would never offer a clue 'because it's much more pleasurable for people to have their own interpretation of a song, novel, film or so on.'[21]

If as vital artistically as Jagger – in that the concept of a Rolling Stones without him was unthinkable – Keith Richards was generally less popular with fans than Mick, Brian and Bill in surveys conducted by *Mirabelle*, *Jackie* and other schoolgirl comics. Perhaps in an endeavour to heighten his profile, he was credited by Andrew Loog Oldham's label Immediate as 'producer' of 1966's *Today's Pop Symphony* by the Aranbee Pop Symphony Orchestra. Open to question, however, is the degree of his involvement in this easy-listening album mélange of current hits by the Beatles, Sonny & Cher, the Four Seasons, the Moody Blues and Wilson Pickett, plus a generous helping of Jagger-Richards compositions. Moreover, while he had been, in 1965, rated fourth in *Beat Instrumental*'s annual readers' poll for best lead guitarist – after Hank B. Marvin of the Shadows, Jeff Beck and George Harrison, but in front of Eric Clapton, Jimmy Page, the Who's Pete Townshend and Dave Davies – Richards had dropped to sixth the following year, overtaken by Clapton and Steve Winwood.

In the rhythm guitarist section, readers ignorant of lines melting between the lead/rhythm roles of the Stones' guitarists, had ensured that

Brian Jones held firm at fourth, but in hard financial terms, he swallowed dust behind Keith who, as well as his share of net income from concerts, was reaping such a harvest from his and Mick's songwriting that, before he had so much as booked a driving lesson, there had been much bowing and scraping in a London car showroom as Richards had paced up and down rows of gleaming Bentleys fitted with two-way mirrors and all the latest electronically operated gadgetry. A week later, a blue Continental model was delivered, delayed by the adjustment of driving-seat contours to Keith's – not his chauffeur's – measurements. From the same source, Doris, Keith's mother, received an Austin 1100 from her son.

For Keith, the city lights had lost much of their allure; giggling fans had winkled out the ex-directory number at the St John's Wood pied-à-terre he had found, after he and Mick had left their previous one in West Hampstead to avoid teenagers congregating outside. Since April 1966, therefore, Keith's principal residence had been far beyond the capital's outer conurbations. He had bought 'Redlands', a spacious Tudor farmhouse with a thatched roof, a moat and foundations dating from the Norman Conquest. The odd poacher and hiker were the only intruders, and expected visitors driving from London would sometimes overshoot the tree-lined driveway along the main road that descended to the village of West Wittering and the Sussex yachting fraternity's sheltered harbour, banked too by Hayling Island and the county town of Chichester.

Brian Jones, still living within the drone of metropolis traffic, may have envied Richards' peninsular isolation, where the only noise to disturb the stillness was the odd chivvying pheasant bursting from a thicket. However, Keith was unashamedly impressed by Brian's new jet-setter girlfriend with her willowy figure and Marlene Dietrich drawl, just the sort of 'bird' he would have liked for himself, especially as his affair with a model named Linda Keith, his first 'serious' girlfriend, was petering out, and would be extinguished altogether after she, supposedly, cuckolded him with Jimi Hendrix.

Richards was to serve Jones likewise with honey-blonde Anita Pallenberg, born in Italy of mingled Swiss, German and Scandinavian stock. Her father, a 'frustrated composer'[22], ran a travel agency in Rome and his two daughters attended a German school there. Gaining a consequent scholarship in graphic design, multi-lingual Anita accompanied painter beau Mario Schifano to New York, where beatnik bards Allen Ginsberg and Gregory Corso were among her social conquests, as was multi-media pop artist Andy Warhol.

Andy had brought humour and topicality back into art through his self-conscious fascination with junk culture – which, as far he was concerned, included pop as much as his soup cans, Brillo pads and comic-strip philosophy. Stimulated by pop celebrity more than the music, he had been sneaked into the backstage area of a Manhattan theatre because, as he put it, 'I wanted to be in the presence of the Yardbirds'[23]. The Stones had warranted some fuss, too, when they visited Warhol's place of work, Studio 54 in downtown New York, where, chortled Keith, 'they ruined a perfectly good theatre by filling it with faggots in boxing shorts, waving champagne bottles in front of your face'[24]. Lou Reed, leader of the Velvet Underground – the house band at Warhol's Factory arts centre – would produce an onstage syringe to simulate the process of mainlining during 'Heroin', a substance he would later say he had never touched.

Pallenberg had not had much to do with heroin – or, indeed, any hard drugs – when she returned to Europe six months later to be employed variously as a disinclined model ('too beautiful to get out of bed', according to her agent)[25], a photography studio assistant and a movie actress, initially with a walk-on in Fellini's symbolism-ridden satire, *La Dolce Vita*. While on an assignment for *Vogue* magazine in Paris, she came to the intrigued attention of Volker Schlondorff, usually based in Munich as a rising director in the revitalization of European art-house film-making. 'I stayed at his flat,' recounted Anita, 'and had a crash course in cinema – but even though I was in the middle of the New Wave, as it were, I was getting into rock'n'roll.'[25]

Brian Jones, meanwhile, had been 'getting into' Zou-Zou, a fancy-free French opposite number to Twiggy, Jean Shrimpton and others in the same mini-skirted, catwalking league. Battle-hardened by the complicated love-life that had shifted into gear in his early teens and had since continued with hardly any interlude, Brian, a most heterosexual young man, had learnt not to spoil a no-strings dalliance by getting jealous and sulky with a girl who needed someone who didn't care anymore than he did. Yet Brian was quite a 'trophy' boyfriend for Zou-Zou as, in France, the Stones were more popular than the Beatles, if behind incumbent luminaries Sylvie Vartan and her singing husband, Johnny Hallyday. Zou-Zou's sexual tastes ran to suggesting troilism with another of her romantic conquests, Dave Davies, who, in a 1996 autobiography, included the enigmatic sentence, 'Marianne Faithfull was Mick Jagger's girlfriend when she wasn't Brian Jones's girlfriend.'[5]

Others too detected a certain friskiness between Jones and mid-1960s singing star Faithfull, who had hooked up with Jagger after he had finished with Chrissie Shrimpton, Jean's younger sister, and stopped debating whether or not to try for a date with someone who was almost-but-not-quite as well-heeled a pop star as himself, say Françoise Hardy – who had figured in plans (which came to nothing) for her and Mick to star in a remake of Jean Cocteau's *Les Enfants Terribles* (1950) – or Dusty Springfield – though it was widely known that Dusty preferred girls.

Despite suffering her first serious flop, Marianne was still a chart combatant in 1966. She was also sufficiently good-looking for Mick not to feel inferior to Brian, proud beyond words when parading around with his new 'bird'. And, damn him, Anita – wasp waist, firm breasts, flawless complexion – was worth more than a second look. The attraction had been mutual from her first – well, it couldn't be described as a 'conversation' – with a vulnerable and alienated Jones backstage at Munich's Cirkus Krone on 14 September 1965, following another of those flare-ups with one or more of the other Stones that had been growing more frequent of late. Dispensing with even perfunctory chivalry, but without a tang of lasciviousness, he had asked Anita point-blank to spend the night with him: 'I can't be alone.'[26]

It did not begin, however, with an ecstasy of bodice-ripping. 'He needed someone to comfort him,' said Anita. 'I held him in my arms, and he couldn't stop crying – like he'd been holding back this pain and now he was able to let it go.'[26] Like a marijuana cigarette, sex was proffered as a gesture of open-spirited friendliness, and Anita tagged along with Brian to the next Stones engagement in Berlin, where she discovered herself shivering with pleasure at the demure smiles he flashed at her from the stage. Her reaction was not lost on Brian, who had been impressed by a disarming self-sufficiency and a well-read aestheticism that put him on his mettle, but would not permit him to be bothered by Anita's 'interesting' past – he had hardly lived like a monk himself – and her Zou-Zou-esque stipulation that, as long as Brian didn't mind her having distractions too, his other *amours* could stay in the picture. Thus she was permitted, if that is the word, to transgress the unwritten machismo code instilled into Jones and, indeed, many adult males throughout Europe at the time, which condoned their own infidelities, but not those of their women.

'He really liked me,' smiled Anita, 'and I responded to him. Basically, I moved in with Brian right away. He was very moody, which I like, and he was physically attractive as well. He looked like a girl in a funny kind of way. Sexually, I like girls as well as men, and Brian seemed to combine both sexes for me. Also, Brian was very outspoken, said everything on his mind, outrageous things, and he had a wonderful inquisitiveness – about new things, new places, everything that was going on. Except for Brian, all the Stones at that time were really suburban squares.'[26]

It would be Brian and Anita for fifteen months before the fairytale went wrong. In the beginning, every day together cemented the two more securely in the same flow of feeling, and they crossed the impalpable barrier between implied companionship and hearsay of Anita telling her parents she wanted to marry the boy. Nevertheless, a frightful row that could be heard all over the Scotch Of St James was not a singular occurrence, and other quarrels frothed and fumed behind closed doors, but Anita made Brian laugh a lot, and healed some areas of his fractured self-esteem: 'Brian was very short, especially his legs. He was a head shorter than I, and he could barely see over the steering wheel of his Rolls. He worried about the look of his teeth, which were capped, but I made him forget his defects, and just think about the positive side of Brian Jones.'[26]

He was inches taller through walking on air as he showed her off round the London clubs. She read books and used long words – a lot of them in German, mind, but long words all the same. With beauty as well as brains, Anita Pallenberg was also just the sort of incredibly sexy blonde out of a foreign film – the pout, the giggle, the whole lot – that secondary schoolboys would invent as a dream date.

After she had settled in, the Jones flat at 1, Courtfield Road emitted a dimly lit aura of either cartoon scariness or fascinating depravity, depending on a given visitor's credulity. Like Dean Moriarty in Jack Kerouac's *On The Road*, Brian was working on becoming oddly fascinating for his mastery of an instinctive and crazed pagan Zen, radiated by the incongruous juxtaposition of Moroccan tapestries and a poster advertising 7 Up on the walls of the living room, and his provocatively creepy face asking to be punched on the front sleeve of *Between The Buttons*. In his and Anita's little world, the mood of the hour might dictate a séance; a cosmic safari to some midnight tor in Cornwall to look for UFOs; 'Satanic spells to dispel thunder and lightning', as a shared girlfriend reported to Jim McCarty; an excursion up west to the Indica – and fireside palavers that swung from incorporeal matters to Brian's shy-making soliloquies about his life, his soul, his agony.

'He was a tortured personality,' discovered Anita, 'insecure as hell, totally paranoiac. He had a volatile temper, and he would react to frustration with physical violence. In his tantrums, he would throw things at me, whatever he could pick up – lamps, clocks, chairs, plates of food. Then, when the storm inside him died down, he'd feel guilty and beg me to forgive him.'[26]

Her *entrée* into the Stones' coterie also gave Pallenberg ample opportunity to log the characteristics of the two members whose songwriting alliance was one of many founts of profound emotional confusion for Brian. She felt most comfortable with the selectively amiable Keith who was 'in many ways, the man Mick wanted to be. Free and easy in his own skin, not uptight like Mick. He was tough when he had to be, never backed down, had a good time, really enjoyed drinking, drugs and carousing, enjoyed sex. Mick envied Keith and was jealous of me.'[26] She gathered too that, on the strength of a one-night stand with him before taking up with Jagger, Marianne Faithfull had concluded that Richards might be the sex stud of the century, and that, in the Stones' gradation of personnel, 'Whoever allied himself with Keith would have the power.'[27]

When he was in London, Richards was omnipresent at Jones and Pallenberg's apartment, and went along for the ride

The Jet Setters: Marianne Faithfull and Anita Pallenberg travel to meet their Rolling Stones boyfriends, in 1967.

when Brian flew to Munich to watch Anita filming. With Mick and Marianne, he tagged along too when John Michell, author of 1967's *The Flying Saucer Mystery* and 1969's *View Over Atlantis*, indulged Brian and Anita's interest in super-sensory matters by conducting them to Woodhope Church, Hertfordshire, to investigate magnetic disturbances in ley lines. In Keith's Bentley Continental, now nicknamed 'the Blue Lena', there was also a small hours outing to Primrose Hill to peer vainly in London's smoggy sky for extra-terrestrials of the kind Keith professed to have seen in the gardens at Redlands.

As an overnight guest in Courtfield Road, Richards was sometimes privy to Jones and Pallenberg's alternate bouts of wounding home truths and abrupt reconciliations. Noises from their bedroom would cover a waterfront from moans of ecstasy to bellowed trading of insults to outbursts of violence. 'Brian was very strong, and his assaults were terrible,' complained Anita, 'For days afterwards, I'd have lumps and bruises all over me.'[26]

Yet Keith couldn't help liking Brian Jones, despite his childish malevolence and need to be admired; the hypersensitivity that steered him into what appeared to others to be needless conflicts; and the way in which he treated Anita – who, he noticed, was more inclined to retaliate than Brian's previous lovers. Richards also made non-committal noises whenever Jones, with bitter intensity, began dissecting the character of Jagger, his principal *bête noire* since 'Brian and I became firm friends again,' perceived Keith. 'I'd managed to break down a lot of barriers, but Brian always had to have an imaginary foe. He was a bit of a Don Quixote, I suppose. All I wanted to do was bring him into the mainstream again, but Brian used that to create a vendetta against Mick.'[28]

If temporarily shaded from the sunshine of Keith's smile, Jagger, looking after Number One more effectively than Brian with his little *Mord Und Totschlag* soundtrack, was searching for an opening in another sphere as soon as a gap appeared in the Stones' demanding schedule. Hardly a week was going by without some pop icon or other, usually a solo entity or the most charismatic member of a group, trying to 'other be' in a non-vacuous film. Dave Clark had been 'Steve' in *Catch Us If You Can* (1965); John Lennon was to be 'Private Gripweed' in *How I Won The War* (1967), and, having just left Manfred Mann, Paul Jones would keep biting his lip as a pop-star-turned-messiah in *Privilege* (1967).

Thus Mick alone – rather than the Stones *en bloc* – was being courted by theatre and movie moguls, either on the lookout for fresh talent or driven by the cynical expediencyof Jagger's pop celebtiry. Yet it was to be a while before Mick committed himself to a film – for, while perusing proffered scripts, a zest for the social whirl and the company of wanted non-pop party invitees had transformed him into 'the most fashionably modish young man in London', in the words of a rather patronizing *Evening Standard* columnist. 'We are told he is the voice of today, a today person, symptomatic of our society. Cecil Beaton paints him, says he is reminded of Nijinsky, of Renaissance angels; magazines report that he is a friend of Princess Margaret; gossip columns tell us what parties he failed to turn up at'.[29]

Most of it was true, even if the Queen's younger sister was a fan of other pop stars too, remarking to Spencer Davis that 'your music has given me a great deal of pleasure'.[30] Mick was also soon to be a neighbour of Commander David Birkin, a hero of Dunkirk, his wife, comedy actress Judy Campbell and their daughter, Jane, listed as 'Blonde' in the closing credits of *Blow Up* (1966), a portrayal of Swinging London that had already become a little antiquated by the time the flick was on general release late in 1966.

In the same cluster of Mews, Places, Walks, Gardens and Rows in Chelsea – though elegant light years away from the ghastly flat along Edith Grove that he, Brian and Keith – and, briefly, Charlie – had occupied during the Stones' early struggles – the Victorian painter James McNeill Whistler's old house along Cheyne Walk had been the setting for *Blow Up*'s orgy scene. On the same side of the road, Jagger set up home with Marianne Faithfull and Nicholas, Faithfull's child from a brief previous marriage, at Number 48, built circa 1710.

Searching for a countryside bolt-hole too, Mick – via a go-between – came across a bargain in 'Stargroves', a property in west Berkshire near the thatched cottage he would buy for Marianne's mother in the village of Aldworth. The grander Stargroves, so he was told by the seller, had been a field headquarters for the Roundheads during the Civil War. Jagger was never able to like Stargroves as much as Cheyne Walk, handy not only for West End nightclubbing, but also for being photographed at the highbrow concert halls, theatres and galleries that he hoped would make more acute his understanding of what was worth absorbing and what was not. Sighting a Rolling Stone in such places would bring puffy smiles of condescension from those for whom 'culture' was second nature (and 'pop music' and its practitioners, therefore, beneath contempt). Such snobs may have assumed that Mick was exhibiting an observed reverence for what he felt he *ought* to appreciate, but did not quite know why. Magnifying the gap between themselves and the common herd, they would not believe that one such as Jagger could glimpse infinity during *Swan Lake*.

While his devouring of new experiences went further than just shallow dropping of

Jagger confronts the camera in 1964.

names, Jagger was not metamorphosing into an emaciated ascetic. His recreational pursuits were both far from sedentary and not always to do with intellectual curiosity. He and the other Stones, with the exception of Charlie Watts, were as prone to untoward nonsense involving drugs and girls as any other in pop's elite, whose disconnection with life out in Dullsville was so complete that their only contact with it most of the time was through personal managers, gofers and narcotics dealers.

Between The Buttons's 'Connection', in which Keith's baritone was louder than Mick's, was an opus that seemed to contain references to the non-prescription drugs that helped the time pass quicker in this bandroom or on that long-haul flight. If all too aware of 'Purple Hearts', 'Black Bombers' and like pep pills, marijuana ('pot') had been a bit too cloak-and-dagger for most 1960s pop stars until no less than the Beatles had giggled through the shooting of their second movie, *Help!*, in the haze of its short-lived magic. Pot then came to be used more and more as a herbal handmaiden to creativity as certain groups started thinking of themselves as more than mere entertainers, but pseudo-mystics whose songs required repeated listening to apprehend what might be veiled but oracular messages. Even the Troggs were to suffer airplay restrictions for 1967's 'Night Of The Long Grass' on the ridiculous premise that it referred to drugs ('grass').

Within the Stones, it was Charlie Watts of all people who had been the first to become aware of marijuana. He had come across it as early as 1957 at the start of his three-year course at Harrow School of Art, when an inexpert reefer was rolled at a *demi-monde* party thrown when someone's parents were away. Charlie was not impressed by that or any of the stronger stimulants that he would see before him as a member of the most notorious pop group of the Swinging Sixties. 'Charlie's not really a Stone, is he?' was the rhetorical question asked by Shirley, his wife since October 1964, by way of explanation. 'Mick, Keith and Brian, *they're* the big, bad Rolling Stones.'[31]

When they asked for his opinion, Charlie – more than Bill or even Ian – was as much the group's still, small voice of reason as he had always been, talking calm sense while the others ran around like headless chickens. Like George Harrison had been categorized for all time as the 'Quiet Beatle' in 1964, so some pressured journalist chronicling the similar mayhem surrounding the Stones had come up with 'the Silent Stone' as a description for Charlie. The phrase stuck, fuelled as it was by media frustration at his reluctant, monosyllabic and, seemingly, bored utterances in interview and when a stick-mic was thrust at his mouth every time the group had threaded through customs after disembarking from an aeroplane. Apparently enduring rather than enjoying pop stardom, Charlie, whose heart was in jazz, was more inclined to saunter rather than run pell-mell from US stadium dug-outs towards the distant stage.

As far as he was able, Watts became almost completely incommunicado to both press and fans for years after he and Shirley had bought their first house in July 1965. Just outside Lewes, East Sussex, the Old Brewery was the seat of a sixteenth-century manor. It had oak beams, a four-poster bed, a fireplace with space for half a tree to blaze in it, a library – the complete olde-tyme, countrified works. There were stables for Shirley's donkey and Energy, a race horse; three cats and three collies roaming here and there; a nook given over to her collection of Victorian dolls, and a cranny for his mementoes of the US Civil War – an abiding interest since childhood – consisting of rifles, revolvers, soldiers' uniforms and other artefacts purchased during stolen afternoon trips to Gettysburg and associated battlegrounds when the Stones were in the States.

The new residents were determined homebodies, who chose not to intervene much in parochial affairs. Nevertheless, the presence of a renowned addressee – one of those Rolling Stones – sent an electric thrill of mingled horror and joy throughout the entire postal district. The Old Brewery was exposed to the attention of a few teenagers who would sink into a languid daze induced by the fixity of gazing up the drive.

A spectator as more public Stones dramas unfolded in 1967, Charlie's ambition was to be unphotographed stepping from an airport lift, to be unchased when out on the street and to be unrecognized when flicking through dog-eared wares in a vintage record shop that specialized in his beloved jazz. All this seemed more far-fetched than getting rich and famous had been when he had joined the group back in January 1963. No matter how much energy he ploughed into protecting his privacy, too soon would come his departure for further long weeks away from Shirley and, these days, 'Hallard', still close to Lewes, but more secluded than the Old Brewery, and with a staff flat and cottage, a swimming pool, farm buildings and thirty-four acres of land. Materially, it was better in every way, but Watts was uneasy about relying on the Stones' management – then in the throes of a takeover – to see to the paying of the mortgage and expenses, especially as there was soon to be another mouth to feed; Shirley was in the final months of a pregnancy that would yield her and Charlie's only offspring, Serafina, born on 18 March 1968.

This coincided with a long period during which the Rolling Stones had downed tools as a touring band for two years – from a date in Athens, Greece, on 17 April 1967 to 7 November 1969 in Colorado. In between, the only 'live' stage appearances would be ten minutes at another *NME* Poll-winners Concert and the fabled memorial to Brian Jones at Hyde Park. Charlie was, therefore, able to give his infant daughter more paternal attention than most – and his friends agreed that fatherhood suited him.

With his purported tally of a least three illegitimate children, fatherhood only suited Brian Jones until the novelty wore off, and for as long as it did not involve too much financial outlay. More important to Brian then was his lost control of the Stones' destiny. One evening in 1966 at the Ad-Lib, he had babbled his vocational fears to John Lennon: 'They're destroying me. I started the band, and now they keep trying to squeeze me out. It's all Jagger-Richards this, Jagger-Richards that. They won't even listen to my songs any more.' The arch-Beatle stared back appraisingly and with not a little exasperation: 'Look, I get sick of Paul sometimes, of the way he's for ever trying to dominate me. You have to stand up to these ego maniacs. You can't just get smashed out of your box. Look, how about if I ask you to play sax or something on some Beatles records? That'll make them all sit up and take notice, won't it?'[32] Gathering strength from this proposal, Brian was to progress from joining in the chorus to 'Yellow Submarine' to honking woodwinds on two Beatles B-sides, 'Baby You're A Rich Man' and knockabout 'You Know My Name'. Of Brian's hand in the latter, Paul McCartney commented, 'He was a really ropey sax player. He played a funny solo. It happened to be exactly what we wanted. Brian was very good like that.'[33]

When Dick Taylor had been a Stone, he too had noted that 'although Brian would despair and get out of his head a bit, he had an acute sense of humour. In the beginning, everyone was great mates, and we used to have lots of laughs.' After a restricted fashion, they still did — for utterances hilarious to no one else would have Richards and Jones howling on the carpet at 1, Courtfield Road, although in studio, aeroplane or tour bus with the Stones, Brian's concentration would split as his ears strained to catch the familiar murmured intrigue as Keith sided with Mick in the resumption of antipathy and further mind games. 'When the Yardbirds toured with the Stones and Ike & Tina Turner in 1966,' noticed Jim McCarty, 'Mick and Keith weren't talking to Brian, and they were pulling faces at him onstage.'

Still, the reminder of 1962 when he and Keith had truly been friends was gratifying while it lasted for Brian, who, having observed instances of Richards' hesitancy with regard to girls, had no reason to suspect ulterior motives. As for Richards, while he may have presumed that a 'suburban square' like himself was out of Anita Pallenberg's league, there were long, dangerous moments between them whenever Brian was out of the room.

Anita and Brian were invited but were unable to attend a house party at Redlands on the weekend of perhaps the most well known drugs bust in pop history – when sufficient substances were found by pouncing police officers to secure the arrest of Keith Richards and Mick Jagger.

While awaiting trial, the two persuaded Jones to come too when they removed themselves to a faraway place where they wouldn't see journalists or further police in the foliage. Mick and Marianne chose to fly, but, with bespectacled Tom Keylock, a Stones road manager, at the wheel of Keith's Blue Lena, Courtfield Road was the starting-off point for the trip to Morocco – where Africa almost touches Spain – via France for Richards, Pallenberg, Jones and a couple of moneyed hangers-on.

The drive was not without incident. Towards the Mediterranean coast, Jones's intake of alcohol and marijuana in the back seat helped aggravate the asthma that had dogged him since childhood. At the close of this first day of travel, just before the Spanish border, he suffered a respiratory seizure of such gravity that, wheezing like a bellows, he had to be half-led, half-carried from the car into a hospital near Toulouse where it was discovered that his eye-crossing coughs had caused both lungs to bleed. Urged to remain there for observation overnight at least, Brian insisted that the journey to Morocco continue without him. This was to prove a historic decision that was to affect the entire course of both the Stones' career and Jones's and Richards' lives.

Throughout the small hours, Jones was engulfed by eddying agitations connected with mistrust and attention-seeking and, during his second day of treatment, he asked a nurse to ring reception at the party's booked hotel in central Spain, instructing Anita to double back to him. Yet, flung together whenever Keylock took bends too fast, Pallenberg and Richards in the back seats were each cherishing a caprice to entice the other into bed. Their yawns at breakfast would indicate that neither had spent the consequent night alone. With retrospective honesty, Anita would aver, 'By the time we reached Valencia, we could no longer resist each other. In the morning, I realized – as did Keith – that we were creating an unmanageable situation – so we pulled back as best we could for the rest of the journey.'[26] Nonetheless, Anita shrugged off both Brian's telephoned message and one frantic telegram after another for four days.

If he was now able to tread the corridors without aid, the man who would be walking towards her with his arms out had every appearance of being seriously ill, and the African idyll was put on ice so that Jones could jet back to London for tests and to recuperate further. Naturally, the person the newspapers referred to as his 'constant companion' had to accompany him. Counselled to avoid stressful situations for a while, a holiday in sunnier climes in congenial company seemed most appropriate. In Morocco, however, tension was in the air, and Brian guessed from subtle signals, split-second looks and awkward lulls in conversation during an excruciating first day round the hotel pool that, no matter how hard they tried to conduct themselves on the same just-friends terms as before, something appeared to be going on between Keith and Anita.

This was also apparent to Jagger, Faithfull and other of the British holidaymakers such as society photographer Cecil Beaton, whose description of Richards' – and Jones's – seedy-flash flower-power attire is worth quoting in passing: 'In eighteenth century suit, long black velvet coat and the tightest pants, everything is shoddy, poorly made, the seams burst. Keith himself had sewn his trousers, lavender and dull rose, with a band of badly-stitched leather dividing the two colours. Brian appears in white pants with a huge black square applied at the back. It is very smart in spite of the fact that the seams are giving way.'[34]

Richards was certain that Jones's nervous manner towards him was because he dreaded finding that his growing suspicions had foundation. Fear, however, was deferring to stoic cynicism and then naked anger. 'Brian kept staring at Keith,' perceived Anita, 'I could sense the rage building up'.[26] If Brian's lovestruck illusions about Anita were now dead, a facade of self-composure continued to be maintained in public, and he and the other male in the triangle remained on terms that were in turns matey and aloof. It was going to be infinitely easier for Brian, a physical coward beneath the bravado, to give Anita a hard time rather than Keith.

In the privacy of the late evening bedroom, his wrath exploded like shrapnel in a slanging match and unflattering comparisons to local prostitutes. The hours of unnerving histrionics and noisome home truths that followed culminated not in Brian's defeatist fists striking Anita – though they certainly did – but his return from a search for vicious amusement in the local bazaar. Looking street-walking whores up and down like a farmer at a cattle auction, he selected two to bring back in order to fuck them, one after the other, in front of an enchanted or disgusted Pallenberg. Either way, a vestige of some code of honour peculiar to himself would be satisfied.

More emotional scum rose to the surface; the sisters-in-shame performed their duties – or at least had been ready to do so – and were paid to go away. It had all gone awry, and Brian lost his temper. Everything went red as hell. He hit harder than ever before for the sake of himself. Then he held Anita to him like a vice, panting and sobbing, and becoming aware of the trickling of blood. She was left with visible minor injuries as well as budgerigar eyes after the remainder of a sleepless night and the incessant sound of his voice.

The next day, Pallenberg's make-up couldn't quite mask the damage, and Jones unzipped a scripted grin on his own drawn face and tried not to betray his own distress. Richards said nothing, but had had all he could endure of both Morocco and the 'fragile monster'[15] that Jones had become. It was time to go anyway as the press had ferreted out his, Brian's and Mick's whereabouts, and tomorrow's curtain would be drawn to reveal a sea of faces and flashbulbs.

That afternoon, when Brian went souvenir-hunting, Keith drew Anita aside and began questioning her about the events of the previous night.

'When Keith realized what Brian had done to me, he tried to console me,' she would recall, '"I can't watch Brian do this to you any more," he said, "I'm going to take you back to London". I was terrified but exhilarated to be freeing myself from Brian's tyranny. I was more than ready to give that up, especially since I was now almost in love with Keith.'[26]

Two days later, the runaways were holed up in the flat he still kept in St John's Wood. In the interim, Brian, bottling up the pain, had boarded the next connecting flight to Heathrow, staring moodily at the clouds as twilight fell on both the countries beneath him and his disjointed thoughts. Eyes bloodshot with tears and fatigue, he went through the motions of storming round to the hideaway to confront a stone-faced Keith and plead with Anita, but an uglier showdown was defused when, with a kind of despairing triumph, it dawned on Brian within minutes that Anita would never cross the abyss that now lay between them – at least, not then.

Of course, he would not have been the Brian Jones of bed-hopping legend if, when people telephoned Courtfield Road, he hadn't made instant light of it, assuring them that he had tired of Anita Pallenberg long ago, and had been on the point of dumping her. Yet what was the point? The truth would out, and everyone would know that Richards had made a fool of him as surely as Richards had already wrested the leadership of the Stones from him.

True love, however, didn't run smoothly, either then or later, for Keith and Anita either. On the subsequent Stones trek across nine countries in continental Europe in April, hope stirred in Jones's breast that Pallenberg might return to him – or at least finish with Richards – when Keith, allegedly, had a fling with another woman during the German leg. However, if Anita got wind of this episode, she came to terms with it as one of the perks of her new boyfriend's job. Yet, though he might have been evasive when the subjects of wedding bells and babies reared up in interview, Richards was, sex on the road notwithstanding, a constant heart. 'Keith was a bit like Charlie,' affirmed Ian Stewart, 'He would find one girl and pretty much stick with her. Maybe a few here and there, but nothing like Brian and Bill, who went potty over birds.'[15]

Anita had had the decency – or work pressure – not to be around much during what turned out to be Brian's final tour with the Stones, during which he would drift like a fakir in a trance on to the boards to unacknowledged screams, reacting instinctively as a tempo announcement pitched him into another Jagger-Richards number with a four-four backbeat that even a halfwit could not lose. Sometimes, banal ritual deferred to the ancient, almost extra-sensory jubilation, but then he would catch sight of Keith with his low-slung Stratocaster.

It wasn't just that. Sometimes, his anguish was non-specific, seeming to hover all over. The entourage had noticed with more than a little concern the frequency with which he was half-closing his eyes as if he was hurting inside. Either backstage or in a hotel bar, he would be seen sitting at a secluded table with fingers pressed against his temples or lost in melancholy thoughts. When the music was over for the day, he would lie with eyes open and temples throbbing as sorrow flooded an already saturated mind. He would long to be at rest, but fingers of despair would reach in and sleep would not come for all the additional potions, tablets and draughts he had been prescribed since Morocco.

While the tour was a peculiar – and ineffective – form of occupational therapy, back in England he seemed to fall back mostly on his own company, albeit shrouded in darkness and rumpled bedclothes at Courtfield Road. Careworn hours passed either in uneasy slumber or, nourished by fast food and worse, in front of the television. Sightings of him on brooding walks or mooching drowsily to a convenience store were not encouraging. Future *Times* correspondent Jonathan Meades would recollect, 'When I was a student, I lived at World's End in Chelsea, and used to see him staggering between the Hung On You and Granny Takes A Trip boutiques, just down the road from my flat. He looked terrible, like some sort of dandy derelict.'

One day, those closest to Brian sensed a change in him, a longing for peace and security not only in his emotional life, but also in his chosen profession, even if it meant continuing to work with Keith. Returning like a prodigal to the Speakeasy or Blaises, he made the effort to throw back his head with laughter at some vulgar joke shared with Richards, demonstrating to all the world that any bad blood between them had been diluted. Holding forth, with a glass filled at regular intervals by one of a bevy of dolly little darlings, his bitter freedom had made him a celebrity jackpot for 'groupies' – once called 'scrubbers' – with raw physical beauty their only asset. Brian knew the type well and was wary, even if the calculating lust for them was as strong as ever.

Yet, while he was partial to variety, this latest library of mostly overnight attachments tended to shelve editions of the same woman – and, however grotesque his exhibitions were with them – apparently, leading one into a soiree on a chain like a dog – he held on to the hope that a situation would arise in which Anita might be unable to resist when he turned on the little-boy-lost charm that had done the trick when they had first met in Munich in 1965. He was evidently not beyond sly machinations to create such a situation; following Pallenberg's completion in Italy of a prominent role in the science fiction movie *Barbarella* (1967), she and Keith arrived at the annual international film exposition in Cannes for the screening of *Mord Und Totschlag*. Benighted in the same hotel, the composer of its music 'tried to engineer some scheme,' glowered Richards, 'Previously, he had tried to engineer a reunion in Paris, but Anita wouldn't have it. During the premiere in Cannes, I just stayed away. Anita came back in tears because Brian had beaten her up.'[15]

Thwarted in this final and vainglorious attempt to win back the love of his life, Brian cried on the shoulders of old girlfriends, among them Nico. Tellingly, her appearance and background had parallels with Anita's. A part in a 'modern times' continental movie, 1963's *Striptease*, came after a spell as a model in Paris and a role in Fellini's *La Dolce Vita* (1960). She also gained a recording contract, largely on the strength of her long blonde hair, high cheekbones, icy hauteur and a rivetingly gutteral German-accented contralto.

In 1965, she crossed the Channel for a slot on *Ready Steady Go!*, singing 'Mr. Tambourine Man' plus 'I'm Not Saying', a one-shot single on Andrew Loog Oldham's Immediate label. Thus Nico came to be connected by affinity to the Stones and, eventually, linked romantically to Brian before Anita – and after Nico had left London to seek a bigger fortune in New York.

After Brian parted from Nico after Monterpy and returned to England, there seemed to be less awkwardness than might be expected about the unavoidable omnipresence of Anita at Stones recording dates and whenever Brian visited Redlands, though he could not help imagining what was happening behind closed doors. He did not need to be told what Anita was like. The scent of diabolical practices that seemed to be emanating from the Stones' songwriting hub nowadays was the legacy of some of his and Anita's antics when they were together. As well as aspects of *Satanic Majesties* and 'Sympathy For The Devil', a new number selected for *Beggars Banquet*, there were undenied rumours leaking to Joe Average of liaisons with both black and white witches – and Kenneth Anger, a former Hollywood child star who, now in middle life, styled himself 'The Most Monstrous Movie Maker In The Underground'.

Modelling both his private life and public persona on that of Satanist wizard Aleister Crowley (who was included in the front cover montage of *Sgt. Pepper*), Anger's livelihood and reputation depended on bleak cult movies such as 1947's homosexual gang rape fantasy, *Fireworks*; *Lord Shiva's Dream*, a coded titular reference to LSD, renamed *The Inauguration of the Pleasure Dome* (1954); and 1963's apocalyptic *Scorpio Rising*, betraying a fascination with the books of Dennis Wheatley. His social circle was commensurate with this, embracing the likes of Anaïs Nin, whose prose poem-cum-novel, *The House Of Incest*, provided the libretto for post-serialist composer Edgard Varese's murkiest work, *Nocturnal* – and, since 1967, Anita Pallenberg and her pop star intimates.

When a guest at Redlands, Anger volunteered to officiate after suggesting in vain that Richards and Pallenberg wed in a pagan ceremony either in the grounds or on Hampstead Heath at dawn. He was also to insert Stones concert footage into *Invocation of My Demon Brother* (1969), and would visualize Keith as Beelzebub in an adaptation of Wheatley's *Lucifer Rising*, another flick then in pre-production. Anger also had a part as big in mind for Jagger, who, holding the decision at arm's length, suggested his younger brother Chris instead to Anger, knowing full well that Chris was then backpacking in India for much of a gap year between Dartford Grammar and university.

These projected film debuts progressed no further than Kenneth talking about them, but, through Pallenberg and her contacts in the film world, Richards would be given a cameo in *Michael Kohlhaus*, starring her and David Warner. The movie was subsequently withdrawn – and would have been lost anyway in the shadow of Anita's next role as female lead in *Performance* (1970), for which Keith and Mick were to provide a song to accompany one of the scenes.

Actually 'in the can' before *Michael Kohlhaus*, *Performance* was regarded by its investors as principally a vehicle for Jagger as a potential screen idol. Shooting was to begin in early autumn 1968 on a screenplay by Donald Cammell, a leading light of the bohemian post-war 'Chelsea Set' of jazzers, painters, debutantes, ex-public schoolboys, the more glamorous criminals – and, by the mid-1960s, the most outré pop musicians too. Cammell was also a godson of Aleister Crowley.

If ostensibly a gangster flick, Cammell's script delved into existentialism and identity crisis, notably when contents merged between Jagger as faded pop icon 'Turner', his lover 'Pherber' (Pallenberg) and 'Chas' – played by James Fox as a departure from his usual upper-class parts – a 'square' but bisexual hit-man, fleeing from both rough justice and the police to Turner's 'right piss-hole' of 'long hairs, beatniks, druggers, free love.... You couldn't find a better little hidey-hole'[35].

When the film was finally on general release, you would find too one of Mick Jagger's most powerful artistic statements. Any argument that his success with the Stones created the opportunity to do so, or that years of playing out his songs on the boards had taught him to act more effectively than most, is irrelevant. Though drawing from the recesses of his own character and personal history, Jagger in *Performance* was to blow away like dust the efforts of Dave Clark, Paul Jones, John Lennon and nearly every other British pop star of his vintage who ever had a go at 'proper' film acting.

His Turner was a mysterious pop hermit – like Bob Dylan, who, in 1966, had banned press interviews and stonewalled more earnest fans. Being so enigmatic was tiresome, and some cynics doubted that the motorcycle accident that ended one phase of Dylan's career that June had actually happened. Nevertheless, by 1968, he had not yet returned from the shadowy refuge from fame that the incident allowed him. Jagger, however, was not to base his portrayal of Turner on such a reclusive and messianic symbol of hipness. 'Turner is supposed to be a great writer like Dylan,' he sniggered, 'but he's completely immersed in himself. He's a horrible person really.'[36]

This perspective approximated Anita Pallenberg's initial impression of Mick, who 'really tried to put me down,' she grimaced, 'but there was no way that this crude guy was going to do a number on me. I found out that if you stand up to Mick, he crumbles.'[26] Yet, during read-throughs and rehearsals emerged the first stirrings of a real-life enactment of that soap-opera cliché whereby the greater the initial antagonism between two characters, the greater the likelihood that they will become lovers.

As this off-camera plot seemed set to develop between him and his best friend's bird, Mick's conscience began to prick after a 'what if?' fashion. Suppose it couldn't be kept between Anita and himself, how would Marianne react? A further complication was that he had also discovered himself thinking more and more about Marsha Hunt. Of mixed race and raised in Pennsylvania, she had been a member of Free At Last, one of Alexis Korner's post-Blues Incorporated combos. Unfinanced, the group struggled to survive from its earliest rehearsals in a Soho basement prior to Hunt's membership of Long John Baldry's Bluesology and then the Ferris Wheel, who specialized in competent workouts of US soul. She also sang with the Soft Machine, a 'progressive' outfit featuring her future husband, Mike Ratledge, on keyboards – though at the time, she was living with John Mayall, whose albums with his Bluesbreakers sold steadily if unremarkably.

Dissatisfied with her artistic progress, Marsha took a six-month break as she contemplated her next move. She considered au pairing and even resuming her poetry studies at the University of California. There were also attempts at learning the bass guitar – borrowed from Fleetwood Mac's John McVie – as an avenue for songwriting. Then someone mentioned that auditions were being held at the Shaftesbury Theatre for *Hair*. If impressing him with her theatrical talent, she was also commensurate with Mick Jagger's apparent penchant for 'girls with long dark hair, who are small and gay. She must be interesting and interested in me. She must be fully aware of the pop scene'[37]. Perhaps calculated to needle Marianne, that was what he told *Boyfriend* magazine.

Marianne Faithfull after her boyfriend Mick Jagger was sentenced for drug possession in the summer of 1967.

While she was not as easily hoisting her records into the charts, Faithfull was making a fair fist of Shakespeare and Chekhov on the stage, and had been approached by director Pierre Koralnik to be a wayward foreign foil to the refined 'Anna' for a musical of the same name, composed by Serge Gainsbourg as the first colour programme on France's new second nationally-networked channel. There were also prominent parts in feature films such as Michael Winner's *I'll Never Forget Whatshisname* (1967) – in which Faithfull was the first to utter the f-word in a mainstream movie – and Roger Vadim's semi-pornographic *Girl on a Motorcycle* (1968)[38], which prompted a reviling in the US Christian publication *Modern Dating* for 'tyrannizing receptive minds with illicit sex, rebellion against parents, rebellion against society, crime, delinquency and romance'[39], and speculation by the *NME's* Alley Cat gossip about what Mick thought of his girlfriend's love scenes with French heart-throb Alain Delon.

Doggedly, Jagger watched *Girl On A Motorcycle* to the closing credits, just as he had been there at every one of 1967's spring evenings when Marianne was in *Three Sisters* at the Chichester Festival Theatre, sending her a potted orange tree instead of a bouquet of first night – because, if there was now less lust in Mick for Marianne, he was still wearily astonished at how much his pride smarted when she made eyes at his friends and associates. He reciprocated with affairs of which the most costly in the long run would be with Marsha (who was to give birth to his first child, Karis, late in 1970).

Both Jagger and Faithfull were not yet beyond dropping urbane public masks and feigning aloofness at home for abrupt reconciliations and making grand gestures of moral and material generosity, if not to rekindle the fire of their courtship then to remind each other of what it had been like. He observed covertly that the strain of life at Cheyne Walk was draining her of her vivacity – and her beauty – but for now there remained an affection that manifested itself in laughter at each other's fantasies, shared recollections, impulsive embraces and the harmless verbal reviling of each other in the way that two old friends who used to be lovers would.

NOTES

1. *The Guardian*, 10 March 2006

2. *2 Stoned* by A.L. Oldham (Vintage, 2002)

3. *Rolling Stones '76* ed. M. Farren (Second Foundation, 1976)

4. *New Musical Express*, 26 March 1965

5. *Kink* by D. Davies (Boxtree, 1996)

6. *Blues In Britain* by B. Brunning (Blandford, 1995)

7. *Stoned: A Memoir Of London In The Sixties* by A.L. Oldham (St Martin's Press, 2000)

8. *Q*, May 1995

9. *Q*, October 1988

10. *New Musical Express*, 4 September 1964

11. *Zigzag*, (date obscured)

12. *Mature Times*, December 2004

13. *Rock And Folk*, May 1984

14. *Keith Richards In His Own Words* ed. M. St Michael (Omnibus, 1994)

15. *Record Collector*, No. 231, November 1998

16. *Record Collector*, No. 212, April 1997

17. *The Record Producers* by J. Tobler and S. Grundy (BBC, 1982)

18. *Melody Maker*, 5 April 1966

19. *Pop Weekly Annual* ed. A. Hand (World Distributors, 1965)

20. *New Musical Express*, 16 April 1965

21. *Rolling Stone*, 5 November 1987

22. *The Correspondent*, 11 February 1990

23. *The Yardbirds* by A. Clayson (Backbeat, 2002)

24. *Loose Talk* ed. L. Botts (Rolling Stone Press, 1980)

25. *Sunday Times*, 2 May 2004

26. *Daily Mail*, 18 July 1990

27. *Faithfull* by M. Faithfull and D. Dalton (Penguin, 1995)

28. *The Rolling Stones In Their Own Words* eds. D. Dalton and M Farren (Omnibus, 1985)

29. *Evening Standard*, 23 October 1966

30. *Midland Beat*, No. 32, May 1966

31. *Rolling Stones A–Z* by S. Weiner and L. Howard (Grove, 1983)

32. *The John Lennon Encyclopaedia* by B. Harry (Virgin, 2000)

33. *Paul McCartney; Many Years From Now* by B. Miles (Vintage, 1998)

34. *Self-Portrait With Friends: The Selected Diaries Of Cecil Beaton 1926–1974* ed. R. Buckle (Book Club Associates, 1980)

35. James Fox as 'Chas' in *Performance* (Warner Bros., 1970)

36. *The Rolling Stone Interviews* ed. J. Wenner (Straight Arrow, 1974)

37. *Trend Boyfriend '68* (City Magazines, 1967). This was before 'gay' came to mean 'homosexual'.

38. US title: *Naked Under Leather*

39. *Modern Dating* by Garner Ted Armstrong (Ambassador, 1969)

Chapter 3
STREET FIGHTING MEN: THE TIMES

*'It's stupid to think that you can start a revolution with
a record. I wish you could.'* Mick Jagger[1]

Across the Atlantic, wonderment at all things British was about to
peak during a week in 1964 when the Beatles occupied nine positions
in the Canadian Top Ten. The Stones, however, were relatively slow to
gain ground in North America. Indeed, the most important consequence
of their first visit was recording at the shrine of Chicago blues, in a
metropolis that seemed to hirsute young Englishmen like a Desperate Dan
cartoon in its contradiction of familiar mystery. A Woolworth's reared up
in North Clark Street – scene of the St. Valentine's Day Massacre – Coca
Cola tasted just the same, and pizza was the Windy City's answer to fish
and chips. Yet the sights and sounds in the streets – the ones the Stones,
most peculiar-looking to passers-by, were able to walk – were so diverting
that they could be hours ambling just a mile from Chess Studios at 2120,
South Michigan Avenue.

As their faces had not been plastered over magazine covers in the
USA for the past six months as they had been at home, it was possible for
a Stone – at the start of the tour anyway – to soak up the sights like
tourists without attracting even the beginnings of a crowd. The next visit
– in autumn – would be, however, a large scale re-run of British beat
hysteria, what with a show at Loew's Theater, Providence on 4

The Stones depart for New York and their 1966 American tour. Top to bottom: Bill Wyman, Brian Jones, Keith Richards, Mick Jagger and Charlie Watts.

November being stopped after four numbers when fans went as crazy as only fans can go. This was not untypical.

After Uncle Sam had capitulated to the Stones, the rest of the world would be a walkover. Once, your group had had as much chance of getting a disc in the charts of even the local newspaper as the lead singer had of being knighted, but these days, if the van had drawn up outside a ballroom on Pluto, it might not have seemed all that odd. There you were, miming your latest hit on *Brisbane Tonight* or, like Frank Allen of the Searchers, touring New Zealand with the Stones: 'I stood watching them, mesmerized by the energy if not overawed by the expertise. A fan by my side remarked that Keith Richards could make his guitar talk. I could see what he meant — and I could almost hear the guitar saying, "Take your hands off me, you clumsy oaf", but it was impressive, of that there was no doubt. This was not so much a demonstration of music as a display of sex and power, and on that level, it worked to perfection.'[3] Keith's riposte to Frank might have been, 'I've always done things on a fairly instinctive basis. I think brains have got in the way of too many things, especially something as basic as what we're doing.'[1]

Primitivism wasn't the way of the Searchers. Yet, in a similar way to the Beatles, while they had wished they were in hell rather than Hamburg at first, it had been punishing seasons in that city's red-light district clubland before the Sixties started Swinging that had toughened them up in readiness for what lay ahead. Similarly, the Stones' first month of hard graft in the States had been their 'Hamburg' in that it was often arduous, but contained hidden blessings. Hitless there, the group had been obliged to unfreeze the cool of non-screaming curiosity seekers – and, though they were judged and found wanting on a couple of poorly attended occasions, other audiences, crucially, when the tour wound up with two performances at New York's prestigious Carnegie Hall, felt a compulsion to dance only a few bars into the first number before a spontaneous rippling stagewards, and were metaphorical putty in Jagger's hand by the finish on the evidence of the bedlam that you could hear back in the dressing rooms. Much of the appeal was that, during a casually cataclysmic performance, the Stones had behaved as if they couldn't give a damn about the paying customers and were just up there having fun amongst themselves.

Nevertheless, the Stones were still struggling as US chart propositions when they finished that second jaunt, having hovered in the lower half of the Top Forty with both 'Tell Me (You're Coming Back)' and 'It's All Over Now', and battled to Number Six with 'Time Is On My Side'. Yet, while each new Stones release at home was a national event in pop terms, what with most of the Union's fifty states comparable in size to the entire British Isles, it did no harm for the group's US record company, London, to hurl at such a wide sales region 45s of any LP tracks that took its fancy. The Stones, therefore, suffered no loss of prestige when another potshot, 'Heart Of Stone' just about made the US Top Twenty before falling backwards. It had been taken from *The Rolling Stones Now!*, the third US album in eight months – possibly symptomatic of London Records sniffing a perishable commodity and shoving out as much Stones product in the first fiscal year as the traffic would allow. To some record executives in the US, the Stones' only distinction was longer hair than any of the other British combos who had toured the States since the Beatles' messianic landing at Kennedy airport in February.

A few snatched hours of serenity round a Savannah swimming pool were interrupted when, recounted Keith Richards, 'we were arrested for topless bathing. Some people were driving by, and swore that there was a load of chicks leaping in and out of the pool with just a pair of drawers on. So the cops came zooming in to bust these "chicks" – and, of course, the closer they got, the more stupid they must have felt – especially when they heard these *sarf* London accents.'[4]

Yet in back street dance halls in Houston or Lexington, you would come across many an outfit that, as far as it dared, had grown out its crew-cuts and ditched stage costumes and big smiles for a motley taciturnity – for, during the interval between their first and second visits, the Stones had amassed widespread grass-roots support. In the North too, there were myriad Anglophile 'garage bands' who, with dubious musical ability clashing with overweening expressive ambition, borrowed elements from the Stones, most blatantly by, say, torturing lengthening male hair into Jones's straight-fringed, shoulder-touching look, and employing vocalists that could ape Mick Jagger's vocal style and side-on microphone stance, broken by handclaps above the head – when he wasn't either blowing mouth organ or wielding maracas – and kicking one leg backwards from the knee.

Diligent private observations of the energetic if sensual stagecraft of James Brown, Tina Turner and similarly motivated soul singers for incorporation into his own turned Jagger into an altogether more physical performer during subsequent North American treks in the mid-1960s, on the vast stages of fifteen thousand-plus capacity venues such as Toronto's Maple Leaf Gardens, the Hollywood Bowl and the Convention Hall in San Diego, to which nowhere in drowsy old England could yet compare. Yet the Stones' stadium-filling impact on North America had less to do with the musicians themselves than the behaviour of a public who, once convinced of something incredible, exhibited a fanaticism for it that left the British swallowing dust.

Alighting in Midwest towns in the graveyard hours, the Stones' aeroplane would still be greeted by hundreds of hot-eyed teenagers, despite parental admonishments that if children had to like Limey beat groups, let it be ones like the clean-cut Dave Clark Five or Herman's Hermits – with a lead vocalist who looked like a young President Kennedy – rather than 'hairy monsters' like the Stones, Pretty Things and Them. 'You walk out of the Amphitheater after seeing the Rolling Stones perform,' exclaimed one Illinois newspaper, 'and suddenly, the Chicago stockyards smell good by comparison.'[5] Derided so by adults as Elvis Presley had been, naturally they were as rabidly worshipped by the young.

Fearing the worst, the middle-aged host of *The Ed Sullivan Show* – the pinnacle of conventional showbiz aspiration in North America – decreed the bleeping out of 'make' in the phrase 'trying to make some girl' in '(I Can't Get No) Satisfaction'.[6] Radio stations across the Union were unhappy about other parts of it as well, and English teachers everywhere were trying to repair the damage caused by the double negative in its very title. Thus 'Satisfaction' would be the Stones' first US Number One and be voted 1965's Best Single Of The Year by readers of *16*, a US teen magazine that never probed deeper than Mick's favourite *color*, what food Chrissie Shrimpton served when the Lennons visited and isn't Dave Clark's smile gorgeous? Still, this was a major feat, considering that the ordained US marketing strategy for keeping up a pop group's momentum was to cast as many records adrift on the vinyl oceans as possible, in the hope that one or more of them might catch on.

Under pressure to capitalize on 'Satisfaction', Jagger and Richards came up with a composition that, if nowhere as disappointing a follow-up as the Beatles' 'Can't Buy Me Love' had been to 'I Want To Hold Your Hand' in 1964, had the record-buying public debating whether the Stones had got into a rut, what with 'Get Off Of My Cloud' having much the same overall sound as 'Satisfaction'. All the same, it tramped a well-trodden path to the top at home, and lasted there a fortnight against a month for 'Satisfaction' in the States. The next single, '19th Nervous Breakdown', however, stalled at Number Two in both charts, after eliciting 'If this hadn't been recorded by the Stones, it wouldn't be a hit' from *Melody Maker*'s reviewer[7]. Its lyricist too 'knew it wouldn't be as good, but so what? I used to write about twelve songs in two weeks on tour. It gives you lots of ideas. You're just totally into it. You get back from a show, have something to eat, a few beers, and just go to your room and write. At home, you don't want to do anything, but read and things like that'.[8]

Within the record industry too, every recording manager outside Decca was alighting with nit-picking hope on the remotest indication of the Stones' fall – and, to Jim McCarty of the Yardbirds, the months after the 'Satisfaction' triumph were symptomatic of 'a bit of a lull artistically then, what with all those hits that were similar, "Satisfaction", "Get Off Of My Cloud", "19th Nervous Breakdown"....'

Jim's Yardbirds, however, were scoring self-penned hits into which were integrated Gregorian chant, symphonic tempo changes and other eruditions. In an otherwise critical autobiography, even a former manager, Simon Napier-Bell, was to admit 'there were four rock bands in the world that really counted, and the Yardbirds was one of them.' He then weighed up the attributes of 'the Rolling Stones – decadent and outrageous; the Who – rebellious and aggressive; the Yardbirds – introverted and moody.'[9]

It was, therefore, cool for the hippest of the hip to dig these groups – with their appeal to the great unwashed only demonstrating to arty illuminati that, firstly, sometimes the multitudes could be right, and also that, however innovative this new breed of British pop stars, they were still commensurate with godhead Andy Warhol's mannered revelling in consumerism, mass production and the emptiness of glamour. Nevertheless, most US pop fans bought Stones records simply because they liked them. Even if they didn't, it was hard not to be aware of the existence of, say, 1965's *Out Of Our Heads*, the first Stones LP to top the *Billboard* list, after a hundred-foot illuminated portrait of its front cover – the group in tight close-up – appeared in New York's Times Square – inscribed 'The Sound, Face And Mind Of Today'.

This also ensured a good turnout at a press conference to kick off the Stones' fourth North American tour. It was alleged by a local guitarist, Lee Underwood, that a freelance photographer named Linda Eastman spent the subsequent night with Jagger 'and wrote about it in an American teen magazine'[10]. Yet the article in question did not come to light during my research – nor proof that any liaison between Mick and the soon-to-be Mrs Paul McCartney went further than a wistful embrace beneath the stars at the conclusion of an evening out.

Even at this stage, as their luck held while other groups came and went, the Stones still expected it to run out. 'I know it won't last,' Jagger had smiled in the aftershock of one US expedition, 'I give the Stones another two years. I'm saving for the future.'[11] Making the most of his time in the limelight too, Dick Taylor agreed that 'everybody was fairly innocent then, a bit of a cottage industry. There was no real sense of career development. We thought the Pretty Things would last two, maybe three years. We never felt we were in the entertainment industry as such.' Neither he nor Jagger were, therefore, so dazzled to think that pop stars were immortal, or that they would never have to wonder about the secure anonymity of a 'proper job' again.

If nothing else, the Stones would recoup golden memories of adulation – though some would be more golden than others. On 22 January 1967, they delivered an allotted four numbers under apparent sufferance when topping the bill on ITV's long-running variety showcase *Sunday Night At The London Palladium*, networked straight after a customary hour of religious programmes. They did so with Jagger singing over pre-recorded backing to which the others mimed. Worse, the Stones refused to join the rest of the cast – which included a comedian, acrobats, a formation dancing team, a lady balladeer and compere Jimmy Tarbuck – at the end when they lined up to wave a cheery goodbye on the Palladium's revolving stage while the pit orchestra sight-read the show's 'Startime' theme tune. By making this stand, the Stones were not only gilding their national notoriety, but identifying with a spreading hippy, anti-establishment sub-culture disturbing enough to warrant a celebrity-laden campaign to curtail it. At a public meeting, Frankie Vaughan – once the Stones to 1950s crooner Dickie Valentine's Beatles – declared, 'Hippies are leeches on society'[12], spurning a flower proffered by one such leech in the audience.

Thus predictable howls of affronted derision from the 'straight' press over the group's behaviour on *Sunday Night At The London Palladium* was resonating still during the next edition's rotating curtain call when Peter Cook and Dudley Moore stood waving next to their cardboard effigies of the Stones. During the intervening week, a couple of newspapers had reminded readers of the previous summer when, via a private prosecution by a local youth club organizer and the manager of a petrol station near Romford, Brian Jones, Mick Jagger and Bill Wyman were fined for 'insulting behaviour', to wit, urinating against a wall of the said garage and, according to the prosecution 'not taking steps to conceal the act'.

On the same tour, singer Dave Berry was in the convoy of cars from which the three desperate men had spilled: 'The pissing in the forecourt was blown out of all proportion of what it was. A *Daily Mail* journalist was travelling with us, and it was his job to find stories – like us, say, getting refused entry to a night club in Scarborough, things like that. He would be straight on the phone as soon as the doorman said, "I'm sorry. You can't come in." We'd get chucked out of hotels too – because, at the time, they weren't geared up to young pop musicians staying in them. Once we were working at a theatre in Manchester on a Sunday, and because the Stones and I were each wearing make-up, the manager brought the curtain down because make-up meant that it was a theatre production – which wasn't allowed on the Sabbath.'

Yet, even after the unpleasantness at both the East End filling station and the Palladium, the more liberal sections of British public seemed to have got over the initial shock of the Rolling Stones, almost accepting them as not a pop group as transient and gimmicky as any other, but a tolerable part of the national furniture like Promenade Concerts, ITV's *Coronation Street*, BBC's *Till Death Us Do Part* and the Beatles. They were even worthy of a modicum of grudging respect as stubborn eccentrics who would not 'go showbiz'. Even fork-brandishing fathers disparaging them in breakfast rooms could differentiate between individual members other than just Mick Jagger.

Crucially, by late 1966, the group was starting to be taken half-seriously in the media. Broadsheets no longer put snooty inverted commas round the 'Rolling Stones', and with-it vicars would slip them into *Five To Ten*, an incongruous five-minute religious broadcast on the BBC Light Programme, linking *Uncle Mac's Children's Favourites* and the *Saturday Club* pop show. From Moscow, the Soviet Ministry of Culture sent an emissary to a Stones concert in Warsaw. He returned so thoroughly horrified by what he had experienced that the department made a firm decision not to let any Western pop into Russia in the foreseeable future. In Australia, Richard Neville, founder of the then Sydney-based magazine, *Oz*, wasn't so alarmist, writing that 'seeing Mick Jagger felt like seeing part of myself – as if the Stones and I, and all our mates, belonged to a secret tribe. The mode of the music was alchemical, Mick's strut signalling a burning impatience with the *ancien regime*.'[12]

Every vicinity across the continent contained an outfit that had reinvented itself as an ersatz British beat group. Sydney's Bee Gees, for instance, mutated from an updated Mills Brothers to quasi-Beatles – while over in Melbourne, a former folk quartet had found a Jagger soundalike in future accountant Rod Turnball and bowdlerized the Rolling Stones' name. What's more, the Spinning Wheels hired Roger Savage, the lately emigrated engineer of the Stones' first Decca session, and worked up a repertoire as rife with, often the same, Diddley, Berry, Wolf, Muddy and Jimmy Reed favourites. A so-so version of 'I Got My Mojo Working' was the first of three singles that prefaced the Wheels' demise in 1966, thus sparing them from being obliged to 'go psychedelic', perhaps without quite getting the point.

'We were on the threshold of this new thing,' Jeff Beck reflected, 'The Yardbirds were the first psychedelic band.'[2] This is arguable, but certainly the influence of psychedelia was beginning to take hold in the music and fashion scenes on both sides of the Atlantic. Many of the early psychedelic-tinged records were not hits, but their creators, depending on where they were performing, drew mixed gatherings of confused fans who had bought pre-psychedelic output: Frankie Vaughan's detested hippies, hangers-on from the London in-crowd and riff-raff from the provinces where college common rooms would fill with tinted smoke from joss sticks, thereby lending ambience to tales of a groovy weekend in London – where nowadays a man was not necessarily asking to be beaten up for walking the streets with beads and bells round his neck, embroidered slippers and floral trousers. Well, the Beatles and Stones dressed like that, so it must be OK.

Innocent of the capital's sang-froid, unabated screaming when a package show like any other over the previous ten years reached the more remote parts of the country indicated that hardline pop was still, well, popular. Yet the appeal of a working band of psychedelic ilk was reliant not so much on big smiles and tight trousers as stamina to sustain incessant extrapolation of tracks from both its last album and the unfamiliar successor being 'laid down' during a studio block-booking of weeks, maybe months.

Singles were regarded as fiddly little things that, even if specifically requested, were not considered a necessary part of the onstage set, even if, among the freak-outs and drug-dazed visions, a vague melody lingered on.

Of the Pink Floyd's 'See Emily Play', for example, a *New Musical Express* critic wrote, 'It's crammed with reverberations, electronic vibrations and fuzzy rumblings. Surprisingly, somewhere amid the happening, there's also a pleasant mid-tempo tune.'[13] Yet the Floyd invited trouble by not bothering to perform either this or their 1967 chart debut, despite back-of-beyond audiences who had paid five shillings' admission to hear 'Arnold Layne' and 'See Emily Play', said so during the group's act, and, on one occasion, hurled pre-decimal pennies at the stage. They didn't think a lot either of group leader Syd Barrett's proneness to spontaneous improvisations onstage that went beyond key and time signature, mixing severe dissonance and serene melody. As intuitive a guitarist as Jeff Beck or Jimi Hendrix, Barrett had earned the esteem of Eric Clapton, Pete Townshend and others who wished that they had the nerve to be as adventurous.

Clapton's high-decibel Cream would soon be spinning out a three-verse blues – Willie Dixon's 'Spoonful' – for nigh on twenty po-faced minutes: 'endless, meaningless solos,' a bemused Eric would reflect, 'We were not indulging ourselves so much as our audience – because that's what they wanted.'[14] This was to be a topic of conversation at Alexis Korner's fortieth birthday celebrations in Bayswater on 19 April 1968, attended by Charlie Watts, Mick Jagger, John Mayall and other old campaigners of the blues crusade back in the era of the Ealing club, the Craw Daddy and Studio 51. Ginger Baker turned up too. He was Cream's drummer and another veteran of Alexis Korner's Blues Incorporated, along with Jack Bruce, the third member of Cream, who had also been with Baker in the Graham Bond Organisation, essentially a Blues Incorporated-related group augmented by guitarist John McLaughlin and then saxophonist Dick Heckstall-Smith. However, after the issue of the outfit's *Sound Of '65* LP, Bruce quit to be a Bluesbreaker. A subsequent sojourn with Manfred Mann had him on *Top of the Pops*, plugging the group's 1966 chart-topper, 'Pretty Flamingo'. With Steve Winwood, Jack Bruce was also in the

Powerhouse, a sextet convened by Paul Jones – when still in Manfred Mann – and pianist Ben Palmer for a jam session after hours in an otherwise deserted Marquee. Among extant tracks issued on a 1967 album, *What's Shakin'*, was 'Crossroads', a song that would later enter Cream's repertoire. At the time of Alexis Korner's party, Cream were in the odd position of being one of the biggest box-office draws in North America while planning an appositely titled farewell album, *Goodbye*.

Instrumental proficiency began to matter more as barriers were broken between rock and jazz. *Fresh Cream* (1967) and *Are You Experienced* (1967), thrived on the musical interplay between their executants. If titivated with vocal harmonies plus an assortment of tambourines, handclaps and other percussion trifles, these and similar albums focused almost exclusively on guitar, bass, drums and lead singing. Among few special effects might be an octave-divider, a vari-speed or a wah-wah pedal, devised originally to make a guitar sound like a muted trumpet.

This production criteria – one that was entirely counter to the mosaic-like making of *Sgt. Pepper, Satanic Majesties, SF Sorrow* et al. – affected, if not song structures, then certainly approaches to soloing as pop artists became aware of, even concerned about, the formal dos and don'ts that traditionally afflict creative flow, and the now debatable usefulness of the blues, jazz and rock'n'roll clichés of old. Among valuable object lessons were the records and, on 23 September 1967, first British concert by the notorious Mothers of Invention, evoking a mixed response for their maelstrom of rock, jazz, classical modernism and parody.

Tastes were divided too over such disparate pop as a Beach Boys estranged from the surf, the Incredible String Band's exotic Gaelic mysticism – and beat groups such as the Zombies, the Poets and Unit 4 + 2 making less conscious 'progress'. Sharing much the same co-existent vision were the 'Waterloo – period Kinks and Procol Harum – once the Paramounts – of ponderous majesty. Not for them either were the elaborate pastiches that were *Sgt. Pepper* and *Satanic Majesties* or the funny noises of the Soft Machine or the Pink Floyd, who when no longer acting as passive vehicles for the ground-breaking songwriting methodology born of the drug-addled and soon-departed Syd Barrett's inner chaos, favoured creating musical moods through improvisation. So did Traffic, who, rehearsing under a starry canopy on the concrete platform outside their cottage, could be perceived miles away as, bathed in swirling colour from a light show, they lost themselves in music till sunrise.

Traffic's was one of countless group names with abstract leanings and lack of preceding article that stressed a collaborative ethos – and were very much *à la mode*; if you were the Ironing Boards, it was kinda groovy in 1967 to change to Ironing Board. After Syd left, the 'the' was symbolically dropped by Pink Floyd as it was too by Soft Machine and Marmalade. From among the more established outfits, the Beach Boys thought briefly of truncating to just 'Beach', but the Beatles and the Rolling Stones considered no like alteration. Both the latter groups had, for the time being anyway in the Stones' case, exempted themselves from having to be 'real' musicians in front of possibly non-screaming customers by nowadays retiring to the studio.

'1967 was the explosion of the drug culture, if there is such a thing,' elucidated Keith, 'It came out into the open from underground, and everybody started talking about it.'[1] When not yet versed in hip jargon, the universal aunt that was the BBC had passed Bob Dylan's 'Rainy Day Women Nos. 12 & 35' (with its 'Everybody must get stoned!' hook-line), though just plain 'Heroin' from the Velvet Underground and 'The Addicted Man' – swiftly deleted – by the Game hadn't a hope of a single Light Programme (soon to be Radio One) spin. The Corporation had frowned too on the Byrds' 'Eight Miles High', and 'Tomorrow Never Knows', the eerie omega of the Beatles' *Revolver* (1966), as the 'us and them' divide between youth and elders over the issue of drugs intensified. It would climax halfway through 1967 – with Keith Richards and Mick Jagger – and then Brian Jones – on the very top of the midsummer bonfire.

It began with a house party at Redlands on a mild February weekend, when the grange was busted by a local narcotics squad. Though he was to surface as the central figure, Jagger began as a mere bystander, almost in the wings, when the curtains rose on the most overt act in a real-life play, hitherto exceptional only for a *divertissement* in which two *News of the World* muck-rakers, mistaking Brian Jones for Mick one evening in Blaises, had banged out a report assuring readers, several months after the fact, that he had obliged them by detailing his drug-taking habits in unholier-than-thou fashion, claiming to have experienced LSD as early as 1963. Then, quite openly, he had swallowed some amphetamine tablets and invited them back to his home to smoke some hashish – or was it LSD? When an outraged Jagger served a libel suit, the editor carpeted the journalists responsible and supposedly plotted a damage limitation scheme whereby the truth – or *a* truth – could be re-timed. The story goes that, by prodding various nerves, he found out about Jagger and Faithfull's visit to Redlands. It was then only a matter of a couple of telephone calls to West Sussex Regional Police Headquarters to arrange for the place to be invaded on the Sunday evening. Sure enough, the officers found enough drugs on the premises to justify cautioning Richards – and, to the *News of the World*'s relief, a subdued Jagger, even if it had to be trumped up from four pep-pills.

Richards' countryside home serves as a retreat following the disclosure of their drug violation sentences, 1967.

A subsequent European tour was blighted by ceaseless harassment from customs officials who had clocked in for work after reading about Keith and Mick's imminent court appearance, and had then tarred the rest of those Rolling Stone scruffbags with the same brush, after every fibre of red tape – including a body search – that bureaucracy could gather.

This was capped by a new worry for Brian Jones. When still exhausted and deeply depressed from the Stones trek round Europe, the most harrowing public ordeal of his stage career, all Brian *ought* to have wanted to do was step aside from the fallout of Mick and Keith's drugs trial, but on 10 May, the very afternoon that they were remanded on bail, 1, Courtfield Road was invaded by Scotland Yard officers who had reason to believe that the premises was being used for the consumption of controlled drugs, contrary to the provision of the 1966 Dangerous Drugs Act, section forty-two.

At four o'clock, the place still slept like the dead, and Brian met plain-clothes Sergeant Norman Pilcher's hammering at the door with bare feet, tousled hair, a kimono and the bewildered pallor of someone 'coming down' from Norman knew not what. Flashing a search warrant and barging in, he aimed to find out, as his men started in the panelled lounge, emptying the ashtrays into polythene bags. The ransacking concluded with Brian and the overnight occupant of the spare bedroom, a young Swiss aristocrat, being arrested for possession of grains of cannabis and minuscule quantities of harder stuff. It had been, philosophized a fatalistic Jones, as foreseeable as the plot of an oft-seen episode in the BBC's recent repeats of *Hancock's Half Hour*. It was almost as if he had willed it to happen. An amateur psychologist might theorize that by putting himself in the same stomach-knotting boat as Mick and Keith, he would be a big wheel in the gang again. Alternatively, perhaps it was to beef up his bad boy image. Whatever those two could do, he could do it worse.

Bare fact is that Brian had answered and ignored telephoned tip-offs of the impending intrusion, possibly from sympathetic journalists who had been told themselves by contacts inside the force. At any rate, a photograph of Brian on the balcony of Courtfield Road during the actual raid was to be published in one tabloid, and a tribe of further press was already crowding the pavement outside Chelsea Police Station when Brian was escorted in for the formal charge.

Soon to bust other long-haired pop stars, Pilcher of the Yard – who, years later, would be jailed for corrupting the course of justice – was regarded by the old and square as a hands-on campaigner against the makers of all this marijuana-smoking music, the depraved cacophony that was subverting all that was good and true. Even if his lookalikes were common enough now in the sticks as well as the bigger cities, Jagger was among 'their' most wanted outlaws – hence the gallery overflowing with press, fans and star-struck legal staff employed elsewhere in the building, who had come to watch the fun when Mick, and Keith, emphatically denied all charges at West Sussex Quarter Sessions in Chichester on 27 June.

Jagger's defence counsel pointed out that those pep-pills were available over the counter in France where they had been acquired, and that his client's doctor had permitted him to retain them to combat work fatigue. This was overruled, and less than ten minutes later, the jury – in which folklore was to include the late TV comedy actor Terry Scott – returned a 'guilty' verdict. Two days later, a harmless and intrinsically law-abiding twenty-three-year-old who only wanted to get to the dock quietly, was steered from his cell in unnecessary handcuffs and, amid extravagant rejoicing and lamentation, sent down for three months.

He managed not to faint, but the famous mouth was almost comical in its gaping shock, and tears were not far away as he was hustled out of the Chichester courtroom and off to Brixton Prison – more convenient than it might have been for visits from his parents in Dartford, who, more than ever, were still, as he would admit long after this particular storm had passed, 'unhappy with what I do'.[16]

Though there were professional and personal interests at stake, Charlie and Shirley, Bill and new girlfriend Astrid, and Ian and Cynthia

Stewart could only watch too as the final scene of what was turning into a fifteen-act tragedy neared. 'The only thing I remember was Mick being in prison up the road to where I lived,' said Watts. 'I went to visit him, but I couldn't get in.'[17]

Looking for a new angle after years of presenting the lead singer as the personification of the Stones, many reporters wondered whether the next one for the chop at this twentieth-century witch-hunt was just as deserving of repellent fascination with his saturnine aspect and crow's nest haircut, now slightly spiked like that of one of men-of-the-moment Procol Harum. Some were taken aback when, taking the witness stand after his friend had already been found guilty, Keith Richards gave remarkably level-headed and articulate answers to prosecution questions, though he may have overplayed his hand as the anti-establishment young rock'n'roller up against the ugly, short-haired old squares: 'When the prosecuting counsel asked me about chicks in nothing but fur rugs, I said, "I'm not concerned with your petty morals". They couldn't take that one.'[1]

It was, more or less, a foregone conclusion that the Crown would enjoy a total victory – with an expressionless Keith receiving his sentence of a year inside. By nefarious means, surprisingly friendly fellow convicts in Wormwood Scrubs offered Prisoner No. 7855 roll-ups containing the very drug that had sent him to jail. He would not have minded. If he was really going to be banged up for that long, a supply of spliffs would help the time pass more quickly in an establishment where 'the food's awful, the wine list is terribly limited, and the library is abysmal'.[18]

Beneath the wryness, Richards was an understandably shaken and downcast man, but his response to the orderliness of prison life was made easier when, during the prescribed counter-clockwise walk around the exercise yard the next day, other inmates, drawing from their own clashes with the law, filled his head surreptitiously with victimization, making an example and further theories of how and why he had ended up there, and how and why he would be out sooner rather than later. Keith was heartened further that afternoon when a thunderous huzzah rent the building as, via a workshop Tannoy, a Stones record was spun on pirate Radio London.

Through the oratory skills of his barrister, Richards would be at liberty by twilight. Likewise, Mr and Mrs Jagger would not be obliged to enter Brixton's high and forbidding walls as, after not quite two days behind bars, their son was granted bail too. He had done his time profitably, having, purportedly, drafted '2000 Light Years From Home', to be *Satanic Majesties pièce de résistance*, and a precursor of the 'space rock' propagated by brand-leaders Hawkwind in the 1970s.

In the interim between conviction and bail, the BBC had wrung its hands over whether or not to pan away from Jagger when that Thursday's *Top of the Pops* transmitted the pre-recording of the Beatles' 'All You Need Is Love', in which the miscreant had been among the turnout of illustrious friends assisting on the chorus hook-lines. That same week, a poster with Mick's image and the paraphrased caption 'LET HE WHO IS WITHOUT SIN JAIL THE FIRST STONE' was in what were becoming known as 'head' shops; protest marches along Fleet Street were broken up with the aid of police Alsatians, and a last-minute insert in the latest edition of *Oz* disclosed the the *News of the World*'s editor's home address – with a sly caution that 'It would be inadvisable for our readers to mail him cannabis resin and then tip off the police in an effort to have him busted'.[19] Its own kind turned on the *News of the World* too. The party line at both *The Sun* and the *Daily Sketch* was that the incarceration was 'too likely to make a martyr of this wretched young man'[20] while the *Sunday Express* weighed in with its opinion that it was 'monstrously out of proportion to the offence'[21].

On the evening of Monday 31 July, hours after Keith was acquitted altogether, and Mick's sentence commuted to a conditional discharge – with the judge reminding him of his 'grave responsibilities' – Jagger was trotted out before ITV cameras to debate the repercussions of his conduct since he had become the kingdom's most reviled and worshipped public figure, with two high-ranking priests, a former Home Secretary and William Rees-Mogg, writer of a fiercely sympathetic editorial in *The Times* that had been influential in Mick and Keith's early releases. Belying both his trembling mind and the assumptions by many viewers that he was some sort of anomalous retard, the former London School of Economics undergraduate gave an intelligent and gently spoken account of himself, not exactly repudiating the taking of illegal drugs, but arguing calmly that he was not the one who had made an issue of it in the first place. As a mere pop singer, he had been unqualified to do so in any case, unconsciously agreeing with the *Daily Express*'s James MacMillan, then sharpening his quill to express indignant wonder that such a discussion had ever wasted television time.

Issued within a fortnight to make the most of all the unlooked-for publicity, 'We Love You' – and, to a lesser degree, its 'Dandelion' coupling – was the most plugged single on Radio London in its final hours. Laying it on with a trowel, the Stones' mock-conciliatory reaction to an ugly situation was bracketed by prison-door sound effects. Still, while 'We Love You' expressed a certain sarcastic humour, the experience of the bust, trial and subsequent sentence was to have a more dramatic effect on the Stones' output; according to Keith Richards, the musical and lyrical styles of *Beggars Banquet* owed much to this eventful period in Stones history: 'I guess it was a reaction to … that severe dose of reality…. I was fucking pissed with being busted. So it was, "Right, we'll go and strip this thing down." There's a lot of anger in the music from that period.'[22]

In the promotional film short, however, Brian Jones's puffed, slitted eyes told their own story. Mick and Keith were now off the hook. He was not.

After Brian's trial date was fixed for 30 October, he bounced thoughts off a designated solicitor. How bad could it be? All right, so he would be fined a couple of hundred quid. Maybe a conditional discharge as well? That had to be the limit. The brief shook his head doubtfully. Despite the ultimate outcome of Keith and Mick's bust, Mr Jones had been caught bang to rights, and the Crown was likely to push for the stiffest possible penalty. It would help, said his advisor, if it could be argued that Brian needed psychiatric treatment rather than jail. As well as being frail and haggard from the arrest and the still-resurgent shockwaves of Anita and Keith, who could regard him as 'normal' after so many years of being under pressures that John Citizen could not begin to understand? Taking this to heart, Jones got himself admitted to a residential clinic in rural London between Richmond and Kew. Set in four thousand acres, it contained uniform, magnolia-coloured single bedrooms that were frugal but bearable enough. The regime was, too. As well as sessions on the couch, inmates were subjected to compulsory exercise, group therapy, confinement to the estate's boundaries and no sex.

In cold print, it reads like prison, but, from an unpromising beginning, the new patient – like Keith in Wormwood Scrubs – reacted well to its discipline. He was also able to re-encounter the outside world with his ways changed – or so both Jones and his legal team assured the bench. Neither this nor the defendant's neat pin-striped suit softened court chairman Robert Seaton's heart. Loudly, as if addressing a mass beyond the stained-glass windows of the Inner London Sessions, he spoke of pop stars setting an example to their admirers, and him failing in his duty if he didn't send Brian down for nine months.

The protests that followed were not on the scale of those provoked by the incarcerations of Jagger and Richards, but a demonstration that snowballed to thirty youthful participants around Sloane Square in the pouring rain was unruly enough to necessitate twelve arrests. This exercise in futility made no difference as the hours dragged by for Jones in Wormwood Scrubs, where he had been issued with regulation ill-fitting garb with the texture of a horse blanket, and allocated a cell. The next day, so he was told by one maliciously gleeful warder, he must endure an enforced visit to the prison barber for the standard short-back-and-sides with electric clippers. However, just as Brian had reached the stage of half-hearted attempts to be pleasant to the guards and the other prisoners, his belongings were returned to him and a thumb jerked at the cell's open door. Twenty minutes later – with all of his hair still on his head – Brian Jones was free.

An expert appointed by a High Court judge had examined him and had been convinced that his mental state was precarious, even suicidal, and this had tipped the balance in favour of an appeal hearing on 12 December 1967. On the day, he appeared contrite but his facial expression might have been more to do with a raging toothache. Nevertheless, it was agreed that Brian had learnt his lesson, and that he had every intention of staying out of trouble for the foreseeable future. He was not, therefore, to receive dental treatment back at the Scrubs, but pay a hefty fine and be put on probation for three years. His behaviour was to be monitored too, via regular consultations with a psychiatrist.

For all his implied promises that he would never touch narcotics again, Brian, weak with relief, celebrated by getting smashed out of his brain almost immediately. A culmination of this escapade, his pulled molar, the eternal asthma and the general strain of that particular week brought about a collapse at Courtfield Road, his body vibrating with shuddering gasps and every pore on an ashen complexion bestowed with a pinprick of sweat. Contrary to medical advice, however, Brian discharged himself from hospital before there was a chance to instigate procedures to find anything in his bloodstream that might interest his probation officer.

Five months later in the throes of the *Beggars Banquet* sessions, Brian's sly resumption of his drug habits was in less secretive focus via another run-in with the law. This time, rather than respond to the relentless knocking – Sergeant Pilcher again – he dialled the Stones' office before the police gained forced access. When an aide's engine died outside, Brian's persecutors were belabouring him about some cannabis uncovered in a ball of wool from the drawer of a desk.

'I don't knit. I don't darn socks. I don't have a girlfriend who darns socks,' he would plead too when, after two nail-biting adjournments, the case came up in autumn. This was true enough, but the jury still thought he was guilty as hell. Under the circumstances, Brian had no right to expect mercy, but those psychological problems of his proved helpful again, and he got away with a fine as inappreciable as the amount of dope with which he had been caught – or he had had planted on him.

'Brian's main preoccupation then was a severe paranoia about being busted,' deduced Keith Richards, 'He had no other thoughts in his head except hiding from the police.'[4] For the proverbial 'moral support', Keith and, more often, Mick had been present at various of Brian's court appearances, and, in the long summer weeks (when *Beggars Banquet* was all but completed) leading up to the last one, he was put up in 'Redlands', out of reach of Pilcher, the newspapers and temptation.

In view of the hippy sub-culture's supposed trafficking in promiscuity and drugs, you could understand police and press's attitude towards the Stones – and what John Lennon called the 'controlled weirdness'[23] of 'Apple Corps', an umbrella term for myriad maverick ventures under the aegis of the Beatles' new self-managed business enterprise. After moustaches, LSD and meditation, the Beatles had not latched onto bourgeois greed all of a sudden. No more qualified to run Apple Corps than the recently deceased Brian Epstein had been to play guitar, 'we had this mad idea of having Apple there,' said George Harrison, 'so that people could come and do artistic stuff and not have a hard time.'[24] Advertisements appeared, therefore, in both national and underground outlets soliciting the public to bring artistic stuff to the Apple Foundation for the Arts in London. Not a postal delivery would go by without a deluge of manuscripts and demo tapes thumping on to its doormat, begging for cases to be heard.

Setting off on his journey to a pathetic end on a gore-splattered New York pavement in 1980, Lennon was to order the issue on Zapple, Apple

Records's short-lived 'experimental' subsidiary label, of his *Unfinished Music No. 2: Life With The Lions* (1968), the second of a trilogy of albums with Yoko Ono, a Japanese-American who many still see as walking evidence of her own conjecture: 'You don't need talent to be an artist.'[25] Its back cover was a photograph of John with his arm round a distressed Yoko in the midst of policemen outside Marylebone Magistrates Court where he had been fined for possession of cannabis.

No longer the Moptop Mersey Marvel of yore, Lennon, with a new penchant for penis display and making his headline-hogging life an open and ludicrous book, had overtaken Mick Jagger as chief representative of all that the likes of Frankie Vaughan feared and despised, particularly after the final outcome of the Stones' drug busts. Though the *Daily Express* — which, since at least the mid-1950s, tended to label a buyer as politically right of centre — had published a cartoon in which a John Bull-like figure voices disgust that 'Mick Jagger, Rolling Stone' had become 'Mick Jagger, Saint!'[26], the heavy handed endeavour to punish Mick Jagger for being Mick Jagger backfired further when his case escalated Caroline Coon's foundation of Release, 'the first youth organization that was really an alternative social service run by young people for young people,' she said with quiet pride. 'I felt people needed to know what to do when they were arrested — that you didn't have to be pressured into a confession. You didn't have to make a statement before you've seen a solicitor. What the police claim to be illegal drugs must be confirmed by analysis. You are legally entitled to a telephone call etc. One of the first practical things we did at Release was put out a know-your-rights Bust Card. We had thousands printed to distribute free.'[15]

When Mick and Keith's freedom had still been in the balance, hundreds of like-minded teenagers had demonstrated in Piccadilly Circus and outside the *News of the World* block; the Who's manager, Kit Lambert, placed an advertisement in a national daily objecting to the two Stones being 'treated as scapegoats for the drug problem'[27], just as the Who themselves were knocking out their revivals of 'The Last Time' and 'Under My Thumb' for a single that would spend three weeks in the lower end of the Top Fifty, in a show of moral support for their fellow musicians.

Less specific dissent was in the air as the Summer of Love was proving to be no more the dawning of the Age of Aquarius than the Twist had been. Collectively, the Stones shared the overall disenchantment of the hippy counter-culture with the dissipation of flower-power idealism – which was to be epitomized in the USA by the Sharon Tate bloodbath in summer 1969. Had it been only the previous October that *International Times* had declared, 'Charlie Manson is just a harmless freak'?[28] Before massacre came to horrify viewers of the six o' clock news no more than a shoot-out in a spaghetti western, an amused Ringo Starr was to ascribe the supplanting of flower-power in Britain by a fad for dressing up as slouch-hatted, tailboard-riding Prohibition hitmen and their molls, to merely 'those lightweight clothes. You'd freeze to death – so flower people are putting on their overcoats again.'[29]

Following Al Capone chic, the next craze appeared to be 'revolution', derided as 'this year's flower-power' by Frank Zappa[30]. Because it exposes a point of view, even the boy-girl couplets of 'The Last Time' might be construed as political, but, after eves of destruction, nineteenth nervous breakdowns and strawberry fields, composers were wringing apocalyptic drops from GIs missing in Indo-China, the Soviet rape of Czechoslovakia and the general upheavals that were in the air now.

John Lennon was putting his mind to an eponymous opus on revolution – which would surface as a B-side to the Beatles' 'Hey Jude' – that, however irresolute, would be his most far-reaching assessment in song of the political undercurrents pertinent to the culmination of the Swinging Sixties. Likewise, the Stones were to come up with 'Street Fighting Man' (partly inspired by the worker and student protests in Paris in May 1968) – and the Pretty Things with 'October 26 (Revolution)'.

Following the end of the students' occupation of the Sorbonne, fighting broke out between the Parisian students and security police in Paris in 1968.

The Stones' old friends and rivals' living still depended on earnings from the road, but they were most amenable to playing for just expenses on a stage erected within the barricades of a sit-in at London's Goldsmith's College at the request of Germaine Greer, then a professor of English there. With New Left radicalism the common denominator, there was so much to spark off such tub-thumping takeovers: the assassinations of Martin Luther King and Robert Kennedy; a compounding of feminism; the continued slaughter and starvation of Mao Tse-tung's cultural purge; Ireland, bloody Ireland; the increasing encroachment of Russian troops on Eastern Europe, and, of course, Vietnam – where a Lieutenant William L Calley, Jnr had just overseen the slaughter of the women and children of an entire village, and had been immortalized in 'Battle Hymn of Lieutenant Calley' by Terry Nelson, which was to go on sale ten days prior to a long-awaited court martial verdict on Calley. Nelson and his record company's prayers that the officer wouldn't be acquitted were answered, and the single flew out of the pressing plant. To the tune of 'John Brown's

Body', it strove to vindicate Calley on the grounds that he and his death squad were merely obeying orders, 'even though they made me out to be a villain, my truth was marching on.' At least a million US music lovers — largely 'rednecks' – agreed.

This ghastly market triumph was a trace of sulphurous vapour on the horizon when kaftans were mothballed as their former wearers trailed along with the crowd to genuinely violent anti-war demonstrations, riots, disruptions of beauty pageants and further student sit-ins. Girls lost their marbles over Daniel Cohn-Bendit – 'Danny The Red' – organizer of the 'situationist' New Left *événements* in France, but not as much as they did over the Cuban revolutionary Che Guevara.

When pressed about the distant hostilities and like inflammable topics, Keith Richards was sufficiently hip to understand that killing people is wrong, and was active after a detached, arm-sweepingly pop-starrish fashion in verbally endorsing both pacifism and Cohn-Bendit's *soixante-huitards*, while enquiring, 'How many times can they use those words – justice, freedom? It's like margarine. You can package and sell that too.'[31] He might also have spoken vaguely, perhaps, about 'unemployment' without going into economic ramifications, but more pointed anger was directed at Decca who, so Keith comprehended, were ploughing back monies amassed through record sales into its radar division – which made parts for air force bombers in Vietnam.

Interviewed by Richard Branson, then editor of the leftish *Student* magazine, Mick Jagger too seemed to be all for dissident popular opinion, though he tended to follow reason as much as his heart, and felt compromised if waylaid by extremist factions who wanted him to join with them. Yet, if he made no doctrinal statement, even under pressure, he would be visible on a traffic island on the periphery of the militant protesters outside the US Embassy in London. Furthermore, while he was to be criticized by agit-prop extremists for not inciting the multitudes at the Stones' celebrated free concert in Hyde Park to take over London, he was to volunteer financial aid when the saga of the notorious 'Schoolkids' edition of *Oz* climaxed at the Old Bailey, and had actually sunk hard cash into and procured premises for the British operation of San Francisco's groovily subversive *Rolling Stone*, until then not readily available outside the States. Hoping that the UK publication was to be developed separately from its Californian template, he would settle down eagerly to his duties as newspaper proprietor. This entrepreneurial sideshow, however, was to be thrust aside as the Stones' business dealings became more and more rife with discord.

NOTES

1. *The Rolling Stones In Their Own Words* eds. D. Dalton and M. Farren (Omnibus, 1980)

2. *Beat Merchants* by A. Clayson (Blandford, 1995)

3. *Travelling Man* by F. Allen (Aureus, 1999)

4. *Keith Richards In His Own Words* ed. M. St Michael (Omnibus, 1994)

5. *Chicago Tribune*, 16 November 1964

6. He was also to insist that Jagger change 'the night' to 'some time' in 1967's 'Let's Spend The Night Together'. On the show, Mick rolled his eyes in mock exasperation whenever he sang the doctored line.

7. *Melody Maker*, 5 February 1966

8. *The Rolling Stone Interviews* ed. J. Wenner (Straight Arrow, 1974)

9. *You Don't Have To Say You Love Me* by S. Napier-Bell (New English Library, 1982)

10. *Blue Melody: Tim Buckley Remembered* by L. Underwood (Backbeat, 2002)

11. *Melody Maker*, 20 July 1964

12. *Playpower* by R. Neville (Jonathan Cape, 1970)

13. *New Musical Express*, 15 June 1967

14. *Behind The Mask*, BBC Radio One, 1985

15. *The Guardian*, 11 February 2004

16. *The Sun*, 25 January 1983

17. *Mojo*, September 2003

18. *Sunday Times,* 17 August 2003

19. *Oz*, June 1967

20. *The Sun*, 29 June 1967

21. *Sunday Express*, 2 July 1967

22. *According to the Rolling Stones* eds Dora Loewenstein and Philip Dodd (Weidenfeld & Nicholson, London 2003)

23. *John Lennon* by A. Clayson (Sanctuary, 2003)

24. *Time Out*, 4 September 1988

25. Excerpt from Yoko Ono's opening address at her exhibition at the Everson Museum of Art, 9 October 1971

26. *Daily Express*, 30 June 1967

27. *The Guardian*, 11 February 2004

28. *The Lamberts* by A. Motion (Chatto and Windus, 1986)

29. *International Times*, October 1968

30. *Disc*, 16 December 1967

31. *Loose Talk* ed. L. Botts (Rolling Stone Press, 1980)

Chapter 4
SALT OF THE EARTH: THE BUSINESS

*'There was a period around 1968 when people objected
to rich rock stars: like, being rich wasn't considered to
be cool – but I wasn't rich then.'* Mick Jagger[1]

'(I Can't Get No) Satisfaction' was still lingering in the US Hot
100 when 'Get Off Of My Cloud' was rush-released in October
1965. It was, thought Keith Richards, 'one of Andrew's worst
productions. Actually, what I wanted to do was slow it down, but
we rocked it up.'[2]

There remains bitter division about Andrew Loog Oldham. Was he
an imaginative and overgrown boy sucked into a vortex of circumstances
he could not resist; one of the cleanest new brooms ever to sweep the UK
pop business; or a music industry version of the conniving and
manipulative Sergeant Bilko, a character who lived on his wits in
television's *The Phil Silvers Show*? Certainly, Oldham's questionable skills
as a record producer had been untried when first he and the Stones had
gathered together in a studio. Yet he seemed to have aspired to be an
English 'answer' to Phil Spector, a weedy New Yorker, who was hot
property in the States for his spatial 'wall of sound' technique, whereby he
would multi-track an apocalyptic mélange – replete with everything,
possibly including the proverbial kitchen sink – behind acts who had
submitted to his master plan.

Andrew Loog Oldham struck it lucky by managing and promoting the Rolling Stones.

Slightly-built Andrew was then only nineteen — younger than any of the Stones — but, since leaving boarding school at sixteen, he had been hovering round the music business in mostly menial capacities in preparation for a grander but yet unknown purpose. When briefly a cog in Brian Epstein's publicity machine, he had understood more thoroughly than many a more experienced British talent scout that Epstein's manipulation of the Beatles and his other chart-busting Liverpool acts was the tip of an iceberg that would make more fortunes than had ever been known in the history of recorded sound.

If even more naïve than Epstein had once been about the ways and means of doing so, Oldham still felt ready to go for the chart jugular as soon as he had found a Beatles-sized vehicle with which to do so. He intended also to not only produce its records but to be more than the customary *éminence grise* behind the group's merchandising, appearing to model himself on fictitious 'Johnny Jackson', the irrepressibly confident Soho agent — who was based on Larry Parnes, and played by Laurence Harvey in 1959's quasi-satirical *Expresso Bongo*. The thrust of the plot was the metamorphosis of Bert Rudge — Cliff Richard's second big screen role — into an overnight Presley figure, via much browbeating hyperbole and media manipulation.

If Andrew did not know much about R&B, he, like Jackson, did know what he would need to exploit – and the Stones seemed as likely to be the next Titans of Teen as any other in this new breed of guitar groups. Thus, in April 1963, a potent combination of vocational boredom, fading business innocence and frustrated artistic aspirations took Andrew Loog Oldham to the suffocating crush of the Craw Daddy and furnished him with the desire to steer the Stones out of it.

Though convinced that he had struck lucky – and had been a nose ahead of an oncoming rush to sign the group –- there followed a week of private anxiety. As Andrew had neither the cash nor sufficient connections to launch the Stones nationally, he supplicated a possible co-manager more steeped in the traditions and lodged conventions of British show business than he. Seventeen years Oldham's senior – and, some might say, the Colonel Hall to his Bilko – Eric Easton was respected and liked by the many prestigious, and principally middle-of-the-road, clients of his cautious West End booking agency, not least because he had been an entertainer himself. When rock'n'roll came along, Eric, a self-confessed 'square'[3], had not let personal dislike of its more transient stars and their teenage devotees prevent him from turning a hard-nosed penny when the opportunity knocked.

Invited to the Craw Daddy by young Andrew, Eric – besuited, middle-aged and balding – stuck out like a sore thumb, but he did not behave as either an unsmiling pedant or as if visiting another planet. Indeed, before it ended in tears, there was enough common ground between Easton and the bombastic Oldham for each to be prone to both thrift and extravagance when presenting the Rolling Stones to the nation.

When the Stones stumbled off after exacting their customary submission from whoever had not wanted to like them, Easton and Oldham struggled through the crowd to suggest a meeting at the agency with Brian Jones, identified already as 'leader'. He was not as nonchalantly indifferent as he may have appeared to be. For some time, he had realized that, while he had proved capable of negotiating bookings with this quizzical pub landlord or that uninterested social secretary, what the group needed desperately was formal management with the contacts to push them up to the next level and beyond.

He arrived at Easton's office with Mick Jagger in tow, and did most of the talking on the Stones' behalf, hearing fine words when Oldham put them on a par with the Beatles. For Brian, the principal upshot was that he would no longer have to write the letters, make the telephone calls and ensure that performers and equipment were in the same place at the same time. Something may have warned him that loss of responsibility meant loss of power, but the overall feeling was one of relief as he signed the official agreement, permitting this odd couple's newly founded Impact Sound management to take charge of his Rolling Stones' professional lives for the next three years.

Mulling over strategies for gaining a recording contract, Eric and Andrew decided that, as the Beatles were proving too lucrative an investment for EMI, they ought to target Decca – especially as Dick Rowe, the label's head recording manager and, intrinsically, as old-fashioned in outlook as Easton, had auditioned and rejected the Beatles the previous year. Although he had been recognized as Decca's chief talent spotter since his 'Broken Wings' by the Stargazers had been the first British disc to top the national chart ten years earlier, Dick's superiors were not quite so sure of him any more. This may have explained why the hit-parade Merseybeat that had followed the ascent of the Beatles had provoked Rowe to saturate Decca with beat groups, in the hope that one of them might catch on like the 'Fab Four' had when grabbed to teeth-gnashing effect by the company's main commercial enemy.

While the Beatles might survive, Eric Easton could foresee the Merseybeat ferry grounding on a mudbank before 1963 was out, and that Dick Rowe could be persuaded that the Stones were the next big fish to hook. This judgement proved all too correct – because, fully aware of the buzz emanating from Richmond, Rowe was ready to make it a point of honour to procure hits for Oldham and Easton's discovery before this beat bubble burst and 'decent' music could reign once more. This was despite finding Andrew a dreadful teenage upstart. While he was old Eric's business partner, Oldham tried Dick's patience as he started calling the shots more or less as soon as he entered Decca's riverside offices and, sprawling disrespectfully in a button-leather armchair when conducted into the presence of Dick Rowe and Decca managing director Bill Townsley, swept aside such obstacles as demo tapes and auditions. No question: Andrew Loog Oldham was obnoxious, but Decca did not want the next Beatles to go with Pye, Philips or, heaven forbid, an EMI subsidiary, did it?

Within days of Rowe's fraught first meeting with Oldham, a Decca recording deal guaranteed the Stones and their handlers a royalty of six per cent between them – a sight more than EMI had granted their precious Beatles. Though it was alien to Decca's policy too, Rowe let Oldham, rather than a house producer, take care of the Stones' maiden A-side, 'Come On' – and, as things turned out, all further releases until the group tired of him.

Whatever Andrew's limits within the spheres of the studio, the Stones had in him the personal manager they deserved. Like Brian Epstein, Oldham made disturbing mistakes while learning his trade, but, when press hounds circled the Stones, whereas Epstein might have cringed if zany merriment about haircuts and mini-skirts swung in seconds to unfunny quips about more inflammable issues, Oldham actively encouraged rather than merely tolerated expletives and gesturing with cigarettes, and endorsed any frankness about drugs and free love, and an overall winding-up of adult rage and derision.

It seemed to do the trick, because when, for instance, 1966's *Aftermath* reached Number One in both the US and Britain, proving once again that sales figures for Stones singles were but a surface manifestation of deeper devotion, it became clear that Bill, Brian, Charlie, Keith and Mick were as sound an investment for Decca as John, George, Paul and Ringo had been for EMI. During negotiations for the renewal of the Stones' contract in 1965, therefore, an unprecedented and jaw-droppingly high advance was bullied most impressively out of the company by the group's recently appointed US business manager, Allen Klein.

A hard-talking New Yorker, Klein knew the complex mumbo-jumbo of US show-business lore backwards, having absorbed much when assistant to Morty Craft, president of MGM in the late 1950s. With a brain that spewed forth estimates at a moment's notice, Klein's growing reputation as 'the Robin Hood of Pop' by the mid-1960s stood on his recouping of disregarded millions for his charges from seemingly impenetrable record company percentages. Through hovering over British pop as a vulture over a dying buffalo, his administrative caress had come to encompass the Dave Clark Five, the Kinks and the uncut rubies – including the Animals and Herman's Hermits – that had been processed for the charts by freelance production whizz-kid Mickie Most. The Stones had also bitten, said Most, after they had 'seen me driving around in the Rolls and owning a yacht, and started wondering where their money was going. Allen got them together and gave them money'.[4]

One of many Goldwyn-esque homilies attributed to him was 'What's the point of Utopia if it don't make a profit?' It went without saying that he wasn't to succumb to kaftans, joss sticks, meditation, Zen macrobiotic cookery or any other paraphernalia indicating a bedazzlement with flower power. Paunchy, short-cropped and an observer of a routine ruled by the clock, Klein had framed family photographs on his desk within the panelled top floor of a Manhattan skyscraper – and, for all his methodically blunt stances on the telephone there, Allen was an impassive, reflective pipe-and-slippers type at home, who liked to distance himself from the office. Everything that Andrew Oldham wasn't, Klein wouldn't be caught, say, nibbling afternoon scones at Redlands or 1, Courtfield Road because he didn't 'bother that much with artists, but you have to develop some sort of rapport – although it's important that you stay away. Otherwise, you can really get on each other's nerves.'[5]

Yet, if pop was a commodity like any other to be bought, sold and replaced when worn out, Klein was not self-deprecating in his knowledge and love of it and, when wooing the Stones via Oldham rather than Easton, he underwent a crash course in their music to better butter them up. Then, with his feet under their table, he was to convince Andrew that too much capital was being wasted on Billy Bunters whose postal orders never arrived – and that Eric Easton's face no longer fitted, just as Ian Stewart's hadn't. However, Eric had been a loyal and essentially honest servant, and it was not surprising that an endeavour to buy out the man who had shared the Stones' fortunes since 1963 was thwarted, and a shower of writs ensued. Subject to the next phase of Klein's seeming divide-and-rule ploy, Oldham would cling on longer until the day in 1968 when he rang Mick Jagger from a telephone kiosk to wish him a nice rest-of-his-life.

Allen, therefore, was not the most popular amongst record industry moguls – and the fawning reverence and terrified admiration of his employees was tempered by innumerable derogatory *bon mots* from former clients. Nevertheless, wasting no time with small talk while driving hard and unrelenting bargains, 'he revolutionized the industry,' believed one Stones accountant with no reason to love him. 'You've heard lots of terrible stories about him, most of which I concur with, but he was a tough American cookie, and he came over here and fought for the artists he was involved with.'[6]

His initial purpose in the Stones' organization was, purely and simply, to help with business affairs so that Andrew Oldham could attend to and expand more creative matters such as his independent record label, Immediate, whose flagship act was the Small Faces. This popular mod quartet had amassed a backlog of hits for Decca, with whom they were persuaded by Andrew not to re-sign. While Andrew was not able to likewise grab the Stones for Immediate, there was nothing to stop individual members from functioning in a behind-the-scenes capacity; the most conspicuous example of this was Mick Jagger as producer of Chris Farlowe, hitherto a blues and soul singer from North London, who had meant next to nothing in the charts, but was appreciated by other artists for a curdled baritone enhanced with strangled gasps and anguished roars. Jagger took charge of all Farlowe recordings for the next two years. 1966 began with Farlowe's 'Think' creating a stir. Next, another Jagger-Richards opus, 'Out Of Time', dragged Georgie Fame from Number One that summer. It did not take long for the going to get rough again for Chris, but his triumph demonstrated that all he had lacked was the right song.

As Farlowe's Top Fifty career went into free fall, Jagger and the other Stones were wondering whether they lacked the right record company. They were Decca's blue-eyed boys, true enough, but they had been disappointed that financial and legal support had not been forthcoming from the company during the 1967 drug busts and consequent trials and imprisonments. Neither did their personal manager pull many strings to get Mick, Keith and Brian out of trouble with the police. Perhaps afraid that he was being lined up by Scotland Yard for the next strike, Andrew Oldham had fled to California.

By autumn, he was no longer representing the group – though he noted that, with indecent haste, any open-handed conviviality around Allen Klein's office desk had given way to the Stones' probing suspicion about how much fiscal wool was being pulled over eyes that used to glaze over during quarterly meetings with accountants, and that their relationship with Allen was becoming more and more rife with discontent and proddings, mostly from Jagger, about where this percentage had come from, and why so-and-so had been granted that franchise. It was a mixed blessing that Klein, now something of a pop personality in his own right, as Andrew Loog Oldham was, had been around less of late, as he was about to be hired to straighten out the Beatles' sprawling Apple empire, a venture that had taken mere weeks to descend into chaos. Yet, once so pleased with Allen's bellicose interventions on the Stones' behalf, Jagger was to take the trouble to call at Apple to dissuade John, George, Ringo and Paul from signing with one he could not yet quite accuse outright of shifty manoeuvres and illicit transfer of cash into his own account. Klein, nonetheless, had arrived before him, and was spieling in top gear.

As no one else was prepared to do so, Mick next applied himself to investigating the Stones' company ledgers, and taking measures to curb what he perceived as embezzlements and fiddles. This was of particular urgency because he, unlike certain other members of the group, did not imagine that his means were limitless. Plain fact was that a metaphorical pistol was being primed to aim with terrifying sureness at the very heart of the Stones by the Inland Revenue – and that the unleashing of another million-selling album could not come a moment too soon to help settle an impending sky-high tax bill that had snowballed over five years of international stardom. On paper, they had made a vast amount of money – but where was that money now?

In a search for plausible avenues for rebate or playing for time, Mick's vocabulary filled with phrases like 'tax concession' and 'convertible debenture'. Moreover, whenever possible, he also stuck to conventional office hours in the group's new headquarters on a single floor of a town house just off Piccadilly. Mr Jagger was a fair-minded if fastidious boss, but his staff could not imagine him after work, relaxing over an after-dinner crossword, or watching *Panorama* whilst sipping a cup of cocoa. He did, however, read the *Financial Times* as well as *Melody Maker*, and was reaping a lasting and beneficial effect of his incomplete degree course at the London School of Economics – or at least the period there when he was alert and interested at lectures, and was applying himself religiously to his essays as if he meant to become a middle-weight financial executive in five years, on the board of directors in ten, and chairman by the time he was forty.

In a peculiar way, the last wish was fulfilled well ahead of schedule, and deservedly so. Walter Yetnikoff, a record-label treasurer with whom Jagger was to have serious dealings as a world-famous Rolling Stone, would deduce that 'his image as the prancing prince of pop belied the side of his character that had seriously studied economics. He was a skilled negotiator who never lost sight of his advantage as a pop icon.' At business lunches concerning multi-million-dollar transactions, Jagger did not show too much eagerness, spoke in riddles and, cried Yetnikoff, 'liked to give the impression of inebriation while retaining control. When it came to numbers, Mick was as sober as St Augustine.' Once, after 'ordering wine that cost more than the GNP of certain countries', he and Walter calculated on cocktail napkins a specific territory's VAT for a given royalty rate and number of albums sold. 'Two minutes later, he had an accurate reading,' goggled Yetnikoff, 'while I was still fumbling.'[7]

When in the process of reducing Allen Klein's say in Stones affairs, Jagger seized the reins of the *Beggars Banquet* promotional campaign. While there was to be no supporting tour, there was a launch party and, like the drugs busts fall-out in microcosm, an unforeseen but welcome opportunity to trumpet it via a frisson of controversy.

Already, there had been long faces over the de-selection of a track entitled 'Jumpin' Jack Flash' (also sometimes pressed as 'Jumping Jack Flash') for *Beggars Banquet,* owing to pressure from Decca that a new single was long overdue. Yet this was not a question of the Stones caving in because a clause in the deal mapped out in 1963 stated that Decca, for all its yearning to sign them, had the final say about release schedules. All the same, the removal of 'Jumpin' Jack Flash' from the shortlist of possible tracks for the new album was as exasperating for the Stones as EMI's insistence in 1967 that the Beatles separate likewise 'Strawberry Fields Forever' and 'Penny Lane' from the yet-unreleased *Sgt. Pepper.*

This annoyance was, however, nowhere as bitter as the issue of the *Beggars Banquet* gatefold sleeve. Keith and Mick had taken the trouble to festoon a dingy section of toilet wall above the seat and cistern in black felt-tipped scrawlings – which embraced disobliging references to the Band ('Music From Big Brown'), Bob Dylan and Frank Zappa as well as world political figures (e.g. 'Lyndon Loves Mao') – and authorize a

photograph of their labour to serve as the outer cover of the album. Both Decca and the US outlet, London Records, washed their hands of it, the Stones dug their heels in, and the release date, first plotted for July 1968, was held at arm's length for nearly six months.

While this was all grist to the publicity mill, it was moderate compared to the

The controversial album cover for *Beggars Banquet*.

shock to come in autumn when the jacket of *Unfinished Music No. 1: Two Virgins* (1968) by John Lennon and his soon-to-be second wife, Yoko Ono, depicted the pair stark naked, front and back. Well, he had a penis, hadn't he? Shortly afterwards, posters were pasted in London's tube stations, that promoted a new film, *Till Death Us Do Part* (1968), based on the BBC television sitcom, and had an unclothed Warren Mitchell as Alf Garnett in pride of place, covering up his genitalia with hands and tobacco-pipe; and what about that murkily lit 'nude scene' there for all to see in *Hair* the very day after stage censorship was abolished in 1968's Theatres Act? Almost exactly a year earlier, *International Times*, Britain's foremost underground organ, had impinged upon the general populace via a centre spread of Frank Zappa bare on the lavatory, but with his modesty strategically hidden – and hadn't there been hearsay of Jagger wanting to be pictured naked on a cross somewhere on *Satanic Majesties*?

If that was more than hearsay, he had been talked out of it, but Mick and the other Stones presented a united front over the *Beggars Banquet* snap. Decca would not budge either – principally because the group (and Allen Klein) knew – and Decca knew they knew – that they would concede defeat, just as they had when obliged to deliver the contractually mandated 'Jumpin' Jack Flash' single, and *Beggars Banquet* was to reach the shops during 1968's Christmas sell-in in a package fronted with the name of the product and the group that created it in elegant copperplate on a white background, not unlike that which the Beatles had just used for their 'White Album'.

In an age when rude words on the printed page and in record grooves, sexual fondling on evening television and truly sick-making commercial strategies had not yet become common, the stalemate over the wretched album sleeve could only have concluded with a face-saving token ritual of roundabout persuasion by creatures from Decca – and, for an especially adamant Keith Richards, open pleas before defiance, hesitation, defiance again and final acceptance chased across the studio-pale countenance of one whose attitude towards any given track could either bring it to completion or sabotage it.

Keith's interest in business affairs was much less intense than Mick's, although his years in the record industry had fostered in him a grasp of financial technicalities that, if opinionated, was less hesitant than most. As the expiry date of the Decca contract edged closer, rumour darkened to a certainty that the Stones were not going to re-sign, owing partly to nonsenses like the *Beggars Banquet* sleeve, but mainly to what was seen by the group as avaricious vacillation over sensed royalty discrepancies. Needless to say, Decca refuted this sullying of its good name, but, swallowing its ire, sent representatives to join other major labels submitting their bids to one of the hottest properties in show business.

Decca also fixed a ghastly corporate smile when 'Cocksucker Blues', obscene doggerel spotlighting just Jagger and an acoustic guitarist, was proffered to an appalled artists-and-repertoire department when the delivery of one more single was the only barrier to the Rolling Stones' complete freedom from the company. The only known precedent to this had been Van Morrison's riposte in 1968 to a small label with similar claims on him. These he relinquished with thirty bursts of voice-and-thrashed-guitar worthlessness, most of them less than a minute long. Then unreleased, the master tapes of both 'Cocksucker Blues' and Morrison's nonsense were not destroyed but locked in safes, where they would lie as forgotten as Serge Gainsbourg and Brigitte Bardot's cancelled 'Je T'Aime...Moi Non Plus' and, also from 1969, 'The Troggs Tape', an illicit recording of a cross-purposes studio discussion with a swear word in nearly every sentence.

Yet when Decca was still clinging to the hope that the foul-mouthed Stones would not be lost to them, its wheeler-dealers continued to up already astronomical offers and express willingness to tack the most preposterous fringe benefits on to the standard clauses, even in the seethe of washroom whisperings that the metaphorical weathervane was turning in the direction of Atlantic Records. This had been indicated in April when Mick and Keith tagged along with the late Ahmet Ertegun, the firm's goateed supremo, when he visited the Speakeasy to catch a recital by Screaming Lord Sutch, the latest acquisition by a company that had been a bystander during the British Invasion, buoyed as it was by a bevy of hit-making black soul singers, before grabbing the Spencer Davis Group in 1966.

More recently, Led Zeppelin, Yes and other British outfits concentrating principally on the US market, had melted into Atlantic's caress too. In a stronger position to dictate terms than they, the Stones were granted their own subsidiary label, Rolling Stones Records, complete with a logo that caricatured Mick Jagger's lips and tongue. If there was the slightest deviation from the ascribed riders, wild horses would not drag the Stones out to utter one solitary syllable or play a single note on a given album's behalf.

It was a tall order, but Atlantic was the label most prepared to obey, and there was too the enticement of its stable of black R&B artists, from the Coasters and the Drifters back in the 1950s to a bevy of hit-making soul singers, among them Wilson Pickett, Carla Thomas, Otis Redding and Don Covay, on both Atlantic itself and its subsidiary outlet, Stax. When the Stones had reached an agreeable compromise between monetary gain and an affiliation to music that had captured the imaginations of their younger selves, the Erteguns (Ahmet and Nesuhi) recognized a sound investment as an in-person slot on *Top of the Pops* oiled the wheels of a domestic chart climb for 'Brown Sugar', the debut Atlantic 45. On the same show, the group also plugged its 'Bitch' coupling – and 'Wild Horses', to be the second US Top Thirty single from *Sticky Fingers* (1971), an album that absorbed just sufficient passing trends not to alienate an older following.

Incidentally, after the inevitable loss of the Stones to another company, Decca was to realign its scruples, using an illustration similar to the toilet cover for *Stone Age* (1971), one of its many catchpenny Stones compilations. This time round, it was the group who objected, expressing their impotent displeasure via sour-faced advertisements in the music press. As a final insult, the original sleeve was printed in full when a digitally remastered *Beggars Banquet* was released decades later – without so much as a syllable of moral protest.

NOTES

1. *The Rolling Stones In Their Own Words* eds. D. Dalton and
   M. Farren (Omnibus, 1985)

2. *Keith Richards In His Own Words* ed. M. St Michael (Omnibus, 1994)

3. *Melody Maker*, 26 September 1964

4. *Disc*, 22 March 1969

5. *Daily Express*, 5 November 1987

6. Roy C. Smith of Saccountants Comins & Son Ltd., who were
   employed by the Rolling Stones (*Q*, March 1989).

7. *Howling At The Moon* by W. Yetnikoff and D. Ritz (Abacus, 2004)

Chapter 5

CHILDREN OF THE MOON: THE SESSIONS

'As soon as Brian stopped adding all those different instruments to Stones tracks, and just played a bit of guitar, he was finished.' Jimmy Miller[1]

Carnal self-interest and other complications of personal alliances had informed the recording of *Their Satanic Majesties Request*, the first Stones album without Andrew Loog Oldham in charge. Now that Sir had left the classroom, the children started doing what they liked. 'It was a really fun moment,' grinned Mick, 'and there were some good songs on it. There's a lot of rubbish too – just too much time on our hands, too many drugs, no producer to tell us "Enough". Anyone let loose in the studio will produce stuff like that. It's like believing everything you do is great and not having any editing – and Andrew had gone by that point. The reason he left was because he thought we weren't concentrating and that we were being childish.'[2]

To brake any further such detours of perceived self-indulgence, the group commissioned Jimmy Miller, a New Yorker headhunted by Chris Blackwell in 1966 to oversee recordings by the Spencer Davis Group, who he had signed to his Island management company on the understanding that their young Steve Winwood, lead vocalist and as gifted a multi-instrumentalist as Brian Jones, would be 'free to go his own way when he had solidified the musical side of his outstanding talent.'[3] Then other British acts became keen on hiring Miller too.

When still at high school, Miller had been the drummer in a modern jazz combo, and became so accomplished before he left his teens that it was to provoke no friction with Charlie Watts when he took over at the kit on the grandiloquent 'You Can't Always Get What You Want', B-side of 'Honky Tonk Women' and the big finish to 1969's *Let It Bleed* album. However, when still an adolescent, Jimmy had once calculated that he could get rich quicker as rock'n'roll singer than a drummer, but this ambition had been thwarted by a saddening fistful of flop singles. Accepting that he was not going to be the East Coast's answer to either Gene Krupa or Elvis Presley, 'I soon realized that the aspect of the business that I liked was being in the studio.'[4]

He had first come to Blackwell's notice as early as 1964 when, what with the Stones, Beatles and further British pop acts invading his native soil, twenty-three-year-old Jimmy – with a small army of other entrepreneurial North Americans (including Allen Klein) – had anticipated correctly a demand for more UK talent and had crossed the Atlantic to stake a claim in the musical diggings. Having recorded the backing track to 1965's feverish 'Incense', his own composition, with a session combo whom he christened the Anglos to indicate breadwinning English connections, Jimmy sought advice about a suitably fiery singer. After furrowing his brow over a competent Midlander named Robert Plant, he gave the task to a pseudonymous Steve Winwood – with whom he was to be reunited in more harrowing circumstances a few weeks later as the original Spencer Davis Group were months away from disbandment. His first task had been to sort out what was to be the Group's US Top Forty breakthrough, 'Gimme Some Lovin''.

After the 'I'm A Man' follow-up, co-written by Miller, barged its way up the Hot 100 too, there could have been no worse time for the Group for Winwood to hand in his notice. Nevertheless, Chris Blackwell retained Jimmy, who became a semi-permanent resident in the secluded two-storey dwelling in Berkshire where Traffic, Steve's next outfit, 'got it together in the country'. The stock publicity angle was the idyll of Winwood and three other groovy guys, united by a sense of purpose and mutual respect, occupying an isolated pad in the English countryside and devoting themselves to creating this beauteous music without outside interference.

Swallowing the jive too, other groups tried 'getting it together in the country' as well. In a colour spread in *Disc and Music Echo*, Humble Pie would be larking about in a haystack while Yes – yet to warrant press attention – experienced communal living to a musical end deep in Devon. Over in the New Forest, future Yes drummer Alan White with ex-Moody Blue Denny Laine, Trevor Burton, once of the Move and, as much a star in Birmingham as Mick Jagger was nationally, Steve Gibbons, named themselves Balls, and tested their stage act in a nearby village hall. Of like genital nomenclature, Hard Meat thrashed it out in the wilds of Cornwall, fulfilling part of the Kinks' Ray Davies' personal hypothesis on the matter: 'If I had all my own way and a country cottage to get together in, I'd write lousy songs and make a lot of money.'[5] With an end result more akin to Traffic than Hard Meat in mind, Jimmy Miller was to encourage the Stones to get the essentials of *Beggars Banquet* together at Redlands, that is, if Keith Richards didn't mind. There, the material stockpiled by Richards and Jagger proved sufficient to fill any new album at least twice over.

On the run around the world, Mick and Keith could not have helped but join one another in this hotel bedroom or that backstage alcove to work up usable songs on a transistorized tape machine. One such example was 'Satisfaction', the riff of which occurred to Keith when he was jerked from sleep and was noted on the transistorized tape recorder that stood perpetually on his bedside table for such a purpose. Amused by the memory, he would recreate how 'The next morning, I listened to the tape, and there was about two minutes of an acoustic guitar playing a very rough riff, and then me snoring for forty minutes'.[6] By 1968, however,

Richards and Jagger – and, under no commercial obligation, Wyman and Jones – were able to work at home on less portable but more sophisticated equipment. At Redlands, this ranged from Keith's cassette recorder – one of the first privately purchased such items in Britain – to the Mobile, the group's freshly assembled transportable studio which, outwardly resembling a dental surgery, was then the most technologically advanced of its kind in the world – so much so that a queue of other outfits, including Led Zeppelin, would form to block-book it.

Keith, Mick and whoever else was around were able, therefore, to potter about with sound, tape the wackiest demos and permit themselves the luxury of commencing a day's work with nothing prepared. When that was done, Keith, like a medieval baron, would preside over dinner at a huge oak table where Jimmy, fingering his moustache, eyed his employers with sly but justifiable satisfaction at work-in-progress. Dishes served *chez* Richards were cooked from the finest meat and vegetables, and were often of quite a gourmet nature – for, during a travelling life of snatched and irregular meals, the Stones' collective palates had not been as coarsened by chips-with-everything in wayside snack bars as might be imagined. Indeed, they had acquired comparatively exotic tastes in a mid-1960s Britain where most restaurants serving a late-night menu were Indian or Chinese. These had mushroomed since the war, especially in the capital where, since 'Not Fade Away' in 1964, the Stones had transgressed Musicians Union stipulations by running over into open-ended graveyard hours.

Furthermore, what fans understood as demarcation lines within the group's division of labour had also been crossed between midnight and six as long ago as 'Play With Fire' from early 1965. On this *lied* to a sophisticate from a well-to-do but dysfunctional London family, the only Stones heard were Jagger and Richards. Bass was thrummed by Phil Spector, by then a Stones confidant, and keyboards were played not by Brian Jones, Bill Wyman or Ian Stewart, but Jack Nitzsche, Spector's arranger, who also tapped a tambourine with, apparently, one of a dozing Bill Wyman's shoes. While the miming of this flip-side to 'The Last Time' on television still paid lip service to Mick on vocals, Keith on guitar, Bill on bass, Charlie on percussion and Brian as general factotum, there would be from then on no constraint on the high command of Jagger, Richards and their newly appointed producer recording tracks to be attributed to the Rolling Stones with whoever happened to be both available and in a fit state to play, with whatever instruments were required and to hand.

After an unfocused manner, such pragmatism pre-empted a trend that reared up later in the decade. 'We feel that today's scene is moving very much away from permanent groups and more towards recognition for individual musicians,' Steve Winwood was to pontificate in royal plural to *Melody Maker* in 1968, 'Going more in the direction of the jazz scene when musicians just jam together as they please.'[7] In tacit endorsement, there came that November an all-day function in a Staines warehouse during which some of the ablest musical technicians of two continents merged the contents of rock and jazz. Among those caught on rarely-seen film was Jack Bruce from the lately sundered Cream, who, with Dick Heckstall-Smith and drummer Jon Hiseman, – each from Colosseum – would tape a one-shot jazz album, *Things We Like*, the following year. The prime mover in a series of less erudite assemblies with the likes of Al Kooper and guitarist Steve Stills – from Crosby, Stills & Nash – was Mike Bloomfield of Electric Flag. The edited result of one of these bashes, modestly entitled *Super Session*, had been among the best-selling albums of 1968.

The clouds parted again on the gods at play when the producer of both the Moody Blues and the Move, Denny Cordell, assembled a star-studded cast to assist windmill-armed Joe Cocker, blues shouter and ex-East Midlands gas fitter who, in the same month as the Staines warehouse bash, had wrenched from Welsh vocalist Mary Hopkin the British Number One position with a funereal-paced and waltz-time overhaul of 'With A Little Help From My Friends' from *Sgt. Pepper*. Cocker's backing Grease Band were augmented by illustrious friends on the consequent LP, among them Jim Capaldi, Dave Mason and Steve Winwood from Traffic; members of Procol Harum, and Jimmy Page, leader of the just-formed Led Zeppelin.

Long before such amalgams became common, studio staff in both London and Los Angeles had long grown accustomed to catalytic familiars and guest musicians adding icing to the Stones' cake too. Jack Nitzsche had continued, for example, to appear on Stones tracks as regularly as rocks in the stream, while the late soul singer Sam Cooke's business partner, Woody Alexander's tambourine rattling had been a trace element on 1965's *Out Of Our Heads* album. If John Lennon and Paul McCartney were delighted to add their voices to 'Sing This All Together', John Paul Jones, when awaiting his destiny with Led Zeppelin, was disgruntled when, after being commissioned to arrange strings for 'She's A Rainbow' – also on *Satanic Majesties* – was kept 'waiting for them forever. I just thought they were unprofessional and boring.'[8]

Almost invariably, Keith Richards would be the last to arrive at Olympic Sound in the leafy south-western suburb of Barnes. If it lacked the reputable antiquity of, say, Joe Meek's ramshackle RGM Sound above a handbag store along Holloway Road or EMI's Abbey Road with its Victorian facade, Olympic was perhaps the most modern and capacious recording facility in London. About to graduate from sixteen- to forty-eight-track, and equipped with the latest state-of-the-art gadgets, its technicians responded to directives dotted with newish jargon like 'pan pots' (stereo channel potentiometers), 'EQ' and 'carbon faders'.

Though about to move to New York, the first among equals there was house engineer Eddie Kramer, a conservatoire-trained South African pianist, who had worked at Pye's Marble Arch studio prior to establishing his own KPS set-up in 1964. After assisting in the complicated refurbishment of Regent Sound, he pledged himself to Olympic where clients included the Small Faces, Traffic, the Jimi Hendrix Experience – and the Rolling Stones, who favoured Olympic more than any other metropolitan complex.

Nevertheless, throughout the making of *Satanic Majesties* and, to a lesser extent, *Beggars Banquet*, Kramer and Glyn Johns grew accustomed to two or even three members of the group missing from any given date. The most consistent absentee was Brian Jones – to the degree that the others were becoming quite used now to life without him. His confidence eroded daily as he had been pushed slowly but surely further into the background, Brian had long realized that not only was he no longer the self-designated leader of the Stones, but also that he was now at the very bottom of the group's hierarchy.

Having moved on from being simply expendable, he was turning into a liability. Though the first autumn leaves were tumbling on his tenure with the Stones, personal anxieties had long turned the easy affability of 1962 into defeated competitiveness with Keith and, especially, Mick. Worse than basking in a less dazzling spotlight was that Jagger with Richards had hogged a near-monopoly of songwriting within the unit structure. Treated now as just a worn-out tool for the masterworks of the fellows who had once been his friends, Brian's penetration of their caste-within-a-caste had been blocked further by the loss of his beloved Anita Pallenberg. More than ever before, as his emotional and professional concord with his fellow Stones shredded, paranoia tormented Brian in the isolation chamber where, with his headphoned ears like mildly braised chops, he might be blowing take after rejected take of harmonica for 'Prodigal Son', and striving to decipher the buzz of murmured intrigue amid the tape spools and blinking dials in the control room. Too frequently, it would occur to him that he was experiencing fatigue without stimulation as he reacted instinctively to the same count-in that pitched him into the nth remake of a track that took as long to complete as an entire album had back in 1964.

Some stretches in Olympic went by as total blurs for Brian, like some run-of-the-mill job he had been doing for years.

He was long past frothing himself into a foot-stamping, door-slamming passion like a spoilt child who cannot get his own way; that had never worked anyway. Somehow, it was easier not to bother his head and, like Charlie and Bill, just linger on the edge of Mick, Jimmy and Keith's occasional contretemps over, say, degree of reverberation on a tambourine track, that would scale such a height of vexation that console assistants would slope off for embarrassed tea breaks until the flare-up subsided to a simmering huff. Yet, for all his forced subservience and biting back hard on his anger, Brian remained the unconscious victim of intensifying character assassinations over venomous whiskey-and-Cokes in the Speakeasy's murkiest corner. The business in Morocco was still one of the most gapingly open wounds. 'The fact that a member of Brian's own group took Anita away poisoned any possibility of the Stones ever functioning the way it had before,' affirmed Marianne Faithfull.[9]

Yet, via perhaps a particular, if accidental, chemical juxtaposition of the over-prescribed tablets he swallowed compulsively to sleep, to stay awake, to calm his nerves, to lift his depressions, he was capable of rallying and delivering musical goods that were as sound as any from happier times. A placatory, even amicable mood persisted now and then when Jones was in the studio; episodes much like a playground situation in which a child teased remorselessly throughout the spring term is suddenly superficially popular

Brian Jones photographed during the recording of the *Beggars Banquet* album.

when he returns to class after the Easter break: a sense of 'Brian has been tormented quite enough. Let's start being nice to him.' Nevertheless, with a face like a Tyneside winter, Jones was present only if his rising, dazed and out-of-sorts, from a bed of dreams coincided with a remembered record date.

'He would turn up for sessions when he felt like it,' concurred Jimmy Miller. 'One night, he showed up after he hadn't bothered to come to the previous four. He had a sitar, and we were doing a blues song. It might have been "No Expectations". There was no way a sitar was going to fit, but I was happy that he was there. Mick and Keith, however, would come up to me and say, "Just tell him to clear off. He hasn't been here for days", and I'd say, "Yeah, but the guy's got problems. Don't you think we have some responsibility to encourage him to show up, and not tell him to clear off when he does get here?" Their reply was, "You're new on the scene. We've been putting up with Brian's nonsense for the past two years."'[10] Even Bill Wyman, the steady older man, had had his fill of Brian Jones: 'I never disliked him as a person, although he was a bastard sometimes, but I found it impossible to get on with him musically. You couldn't rely on him, but he wasn't unique in that he was messed up. A lot of people in bands were messed up then.'[11]

Miller, however, was to praise Brian's slide guitar playing on *Beggars Banquet* – though it surfaced on few tracks: 'No Expectations', 'Stray Cat Blues' and possibly 'Prodigal Son' in duet with Keith, now secure enough as the Napoleon to Brian's Snowball not only to plan to take a lead vocal on the next album, but also to gatecrash what had been Jones's exclusive preserve by applying the careen of his own recently acquired slide/bottleneck technique wherever he felt appropriate. It was, however, never as distinctive as Brian's – or even that of George Harrison after the soon-to-be ex-Beatle took up the style on tour with the US outfit, Delaney & Bonnie & Friends in December 1969. There were now instruments like the Dobro that had been manufactured specifically for slide and, while

George was to start with a piece hacksawed from an old hollow-tubed amplifier stand, it was no longer necessary for non-specialists like Keith to make do with bits of piping and test tubes. 'I had some glass slides made too,' Harrison was to explain, 'I find they tend to be a warmer sound, whereas the metal one is more slippery and brighter.'[11]

Richards agreed, but was inclined to favour a metal slide. Furthermore, rather than a direct absorption of Elmore James, Muddy Waters and the other black exponents that had determined Jones's methodology way back when, he favoured the more academic approach of his new pal Gram Parsons and, to a greater extent, Ry Cooder, a Californian he had met via Jack Nitzsche. A music archivist and a bottleneck – and mandolin – virtuoso, fresh from Captain Beefheart's Magic Band, Cooder was then in London with Nitzsche to assist with the incidental music to *Performance* – which, so he understood, had to include a Jagger-Richards opus with a contractually mandated lead vocal from Mick and, hopefully, an accompanying quorum containing sufficient Rolling Stones to justify crediting it to the group on the soundtrack album. If it was completed by the deadline, perhaps they would consider selecting it for *Beggars Banquet* too.

Cooder could not understand immediately why, first of all, nothing was seen of Brian Jones at any of the sessions and, next, that the studio time for the original by Keith and Mick for the film, 'Memo From Turner', kept being either abandoned after the most desultory attempt or reallocated to the ongoing completion of *Beggars Banquet*. The subtext of all the excuses presented to screenwriter and co-producer Donald Cammell was that Keith, still in the first flush of his romance with Anita, was filled with jealous confusion because the shooting of the movie required her to cavort between the sheets with Jagger. Worse, as the gradually more non-functional Brian had been ready to believe with a kind of despairing triumph, the scripted sexual intimacy was likely to go beyond dramatic simulation, Pallenberg passing this off as 'method acting'. Educated guesses and alarmist reports flying up and down that his 'old lady' was going to do the dirty deed with his best pal were too much for Keith, who chose to sulk gently in a parked car outside the house where the cameras were set up for the evil moment.

Richards was to be discountenanced even further when *Performance* was presented to Warner Brothers, its investors. Because it was not the expected happy-go-lucky crime caper set in the Swinging London of *Blow Up*, Warners did not accept the director's cut of X-certificate *Performance* without comment. The violence was too sickening and the sex too weird and graphic. It was to be postponed indefinitely, and the re-editing – in which a scene of Jagger and James Fox kissing had to be scissored – was to be subjected to the closest scrutiny, with extra special attention paid to the goings-on between Mick, Anita and the other female lead, Michèle Breton.

Scene from the cult film *Performance* featuring (left to right) Anita Pallenberg, Michèle Breton and Mick Jagger in 1970.

Passionate social adversaries as they were, previous derisive comments between Pallenberg and Jagger were a sublimation of a physical attraction that had been unleashed in the huge bed on set where they were required to simulate sexual congress. To the crew projecting lenses beneath the sheets, there was more than enough realism in the pair's 'method acting', certainly enough to persuade a pregnant Marianne Faithfull – who was to miscarry days after filming was completed – that Jagger and Pallenberg had actually screwed.

Was it, Keith may have wondered, the karma for his brief *amour* with Marianne? Consumed with at least a glimmer of what Mick might have felt about that – and Brian about the loss of Anita – Richards expressed his soul-torture with negative expediency by making 'Memo From Turner' sound amateurish when he deigned to turn up at sessions that, into the bargain, he had been responsible for delaying as long as possible. When he finally arrived, he would hold things up further by being pernickety about the volume, tone and tuning of his guitar; drag out breaks with one more cup of coffee, and drip-dripping Jimmy Miller and Mick with enough little problems to start a Third World War, forcing them to chat him up to get him to buckle down to work. It was fun winding them up. Basically, all he had to do was be laid-back if Mick was uptight and vice versa.

In desperation, Jagger and Miller may have attempted to lift the strike-happy mood by bringing in an outside party of sufficient eminence that – like a parson in a BBC situation comedy – his mere presence would compel Keith to rein in his nonsense. The chosen one was Al Kooper, who, as well as playing organ for Bob Dylan, was also the mainstay of Blood, Sweat & Tears. With Electric Flag and Chicago, they were the most famous rock equivalent of a 'brass band' – Kooper's own description in the sleeve notes of the combo's first LP, 1968's *Child Is Father To The Man*.

Yet, thanks to Richards, the effort by the group and Kooper – on guitar – was so unsatisfactory that all hope (if there had ever been any) was lost of its inclusion on *Beggars Banquet*. Jagger tried again to no avail with personnel from Traffic, but then his impossibly tight *Performance* schedule became such that Miller was left with the exacting and eleventh-hour task of salvaging and isolating the lead vocals from the most viable Stones take and layering a more acceptable arrangement on to them via a session crew. It was this cobbled-together version that was issued as a Decca 45 – Jagger's first official essay as a solo recording artist – in November 1970 to teeter on the edge of the British Top Thirty.

The most prominent instrumentalist on this 'Memo From Turner' was Ry Cooder who, invited to Redlands, had been flattered but not quite comfortable with the close attention the host paid to his picking, but was still amenable to being escorted to several *Beggars Banquet* sessions, purportedly applying his uncredited fretboard skills in less brutalized fashion than a relative newcomer to bottleneck, who prized the exhilaration of rough-and-ready spontaneity and endearing imperfections more than technical accuracy.

The open chord to which Keith tuned his instrument was most commonly G major, requiring the removal of a string so that the dominant would not, well, dominate. During the transition between *Satanic Majesties* and *Beggars Banquet*, the conducting of such experiments had 'rejuvenated my enthusiasm for playing guitar – because you'd put your fingers where you thought they'd go, and you'd get accidents happening.'[13] His high office in the Stones' hierarchy enabled Keith also to play both bass and lead guitar on *Beggars Banquet*'s most renowned track, 'Sympathy For The Devil' – on which the unreliable Brian was permitted to fret negligible acoustic chords when the track was recorded in June 1968.

Becoming more and more morose as the sessions had advanced through February and March 1968 and resumed in a dull, cold May, he had given up imposing even the mildest unsolicited suggestion upon the established status quo, and a shaken and downcast man occupied himself instead with an increasing intake of hard drugs, booze and sexual adventure. Maybe because Brian was their *bête noire*, Keith and Mick had not *wanted* to be keen on his idea of incorporating the Joujouka hand-drummers and pan pipes into *Beggars Banquet*, most obviously on 'Sympathy For The Devil', which was to lend itself admirably to a pot-pourri of percussion, pattered by Bill Wyman – and Rocky Dijon (Dzidzorna), whose commercial discography had started with 'Citadel', the contradiction of a nostalgic look at an unnerving inner-city future, on *Satanic Majesties*.

His conga-thudding was to enliven many other Stones tracks, just as, decades later, the tribal ensemble of Joujouka would infuse 'Continental Drift' on *Steel Wheels* (1989) with an essential ingredient of North African mysticism. 'Brian Jones turned us on to it,' Jagger confessed at last, 'and I wanted to try something in the same vein myself. To be honest, I thought it would end up on one of my solo records, but Keith was well into it. We worked something out on a keyboard and then went to Morocco to record the real thing, heading off into Brian's territory.'[14]

'It is as though the spirit of Brian Jones has entered into the music,' agreed a *New Musical Express* appraisal, 'It is both a moving and an honest tribute to another master musician.'[14]

Back in the desperate hours of *Beggars Banquet*, however, Jones was becoming – or pretending to become – impervious to Mick or Keith questioning his very proficiency as a player to his face now. An instance of this was there for all to see when the making of 'Sympathy For The Devil' was documented in a film of the same name by Jean-Luc Godard, who, during long weeks of daily scrutiny of the accumulated celluloid miles, caught Jones asking Jagger, 'What can I play?' 'Good question,' was the cutting reply, 'What *can* you play, Brian?'

It was scarcely surprising that Jones was dropping out of more studio commitments than ever – and that the group were waving in not so much auxiliary players as overt substitutes. When Brian was in danger of going to jail for his second drugs offence, Decca insiders had kept their peace when Allen Klein had calmed press friction with 'There is absolutely no question of bringing in a replacement.'[15] It was not yet public knowledge that other guitarists were cropping up in heated discussions about a Stones US tour pencilled in for autumn 1969, including Dave Mason who, highly recommended by Jimmy Miller, helped out on *Beggars Banquet*. As well as acoustic and electric guitars, he was also adding percussion, mandolin (on 'Factory Girl') and, on 'Street Fighting Man', the *shehani*, an Oriental woodwind instrument.

Dave was then at something of a loose end, having left Traffic from December 1967 to the following April to strike out on his own as both a freelance record producer and maker of a solo 45, 'Little Woman', with the assistance of Family, a Leicester outfit who had emerged as darlings of London's underground movement via regular appearances amid the light-shows and tinted smoke at metropolitan clubs like Middle Earth and UFO. With Jimmy Miller, Mason had overseen Family's debut LP, *Music In A Doll's House* (1968) – recorded in an Olympic studio adjacent to the one where *Beggars Banquet* was being forged – taking the opportunity to off-load on to it one of his compositions, 'Never Like This'. Vague parallels might be drawn, one could argue, between Dave and Brian Jones – or, less obliquely, Bill Wyman, driven to placing his songs with the End and other of his production and managerial clients. Yet, unlike Bill and Brian, Mason had not moaned ineffectually before resigning himself to just supplying power to the chord sequences and rhymes of members of his group deemed by investors to be less dispensable. To Chris Blackwell, Traffic without Boy Wonder Steve Winwood was as unthinkable as the Stones minus Jagger. By the same token, just as the Stones were, to almost all intents and purposes, operating without Brian Jones, so Traffic might be able to operate without Dave Mason.

Thus it was that matters reached a stage where Mason no longer belonged in the group that he had helped Winwood to 'get together'.[16] A chief bone of contention had been that Dave's presentation of his compositions as rigid *faits accomplis* had been counter to his outfit's collaborative ethos. Artistically, he had been as solitary a mister as Brian, and his attempts at using Traffic as a passive vehicle for his own firm notions generated increasingly more unrest, especially for X-factor Winwood – to whom perhaps a green-eyed monster had whispered that Mason, whose 'Hole In My Shoe' had been the closest Traffic came to a chart-topper, was the most self-contained, prolific and marketable songwriter in the group and, if given his head, might outshine not only Steve's Spencer Davis Group backlog, but also his Traffic heritage. 'When Dave started coming on strong, Steve couldn't handle it,' shrugged Jim Capaldi, 'and there was a clash of personalities, especially musically.'[17]

Jimmy Miller had been Dave Mason's most fervent ally in Traffic as he was Brian Jones's in the Stones – though, against the opposition, that wasn't saying very much. It was not long before Jimmy too was treating Brian as a passenger. Yet Jones's face still vied with Jagger's as the one to which fans were drawn at first glance in most Stones publicity photographs. For a while, this had allayed any fears in Jones that he was in danger of going the way of Pete Best, replaced by Ringo Starr in the Beatles. Nevertheless, the chemistry of the Stones' corporate public persona apart, Bill, Charlie, Keith and Mick were as fed up with Brian as he was with them.

Emitting an almost palpable aura of self-loathing now, as he sat down to overdub some trifling *Beggars Banquet* guitar fill, Brian's mind would drift off from the task in hand, and a glazed listlessness would set in. Meanwhile, an engineer occupied himself for long periods with switches, faders and editing blocks, and, on the other side of the glass-fronted booth, Jagger collated the rest of the lyrics of another of his compositions as co-writer Richards teased a melodic phrase or chord cycle from his guitar, like painters dabbing at a hanging canvas minutes before the gallery opens.

One intended track had been started before the present sessions had been block-booked. Featuring Nicky Hopkins on piano and organ, Jimmy sharing backing vocals with Mick, and the still-versatile Brian on soprano saxophone, 'Child Of The Moon' dated from October 1967 – the tail end of the *Satanic Majesties* era – though the finishing touches were made the following March. It bridged a gap between psychedelia and the pastoral element embraced on *Beggars Banquet*, albeit with a hint that someone had skip-read black magician Aleister Crowley's *Moonchild*.

For a very short while, 'Child Of The Moon' shared A-side status with 'Jumpin' Jack Flash'. The general post-psychedelic rejection of musical insights that were not immediately comprehensible reared up in this single, in which any kowtowing to either 'meaningful' lyrics or standard changes within a three-chord structure did not seem too premeditated. Rock'n'roll revival was in the air too – and, as company directors, it was incumbent upon the Stones to supply sturdy goods commensurate with the intimations of market research. 'Jumpin' Jack Flash' was, therefore, as unvarnished and as *au naturel* as it was possible to be by marrying a return to the Craw Daddy primeval to advanced technology and gutter-poetic metaphysics. Into the bargain, rather than lose the drive inherent in the take used, a discordant couple of bars from the guitars in the middle instrumental passage were preserved as an 'irritant factor'.

Bill Wyman continued to be annoyed that, while it was he who had stumbled upon the song's central riff when seated at a piano in a rehearsal studio in Morden, he was not credited as composer with Jagger and Richards. Was it ever thus? How many black bluesmen with a disregard for business affairs failed to receive not only payment but also acknowledgement due to them from white rock outfits like Led Zeppelin, who seemed to have rewritten Howlin' Wolf's 'How Many More Years' as 'How Many More Times'? More germane to this discussion, a typing error had just attributed a version of the Yardbirds' 'Shapes Of Things' on a 1968 album by the Jeff Beck Group to bass player Paul Samwell-Smith alone rather than co-writers Jim McCarty and Keith Relf. Then there was the earlier – and more serious – case of the Animals' 'House Of The Rising Sun'. This joint overhaul of a traditional ballad topped international charts, but as there was not sufficient space on the single's label to print all five Animals' names, only one was used – that of organist Alan Price, who had had, apparently, the least to do with the arrangement of the number. The others were soothed with the promise that it wouldn't make any difference to shares in the royalties, but, insists drummer John Steel today, 'We never saw any of the money. Alan still earns on it now.'

Bill wanted to lead a deputation of himself, Charlie and Brian to confront the other two about 'Jumpin' Jack Flash' and related matters, but threw in the towel after a registered protest that 'the part I'd composed worked perfectly – but the credit for this, one of our best tracks ever, reads "Jagger-Richards".'[18]

With no axe to grind, the Who's Pete Townshend was so excited by the Stones' latest that he advised recalling the thrill you got the first time you heard it as an aid to reaching a state of meditative bliss. 'It's the one that I would immediately go to if I wanted to approach a state of nirvana,' agreed Keith. 'The feeling's one of exhilaration. As soon as I play that riff, something happens in your stomach. It's an amazing, superhuman feeling. An explosion would be the best way to describe it.'[13] For most other Stones consumers too, 'Jumpin' Jack Flash' endures as perhaps the group's most lasting – and exciting – artistic statement. Certainly, it surfaces as frequently in 'Sounds of the Sixties' nights as the Beatles' 'Yesterday' does in 'quality' cabaret.

The Stones' re-emergence as in-person entertainers may be dated from this first domestic chart-topper since 'Paint It Black' aeons ago in 1966. As a welcome break from the day-in, day-out *Beggars Banquet* sessions, they had previewed 'Jumpin' Jack Flash' a fortnight before its release on 23 May 1968 when a rumour swept music lovers at an otherwise routine *New Musical Express* Poll Winners' concert at Wembley's Empire Pool that an attraction far more famous than any group or solo star on the rest of the bill – the Move; Dusty Springfield; the Bee Gees; Cliff Richard & the Shadows; the Tremeloes; Love Affair; Dave Dee, Dozy, Beaky, Mick and Tich; Amen Corner; you name 'em – was to make a surprise appearance – their first spell on stage for almost two years. Some smart alec, while not wanting to build anyone's hopes up, reckoned he had just noticed three of the Downliners Sect backstage, and that Frankie Vaughan was stuck in a traffic jam on the North Circular. With credulity stretched to the limit, some were weeping with anticipation when master of ceremonies Jimmy Savile announced the Rolling Stones.

Walls trembled, circle stalls buckled and the place exploded generally as the majority of girls in the crowd of ten thousand went berserk, tearing their hair, bursting into tears, rocking foetally, wetting themselves, flapping scarves and programmes in the air, and sometimes fainting with the thrill of it all. Somehow, the already ear-stinging decibels of screams climbed higher when the five Stones sauntered on, the guitarists plugged in, Charlie settled behind his kit and Mick unclipped the microphone from its stand.

The volume rose momentarily to its loudest – as if the whole audience had sat on tin-tacks – when Jagger came as belligerently alive as he had ever been when the lights hit him. Then there came a spontaneous surge towards the crash barriers in front of the wide stage, where rampaging fans were hurled back again by exultant bouncers, shirt-sleeved in the heat, and aggravatingly nearer to Bill, Brian, Charlie, Keith and Mick than those who would give their souls to be so close. Barely a note was heard during ten sensational minutes of 'Jumpin' Jack Flash' and, next, 'Satisfaction' – when one of Jagger's shoes sailed into the boiling mêlée with one particularly energetic Tiller Girl-esque goose step. In the press enclosure with Anita Pallenberg, Marianne Faithfull tossed tulips at her prancing boyfriend and his colleagues.

Ostensibly, it was just like another such extravaganza they had done what seemed like endless centuries ago on 11 April 1965, when another predominantly female audience had gone crazy over them. They had shared the stage then with the Kinks, the Animals, the Beatles, Dusty Springfield again, the Searchers, Georgie Fame, Tom Jones, Wayne Fontana & the Mindbenders, the Moody Blues. Donovan, Herman's Hermits, Freddie & the Dreamers, Cilla Black – the very upper crust of British pop – when the beat boom was basking in its electric high summer.

Three years on, a petrification of rock'n'roll's turbulent if unending adolescence was underway. *Top of the Pops* had brushed a nadir one schmaltzy weekly edition in spring when the only group featured was the Tremeloes who were to be, with Love Affair and Marmalade, a prong of a grinning triumvirate that ruled this silver age of British beat groups. Beneath them, the charts would be constipated with further harmless purveyors of popular song such as Plastic Penny, the Paper Dolls, Springwater, Cupid's Inspiration, the Casuals, the Pipkins and all the rest for whom it was good going if they lasted for maybe two Top Forty showings. With a nod towards North America's cartoon Archies and the Don Kirschner 'bubblegum' factory, some of these acts had no physical form beyond television. No wonder the Stones sent Wembley into turmoil like gin-sops at a temperance meeting.

This blink-and-you'll-miss-'em slot was the sum total of direct hard-sell plugging of 'Jumpin' Jack Flash' in Britain and, indeed, everywhere else. However, a promotional film short was memorable for Jones's orange pancake make-up and the cavortings of a Jagger war-painted *à la* Arthur Brown in a straightforward synchronization of a performance of the song. It was seen on television screens across the globe, and, while it did not provide enough push for the Stones to duplicate the UK chart feat of 'Jumpin' Jack Flash' in other territories – where it stopped, for example, at Number Two in Australia, and Three in the Irish Republic and the USA – it was clear that the paring down to just vocals, guitars, bass and drums, plus keyboards and secondary percussion where needed, met with the approval of a public that expected the same of the interrelated LP still being completed.

More than possibly Jagger and Miller, Richards was now very much 'in charge of recording sessions, more or less, in an oblique way,' perceived Ian Stewart, 'He doesn't march into the studio and say, "Right! It's going to be this, that and the other". He just kicks off into something, and most people follow him. He usually decides how each song is going to shape up.'[13]

Richards left his mark at the most bedrock level. It was to come to the fore when, as the decade turned, the advent of monitor speakers, programmable desks, graphic equalizers, megawatt public address systems et al. emphasized like never before the idiosyncrasies of the Stones' approach to corporate rhythm. The concept of the guitarists and singer being controlled *en bloc* by tempos defined by bass and drums had always been a misnomer – as it was in other famous groups. 'It's the way I place the lyric on the beat,' was vocalist Reg Presley's assessment of how it was with his Troggs, 'Ronnie [Bond] hits his snare a fraction behind, and Chris [Britton]'s guitar is somewhere in between. There's such a closeness in how that happens, a matter of a split second.'

In the Stones' case, it had boiled down to an interaction hinged on the good-bad rawness of Keith Richards' chord-slashing, compulsively exquisite, even to more proficient guitarists who could hear what was technically askew. Bill Wyman's elucidation is worth quoting at length: 'Our band does not follow the drummer. Our drummer follows the rhythm guitarist. Immediately, you've got something like a one-hundredth of a second delay between the guitar and Charlie's lovely drumming. Onstage, you have to follow Keith. You have no way of not following him. With Charlie following Keith, you have that very minute delay. The net result is that loose type of pulse that goes between Keith, Charlie and me.'[19]

'Keith knows in general that we're following him, so he doesn't care if he changes the beat around or isn't really aware of it. He'll drop a half- or quarter-bar somewhere, and suddenly Charlie's playing on the beat instead of the backbeat. He'll be so surprised, and be very uptight to get back in, because it's very hard for a drummer to swap the beat, especially on the intros. He's got monitors, but, if you're not hearing too well with the screaming crowds, it's very difficult to hear the accents, the difference between the soft and hard strokes. The problem is that he's often totally unaware that he's on the wrong beat, and he shuts his eyes and he's gone. Someone has to go up and kick the cymbal – but I think that's a little of the charm of the Stones.'[20]

On the boards, the Stones – like virtually every other rock group – were inclined to accelerate and slow down *en bloc* to inconsistencies of tempo motivated by the mood of the hour, but a different discipline had to be enforced in the studio. Nevertheless, Keith held the whip hand as the Robespierre of rhythm as much at Olympic Sound as he had at the

Wembley Empire Pool recital. If his methods within the slicker, even sterile, exactitudes of the studio seemed slapdash – as if he was making it up as he went along – to outsiders, those in the know exercised patience, aware as they were that, within his shell, the poker-faced guitarist and composer functioned on what Glyn Johns, one of *Beggars Banquet*'s two engineers, called 'his own emotional rhythm pattern. If he thinks its necessary to spend three hours working on a riff, he'll do it while everyone else picks their nose. I've never seen him stop and explain something.'[13]

'If things don't suit Keith, he won't go along with it,' guffawed Bill Wyman again, 'and that's the end of the subject. When asked why not, Keith would reply, "Because I don't want to."'[13] Via a monosyllabic obstinacy rather than bossy hauteur, Richards facilitated the discarding of musical clutter, and direction and final result would, like a painting by Rolf 'Can you tell what it is yet?' Harris, shine through with sudden clarity.

As it unfolded, the unvarnished directness of *Beggars Banquet* became, with *John Wesley Harding* and *Music From Big Pink*, part of the movement that was steering pop away from backwards-running tapes, exotic instruments and self-conscious superficiality that disguised many essentially inane artistic perceptions. Nonetheless, much of its rough edge was contrived via refinements in recorded sound since the first Rolling Stones album back in 1964.

Employed on both 'Jumpin' Jack Flash' and the album, one approach developed by Keith Richards was taping an acoustic guitar, with attached magnetic pick-up, through an amplifier on to his cassette recorder with so much overdrive that it sounded electric. On transference to the eight-track mixing desk in Olympic, it also lent a gritty quality to finished products such as 'Street Fighting Man' – on which the only solid-body instrument heard was the upfront bumble-bee bass, also thrummed by Richards.

Through their comprehensive shadowing of the procedures and varying abilities of the likes of Andrew Loog Oldham and Phil Spector since 1963 – as well as their own ventures into record production with

Immediate artists and *Satanic Majesties* – Keith and Mick especially had become sufficiently familiar with the workings of the console not only to make learned recommendations, but even to turn knobs and push faders. Indeed, when he first removed his jacket and loosened his tie in the producer's chair for *Beggars Banquet*, Jimmy Miller had accepted quickly that the group too should have a pronounced say in activities behind the glass-fronted booth of buttons and lights. The fellows also felt entitled to bring along girlfriends and wives to the sessions, not only to watch the fun nowadays but to join in too. Anita Pallenberg, for instance, was loud and clear on the *oo-oooo* background chant on the celebrated 'Sympathy For The Devil', which clocking in at almost seven minutes, was to be the album's longest opus – and its most wordy.

'If you have a question about the lyric, ask Mick. That's his department,' was still Keith's stock reply to enquiries about division of songwriting labour[21]. While the partnership had become less cut-and-dried Rodgers & Hammerstein (or, if you prefer, Lloyd-Webber & Rice), Richards would continue to suggest that, though creative functions dissolved and merged, he was chiefly responsible for the music, and Jagger the words.

In 'Sympathy For The Devil', the guitarist delivered a startling needle-sharp solo while the singer portrayed himself as a *comme il faut* but fiendish figure, on the fringe of events but sufficiently well placed to stir kettles of fish for private amusement, whether a face in the crowd at Golgotha for the Crucifixion, in conference with Adolf Hitler 'when the blitzkrieg raged and the bodies stank', or behind the steering wheel of JFK's Lincoln Limousine at Dallas. When the President's younger brother died at the trigger-jerk of another maniac in June 1968, the infallibly practical Jagger had made the line 'I shouted out, "Who killed John Kennedy!"' plural ('the Kennedys').

While *Beggars Banquet* was seen as a new beginning, its 'pure papier-mâché satanism'[22] – as Marianne Faithfull would describe it – also embodied aspects of much that had gone before as exemplified by Lucifer's presence in spirit on and in the very title of *Satanic Majesties*

Request. In parenthesis, as the opening track, 'Sympathy For The Devil' framed the unveiling of a shouted 'Get down with it!'. Turning into a catchphrase of a kind on *Beggars Banquet*, it had come from the title of a Little Richard single, 1966's 'Get Down With It' (which was to be reworked as 'Get Down And Get With It' as Slade's maiden Top Twenty entry in 1971), and Jagger was to use it again – in truncated form ('get down!') during the 'Sympathy For The Devil' coda and in 'Street Fighting Man'.

As a testament to the standing of 'Sympathy For The Devil' as one of Jagger's cleverest librettos, Bryan Ferry, a more erudite singing wordsmith, if deploring the overall quality of Mick's lyrics, was to exhume 'Sympathy For The Devil' in quasi-'Monster Mash' fashion on a 1973 solo LP. That same year, the Stones themselves created a belated sequel in 'Dancing With Mr. D', which led off *Goat's Head Soup*, an overall miscellany of recycled ideas.

À propos nothing in particular, Jimmy Miller was poleaxed with a digestive complaint, but managed to complete this album – though he was never to work with the Stones again, and was to die of liver failure in 1994. The sharp-eyed had either recognized or guessed who Miller was after Jean-Luc Godard's film reached cinemas. Every unforgiving minute of the gradual flowering of 'Sympathy For The Devil', or 'The Devil Is My Name', to give the song its working title, from plug-in to trial mix – over 'two very good nights' at Olympic, estimated Jagger[23] – was immortalized by an omnipresent camera crew for editing by Jean-Luc, who, though approaching his forties, was still seen as an *enfant terrible* of European cinema. 'Godard understands music better than any director, alive or dead',[23] reckoned Mike Figgis, an acquaintance of Charlie Watts, and then an aspiring film-maker himself.

On the strength of an exploratory acoustic arrangement, 'Sympathy For The Devil' seemed to have been conceived almost as a country number along the lines of those Dylan had written for *John Wesley Harding*. However, hints of the crazed energy to come crept in via Nicky Hopkins' prominent keyboard vamping over a sparse rhythm centred eventually on a potpourri of minor percussion instruments – one of them courtesy of Bill Wyman, who surrendered his bass lines to the tender and experimental mercies of Keith. As the film developed, so did the song, most conspicuously when the beat shifted to the familiar samba; Hopkins focused exclusively on piano, and an unruly chorale – which roped in Hopkins, Glyn Johns and Anita Pallenberg as well as Brian and Keith – added a simple but sardonically appropriate 'oo-oooo' chant.

Godard had been so captivated by the new Jagger-Richards number that he had abandoned the flick's working title, *One Plus One*, for *Sympathy For The Devil* before the picture was shown at the London Film Festival in November 1968, a fortnight before the release of *Beggars Banquet* (on 6 December 1968 in Britain, a day later in the USA). A slow-moving ninety-nine minutes, *Sympathy For The Devil* had been intended to contrast construction (i.e. the Stones creating the song) and destruction (a girl's suicide when deserted by her lover), but was now remodelled with no linking narrative between footage from the shuttered Olympic encampment with mains leads fanning out in all directions; Black Power militants in a Battersea car dump; a television interview with some woman ('Eve Democracy') in a forest; her spraying graffiti all over London; and a bloke reading excerpts from Hitler's *Mein Kampf* in a pornographic bookshop. It was an Art Statement, like – and very much of its era, fading swiftly from circulation after its general release in 1969. Too much for the ordinary moviegoer to render an Art Reply, it has since received viewings only in film clubs and arts centres (although a DVD was given away free with the *Sunday Times* in 2006).

Disregarding the abstract vignettes, *Sympathy For The Devil* may be seen now to both anticipate and mirror the Beatles' silver screen 'reality' project, 1970's *Let It Be*. The third (and final) film John, Paul, George and Ringo still owed to United Artists, this feature would be directed by Michael Lindsay-Hogg whose curriculum vitae included overseeing *Ready Steady Go!*, the most atmospheric TV pop series of the 1960s, and the *Rolling Stones*

Rock And Roll Circus. Most would watch it to the bitter end but, as it was with *Sympathy For The Devil*, you couldn't help wondering if they would have bothered had it featured a band like, say, Love Affair bickering, running through old songs, hitting trouble as soon as they tried anything new – and hastening their freedom from each other.

While Brian Jones was either studiously avoiding or oblivious to confrontation, what had fluttered on to the cutting room floor between a scene in which Wyman is at his usual instrument and the next with him wielding maracas while Richards has taken over on bass? It is difficult to guess on the evidence of between-take mutterings and wry shallowness in which little that was notably droll, provocative or even significant comes from the lips of any of the dramatis personae.

How typical was this of the overall ambience that resulted in *Beggars Banquet* – or any recording session by anyone? Surfacing on bootlegs but

The Stones in July 1968, during a recording session for 'Sympathy For The Devil'.

otherwise unreleased were instances of when the tape was kept rolling during loose jamming round antique blues and soul numbers, nameless instrumentals and nascent originals, mostly when rehearsing in the inexpensive RG Jones Studio in Morden, Surrey – first used by the Stones (and the Yardbirds) in 1963 – prior to transfer to Olympic. Nigh on ten minutes of Muddy Waters' 'Still A Fool' and like ambles down memory lane consumed time as late arrivals set up their gear or engineers twiddled through some boring mechanical process. In the teeth of intriguing titles – 'Hamburger To Go', 'Blood Red Wine', 'Highway Child'[24], Stax duo Sam & Dave's 'Hold On I'm Coming' or 'Shoot Me Baby' from Jimmy Reed – it revealed nothing more remarkable than any idle bunch of musicians' ramblings not intended for public ears, after one of them kicks off an extemporization hinged on a riff and standard chord patterns. Some more formal pieces petered out if bedevilled by a forgotten middle eight or verses that Jagger could not be bothered to la-la any more.

Tedious listening it made for all but Stones collectors, for whom no shared or audible information about the band is without value. On occasion, it may have proved to be the wellspring of useful reference for the group itself. A go at 'I'm Coming Home', a blues from time immemorial, by Charlie, Ian, Keith and Mick in Morden concluded with strains of what would smoulder with surprising swiftness into less amorphous form as 'No Expectations'. This was to become the second track of side one, the following evening at Olympic when a Dickensian-sounding title was married to a rural blues reminiscent of Robert Johnson, in which some of the deliberation of a dream's slow motion owed much to Brian's contribution on a bottleneck guitar that rolled like treacle (and was, opined Mick, his last major contribution to the Stones *oeuvre*). Reportedly, it was taped with the entire group seated round an omni-directional microphone, with the additional presence of Nicky Hopkins. Having studied at London's Royal Academy of Music, Hopkins had worked his notice with Lord Sutch's Savages and then Cyril Davies' All Stars before becoming so omnipresent in London studios that he'd been immortalized by the Kinks in the 1966 LP track, 'Session Man'.

Reposeful 'No Expectations' contrasted with both 'Sympathy For The Devil' and the selection that followed, 'Dear Doctor'. With a lyric that wavers and springs between the sadness and gladness of an unwilling groom, desensitized with an injudicious quantity of Bourbon, jilted by his repulsive bride, this was a waltz-time comedy number epitomized by Jagger's idea of a Deep South drawl, ascending into mocking falsetto on the take selected for the album. Like Chuck Berry's 'Maybelline', it owed as much to C&W as blues. Crucially, it sounds as if the Stones enjoyed recording it, conjuring up visions as it does of ale-choked mouths and flushed, happy faces in Olympic Sound as well as the one-shot novelty of songs such as the Beatles' 'Yellow Submarine' or the Stones' own 'Something Happened To Me Yesterday', played for laughs too on *Between The Buttons* – and featuring both the twelve-string acoustic guitar of Dave Mason and, added later, Brian Jones's harmonica.

Jagger blew harp on the lewd 'Parachute Woman' that, as not so much a song per se as an organized jam, echoed the looser and much lengthier 'Goin' Home' (from *Aftermath*), John Lee Hooker's 'Boom Boom' and, perhaps more closely, Skip James's 'Special Rider Blues' (a.k.a. 'Hurry Sundown'), a late 1960s 'blues boom' standard revived by New York's Insect Trust in 1968 and, two years later, by Hawkwind (produced by former Stone and founder of the Pretty Things, Dick Taylor).

There was also a shadowy link to 'Satisfaction' in there too; part of the Otis Redding arrangement's appeal to Keith had been the brass section punching out the riff – as the resident band did on the final bars when the Stones premiered this, their first US chart-topper, on the networked pop showcase, *Shindig*. On the disc, an attempt to approximate this effect had been made with the aid of a device called a 'fuzzbox' – reputedly, the first in Britain – attached to the 1959 Les Paul Standard that Richards had brought back from the Stones' first US trip. When designed by Gibson in 1962, the Maestro Fuzztone had been intended to make a guitar sound like a saxophone but largely through Keith, would assume a personality of its own. Further endorsements would come from the Beatles, who fed a bass guitar through one when preparing their winter album, *Rubber Soul*, on hit singles by the Spencer Davis Group and Dave Dee, Dozy, Beaky, Mick and Titch. When Keith dusted it off for 'Parachute Woman', he enhanced its blackboard-scratching hoarseness by recording the overdubbed two-note riff on his ubiquitous cassette machine, and letting it gnaw at the number as horns in unison might have done.

Over and done in slightly more than two minutes, 'Parachute Woman' was as succinct as 'Jigsaw Puzzle', around the six minute mark, was not. Mostly the work of Jagger, it was triggered maybe by him peering glumly from a window of his elegant Chelsea mews at a rain-sodden early evening street where a vagrant, his mind rotted by methylated spirits, trudges off to sleep on the Embankment in cardboard-boxed squalor. Next up is a gangster who, in private life, is a devoted husband and father. Then, via some incongruous connection, a deadbeat pop group lurches from gig to gig with no choice but to go right on performing just to maintain a tolerable standard of living. Overall, the song comes across as an overlong and disjointed piece of quasi-Dylan-esque musical word-play, muddled through a marathon fourteen remakes before arriving at a version with an increasingly more disinclined Richards' swooping slide guitar to the fore and Hopkins' bluesy pounded piano triplets utilized almost like tuned percussion. It was feasible that everyone at Olympic and during the album's mixing and mastering in July at Los Angeles' Sunset Sound could stand only so many fantastic versions of 'Jigsaw Puzzle'.

Brian Jones did not fly across the ocean for any of the last details of the album, and no one endeavoured to persuade him to do so, for fear that he might. Yet Brian was not making any tangible long-term plans should he take a leap in the dark as a non-Stone as much as an ex-Stone. How could he? Nonetheless, it may have crossed his mind to quit pop altogether, fling all of it back in their faces, so that there would be one less poor sod to be reduced to a dogsbody-cum-scapegoat. 'Even if he was thinking about getting a new band together,' speculated Keith Richards with mildly facetious hindsight, 'I don't feel that's what he would have ended up doing. I think he would have gone into maybe something completely different, collecting butterflies or something.'[13]

A rapid disenchantment with the shabbier aspects of the record business had led already to Brian's now distant friend, guitarist Brian Pendleton, leaving the Pretty Things in 1965 when he got off a train en route to some one-nighters up north. 'We went round to his flat afterwards,' sighed singer Phil May, 'and it was like the *Marie Celeste*. We next saw him at a business meeting four years later.' Something-in-the-City now, Pendleton stonewalled a Things trainspotter who accosted him in a West End record shop. Like completing National Service, your old job was often waiting for you when you got back from the disorientating world of the music business. 'As I'd been in an insurance office on leaving school,' recalled Colin Blunstone – whose Zombies were to disband in 1969 with a record high in the US charts – 'it seemed a natural thing to do. After the Zombies, it was refreshing to have a structured day.'

A hidden statistic of 1960s pop is the number of pop artists who, on growing to adulthood in the hothouse of its turbulent and endless adolescence, made similar deliberate decisions to jump the gun and become nobodies again before their time in the limelight was up. As well as Brian Pendleton, known to Jones was Chris 'Ace' Kefford whose drug-addled condition had brought into sharper focus the discord and intrigues that make pop groups what they are, and had driven him from the Move in the midst of their five-year chart run. Next up was Syd Barrett, whose departure from the Pink Floyd in 1968 was on a par with, say, Brian, unable to cope with being a Stone after 'Not Fade Away', their third single, scurrying back to Cheltenham to live quietly with his parents and their 'I told you so' recrimination, or – as actually happened – Chris Curtis, the Searchers' drummer-leader during their chartbusting zenith, dismissing show business altogether for the security of the civil service. Like an inverse of the 'happy ending' in a Victorian novel, they seemed to live outwardly unproductive lives artistically, in which nothing much was calculated to happen – though Blunstone was to rise from his swivel chair in 1972 to clock up more UK entries than he ever did as a Zombie.

To hell, anyway, with the music industry, ruminated Brian, with its short-sightedness, its mental sluggishness, its cloth-eared ignorance. Who needed the time-serving incompetence, the fake sincerity, the contradiction of excessive thrift and heedless expenditure – and the backstabbing? Far beyond Bill Wyman's disgruntlement at the theft of his 'Jumpin' Jack Flash' riff, venerable old heroes of Brian had died in poverty, playing for dimes from passers-by while waiting in vain for fat royalty cheques as Arthur Crudup did for those for Elvis Presley's million-selling covers of his 'That's All Right' and 'My Baby Left Me', and Junior Parker for the King's success with 'Mystery Train'.

Keith and Mick, however inadvertently, seemed to be serving Robert Wilkins in the same fashion, treating him as the rascally music publisher did the main character in the 1943 film version of 'Phantom Of The Opera'. Snide remarks were rife within publishers' glass palaces about Jagger and Richards 'stealing' the composing credit for 'Prodigal Son' (titled originally 'That's No Way To Get Along' and conceived initially as a paean to a girl), still-living Great War veteran Robert's 'holy blues' that embraced a straightforward account of the New Testament parable, with an arrangement by the Stones for acoustic guitars and harmonica – and harking back to that of *Aftermath's* neo-skiffle 'High And Dry'. Thus it read '(Jagger-Richards)' beneath where 'Prodigal Son' was listed among the other selections on side two on the circular Decca label on the first vinyl pressing of *Beggars Banquet* in December 1968. The mistake was rectified for subsequent editions when brought to the attention of the Performing Rights Society.

There were no other avenues for outright accusations of plagiarism elsewhere on *Beggars Banquet*, though general influences screamed out of particular tracks – as they did in 'Factory Girl', the Stones' close approximation of the sound of a Dust Bowl string band of the Depression, albeit with Rocky Dijon's congas, Charlie Watts rapping a tabla – with aberrant sticks instead of fingers, denting them as he had those on 1966's 'Paint It Black' – and with Jagger lyrics that might have been an articulation of a scenario in, say, industrial Lancashire at any time in the previous half-century. Certainly, there were vague traces of Walter Greenwood's *Love On The Dole*, a novel that was turned into a social melodrama in a 1941 film that was for ever being screened on Sunday afternoon television from the mid-1970s.

'Factory Girl' is distinctive too for the presence of Rick Grech, whose quirky fiddle overdubs were an ingredient of the affected 'weirdness' of Family's *Music In A Doll's House*. His had become a fashionable name to drop in the inward-looking world of English rock's ruling classes. Born in Bordeaux, Rick had moved with his family in 1953 to Leicester where he played violin in the city's Symphony Orchestra. In 1965, he was bass guitarist in what was to become Family, after the onset of puberty had found him looking for an opening in pop. A strong motive for any red-blooded lad to do so is that no matter what you look like, you can still be popular with young ladies.

The eventual rise of Family's *Music In A Doll's House* to Number 35 in the UK album chart was aided by sessions on John Peel's *Top Gear* series on BBC Radio One, and the band's off-duty frolics being chronicled in Johnny Byrne and Jenny Fabian's racy *roman à clef, Groupie* – for, though admirable young men in many ways, Family had their share of young men's vices. Yet temptation did not come their way anywhere as often as it did the Rolling Stones. During the loading up after one-night stands back in 1963, one of them might have been pawing some available girl either against the shaded side of the van or in the romantic seclusion of a backstage broom cupboard. Coming on erroneously as the rough, untamed East Ender, Jagger in particular had been discovering that a fledgling pop star's life brought more than mere money, but with the condition implied in his 'Ugh! We used to attract such big, ugly ones. Dreadful birds with long, black hair, plastic boots and macs.'[26]

Matters improved, and tatty Jezebels up for a knee-trembler when the Stones were still humping their own equipment would give way to more pulchritudinous, if often disreputable, female fans skilled at evading the most stringent security measures to impose themselves on the group's touring party in hotel suites and backstage areas theoretically as impregnable as Howard Hughes' Las Vegas penthouse. Fame is a powerful aphrodisiac, and time which hung heavy between one Stones concert and the next was not only killed with, say, chess tournaments, shaving at a band-room wash-basin, reading a challenging book or practising guitar. Sometimes, it might have been like that, and, in any case, shadowy thighs and ribald sniggering did not leap out of the pages of letters home, even if their nearest and dearest could not quite shut out of their minds imagined grapplings with this or that super-groupie.

As *omertà* is to the Mafia, a vow of silence concerning illicit sex seems to persist among bands of roaming minstrels. Nevertheless, scum-press gossips had no such qualms – especially after the Redlands bust – about bringing to public notice the Stones' effortless procurement of erotic gratification from too many young women. Once, a tryst could be sealed with a boyish grin, a flood of libido and an 'All right then. I'll see you later', but, by 1966, when the Stones embarked on their last tour for almost three years, they were cutting out even perfunctory chivalry during imprisonment in luxury hotel torpor. After trying to guess whether or not a selected girl in the lounge was underage, a Stone might just seize her by the arm and manoeuvre her into the nearest lift for tea-and-biscuits upstairs. If already ensconced there, he would simply instruct the road crew to summon one (or more) of the 'skirt' that had taken his fancy either from among the screaming mass as amorphous as frogspawn at the theatre, perpetual loiterers in the foyer or those clogging the pavements in the hotel environs during marathon vigils for just the slightest attention from their idols, just a smile from a Stone as he dashed from revolving door to limousine. Quite what such a girl would have done had she succeeded in shoving a hand through a gap in the wall of bodies mobbing the group to grab the belt of Charlie's trousers and pull is open to debate, especially as there is no evidence whatsoever that Watts was ever unfaithful to his missus.

Yet, the Stones had been feted wherever they went since hitting the big-time in 1964, and the most debauched Roman emperor might never have had it so good. A mythical aura of sometimes arcane sexual excess had always emanated from the group since they became internationally renowned – and, in the case of certain individuals, long before. The teenage Jagger had spoken confidentially to sceptical Dartford Grammar classmates about sex as if he had inside knowledge about it. This overriding interest would manifest itself in a constant and relentless search for 'birds' more dauntingly free-spirited than the usual 'nice' girl of the mid-1950s, 'saving herself' for the wedding night. Little had changed by the later 1960s, and, while not as active in that department as Bill Wyman and Brian Jones, his alleged exploits on the road had earned him the nickname 'Mick Shagger' among the kind of British girls who were proud of love bites.

His first in-yer-face voicing in song on the subject was 'Stray Cat Blues'. Jagger had attempted to steer the song towards a sound akin to the early Velvet Underground – as evidenced by rawer demos in Morden – but there remained only a vague link to Lou Reed et al. on the final version in which Brian's bottleneck and subtle legato mellotron counters Keith's

'Citadel'-esque rhythm guitar offbeat and unusually Albert King-like passagework, underlining couplets about what a lawyer might interpret as the molestation of pliant minors, that were the only barrier to this track making, had the Stones wished, a most marketable single.

The same could not be said of the less routine 'Family', a remaindered *Beggars Banquet* item, with a narrative – taking on two tempo variations – of off-colour doings within a domestic circle, which could be interpreted by the-man-in-the-pub as an unfunny serenade to incest or 'darkly humorous' by a rock scribe trying to be cool. Perhaps the funniest opus in the entire Stones canon is another sex-freighted *Beggars Banquet* reject, 'Downtown Suzie' (alternative title: 'Downtown Lucy'). Penned by Bill Wyman – if sung by Jagger – this appears to be an upbeat, blues-tinged call-and-response account of the morning after a bender in some peculiar house of ill repute. Maybe there was space for only one jokey number on *Beggars Banquet*. Nonetheless – and this may sound like a stretch – if radically re-arranged, it might have been suitable for Frank Sinatra, jackpot of all songwriters. Certainly, Bill's oft-thwarted ambition as a composer provokes sympathy.

There were no laughs whatsoever in the five-plus minutes of 'Sister Morphine'. Marianne Faithfull claimed authorship of lyrics proffered when Richards and Jagger were tinkering with the slow but ear-catching melody. With Mick on acoustic guitar, she was to record her own version of 'Sister Morphine' as the B-side of her last single of the 1960s, after a Stones version had been given the thumbs-down for *Beggars Banquet*.

Prescribed drugs had previously come under the Stones' scrutiny in 1966's 'Mother's Little Helper' (on *Aftermath*) – concerning habit-forming tablets which hasten a frantic housewife's 'busy dying day'. This time, 'Sister Morphine', smelling of hospitals, depicted a fragile accident victim on a ward mattress after arrival to the agitated clang of an ambulance bell. While the surroundings fill him/her with nightmare reflections – 'why does the doctor have no face?', 'tomorrow I'll be dead', 'clean, white sheets stained red' – a sense of longing as much as wretchedness also permeates the atmosphere.

On the orders of a hand-wringing Decca executive who had taken the trouble to listen to it, the Faithfull 45 was withdrawn from circulation. Not only was it, in his misinformed view, 'drug music', but the image of the artist and, indirectly, that of the record company, had been tarnished too much already by her frank opinions on free love, her cohabitation with Jagger and the identification by innuendo of her as the 'nude girl' noted by the police when they had raided Redlands.

Although Keith Richards was to find the emotional detachment to permit the Stones' crack at 'Sister Morphine' to be exhumed and re-recorded three years later for inclusion on *Sticky Fingers*, it was nearer the knuckle for him than it had been in 1968.[27] For some time, he – and Anita and Marianne – had been escaping into reveries induced by cocktails of cocaine and its sister narcotic, heroin. Its needle still sending him into a state of existential grace, Keith imagined that he could give it up any time he liked. However, if not yet breakneck, the slide into dependency had become unstoppable. His addiction was intensifying, and would continue to do so until it all but killed him: 'I never considered I was actually pushing it anywhere near the danger limit, although later on, I realized that I was probably a lot closer than I ever admitted – but it kept my feet on the ground, nearly underground in fact.'[13]

This was years away in 1968, although hallucinogens were becoming less popular than heroin as an extreme recreational stimulant for those for whom being this type of junkie was the coolest thing in the world, membership of an exclusive sect of the damned. David Bowie's 1969 chart debut 'Space Oddity' was seen in some quarters as a paean to the muck – which would be seizing Keith, gradually if unknowingly, during that autumn's US tour.

Conversely, Jagger was able, when needs must, to brake 'the typical dissipated life of a rock star, full of drugs and booze and chaos. My health is my most treasured possession. When I'm on tour, I never touch hard liquor, and I try to get as much sleep as I can.'[28] Daily voice-coaching was on a distant horizon, but in the retractable sphere of the studio in 1968, he likewise got a professional grip on himself. Indeed, never before had his pipes been more adept than on *Beggars Banquet*, which drew from him a wide range of vocal expression from jocular 'Dear Doctor' to fundamentally sinister 'Stray Cat Blues'. When about to move beyond a natural vocal compass, he either veered cleanly into falsetto – as exemplified towards the close of 'Sympathy For The Devil' – or, rather than try and fail to hit notes without cracking, extemporize huskily like a soul man, as though a random verse's sentiments could not come across through orthodox means.

A Caruso-loving fly on an Olympic Sound wall may well have blocked its ears because, by European bel canto standards, Mick Jagger had a horrible voice, devoid of vowel purity, plummy eloquence and nicety of enunciation. Instead, you got slovenly diction, stentorian nasalings and an often strangled vehemence dredged up from the throat rather than the diaphragm, his vocal muscles beyond remedy through tearing the cellophane off at least one daily packet of cigarettes since adolescence, and seven years of ranting any old how through variable PA set-ups during a medieval period of amplified sound, in which vocal balance was achieved by simply moving back and forth on the microphone.

However, despite being inaudible without electronic assistance, Mick's battered nuances, yet-untutored phrasing and an inability to stray far beyond his central two octaves reinforced an idiosyncratic charm peculiar to certain singers who warp an intrinsically restricted range and eccentric delivery to their own devices. Mick was one of this oligarchy, as were Bob Dylan, Ray Davies, Phil May, weedily androgenous Adam Faith, asthmatic Keith Relf, laconic Dave Berry, and Reg Presley with his Long John Silver burr. Who cares if, in a Scott Walker sense, he was not much of a singer – at least Mick Jagger always sounded like Mick Jagger.

Furthermore, the Walker Brothers' euphonious *chanteur* had been magnanimous about him after a fashion when, following a vitriolic swipe at Tom Jones, he added, 'I'd sooner hear somebody who doesn't claim to be a great singer – like Mick Jagger'.[29]

If Jagger never sacrificed impassioned content for pitch-perfect virtuosity, Richards had been finicky about tonality from earliest youth when, as a primary school chorister, he had sung in the finals of an inter-choir competition at no less than the Royal Albert Hall. During 'musical evenings' at his grandfather's home in north London, 'If I didn't sing a grace note,' remembered Doris, Keith's mother, 'he would tell me to do it properly. He'd know it was wrong. It's something that's just built into him.'[13] It had been the choirboy in Richards that had caused him to shy away from the microphone during the Stones' exploratory engagements, dejected as he was by having to virtually gulp it when striving to hear himself through puny house sound systems. Yet, if lacking Jagger's individuality, his baritone was found to be strong and tuneful enough after a nicotine-aggravated fashion to harmonize and engage in call-and-response with Mick, following the brutal resolving in late 1964 of a running debate about who was and who was not allowed to sing onstage. 'Brian could sing,' gloomed Pat Andrews, 'but he was informed by Mick, Keith and Andrew Oldham that he wasn't to do backing vocals any more. They more or less told him he was rubbish at it.' Less abruptly, Wyman too ceased to contribute and, resplendent in his victory, Richards concentrated on harmonies that were integrations into the lead vocal rather than unison antiphony, indicating lessons learnt from the small chorales of the Beatles, the Hollies, the Searchers, the Byrds, the Beach Boys and, more recently, the *SF Sorrow*-period Pretty Things.

He had ensured too that his voice was more prominent than Mick's on 'Connection', and that 'Something Happened To Me Yesterday' on the same 1967 album, *Between The Buttons*, amounted to a Richards-Jagger duet. On *Beggars Banquet*, to his own acoustic strumming, he took the entire first verse of the singalong 'Salt Of The Earth' finale, while leaving Jagger to handle the rest of this stirring anthem to the working classes by rich, sophisticated men, long and, perhaps, guiltily detached from the everyday. Yet, because the Stones didn't pretend to be anything else, the song did not inflame raw nerves in the queue at the labour exchange as the British government continued its battle against a formidable balance of payments deficit.

As a convenient gesture of authenticity for consumers in the USA – where Martin Luther King had died a hero's public death in April, sparking off further black-white confrontations and where, during a New Year's Eve concert in New York, Jimi Hendrix was to dedicate 'Machine Gun' to 'the soldiers fighting in Chicago, Milwaukee, New York and Vietnam'[30] – the all-female Watts Street Gospel Choir, added to 'Salt Of The Earth' just before the definitive mixing of *Beggars Banquet* in Los Angeles, were from the depressed suburb of the city where racial tension had flamed into open riot during 1965's humid August.[31]

The difficulty with topical ditties is this: what becomes of them when they are no longer topical or the topic gets tedious? Fortunately for Mick and Keith, 'Salt Of The Earth' was all-purpose enough to be put to use after the third millennium began not on New Year's Day 2000, but 11 September 2001 when hijacked aeroplanes had torn into New York's World Trade Center. On an October Saturday six weeks after 'nine-eleven', Richards and Jagger gave 'em 'Salt Of The Earth' when among Billy Idol, Destiny's Child, the Who, Bon Jovi, David Bowie and the other artistes doing their bit at Madison Square Gardens, celebrating the work of the New York firefighters and shaking fund-raising buckets against the terrorists.

Just as lyrically direct, 'Street Fighting Man', the spin-off US single from *Beggars Banquet*, had been born of another generally murderous mood many summers earlier, and Jagger had endorsed its sentiments with 'They told me "Street Fighting Man" was subversive. Of course it's subversive!'[32] However, it did not start out like that. Not sure whether to call it 'Did Everybody Pay Their Dues' or just plain 'Pay Their Dues', Jagger struggled over jarring lyrics that coalesced a March 1968 demo with contributions from Dave Mason and personnel from Family. From this, the general musical undercurrent – hinged on piano, Keith's acoustic six-string and Charlie at a tiny antique drum kit from his vast collection – survived, but the words were completely different when the group tried again two months later.

If not as pointed a rallying cry as, say, the Kinks' 'Every Mother's Son' – which peaceniks sang en masse outside the White House during the Vietnam moratorium – 'Street Fighting Man' acquired million-selling outsider chic when banned by both the BBC – probably because of the demonstrations in London and the *événements* just across the Channel – and, in the light of alarmist talk about the forthcoming 1968 National Democratic Convention, by various radio stations in Chicago where Mayor Daley had ordered police to 'shoot to kill' marching troublemakers.

Towards the fade-out was heard a plink-plonk emulation of Big Ben's chimes on a piano beneath the fingers of Nicky Hopkins, who was actually more contributory to the album than Brian Jones, whose semi-percussive tamboura and long twangs of sitar were faint reminders of how multi-faceted and crucial he had been on *Aftermath* through to *Satanic Majesties* – and how unwilling or unable he now was to so minister to *Beggars Banquet*. For those insensible to the shift of his status within the group from co-navigator to back-seat passenger, it seemed that it was business as usual for Brian, Charlie, Bill, Mick and Keith, as, with the ugly moments in court behind them, they would be soundtracking the 1970s as they already had the Swinging Sixties, and they had saved themselves if not the world. For one of their number, however, his valedictory humiliation on *Beggars Banquet* was to be seen from the distance of years by a public ignorant of what actually went on behind Olympic's closed doors, like Debussy said of Wagner's *Das Rheingold*, 'a glorious sunset mistaken for a dawn'.

NOTES

1. Among fleeting telephoned comments on his time as the Rolling Stones' producer.

2. *Sunday Times,* 10 August 2003

3. *Melody Maker*, 4 March 1967

4. *Beat Instrumental*, April 1968

5. *Record Mirror*, 30 July 1970

6. *Behind The Songs* by M. Heatley and S. Leigh (Blandford, 1998)

7. *Melody Maker,* 7 December 1968

8. *Stoned* by A.L. Oldham (Vintage, 2000)

9. *Daily Mail*, 18 July 1990

10. *Record Collector*, November 1993

11. *Q*, October 1989

12. *Musician*, November 1987

13. *Keith Richards In His Own Words* ed. M. St Michael (Omnibus, 1994)

14. *New Musical Express*, 2 September 1989

15. *New Musical Express*, 14 November 1967

16. Dave was to leave Traffic permanently in autumn 1968.

17. *Trouser Press*, January 1978

18. *Stone Alone* by B. Wyman and R. Coleman (Viking, 1990)

19. *Best Of Guitar Player*, November 1994

20. *The Rolling Stones In Their Own Words* eds. D. Dalton and M. Farren (Omnibus, 1980)

21. *New Musical Express*, 23 September 1966

22. *Faithfull* by M. Faithfull and D. Dalton (Penguin, 1994)

23. *The Guardian*, 7 July 2004

24. Nothing to do with the 1967 Jimi Hendrix B-side 'Highway Chile'.

25. *Record Collector*, November 1993

26. *Who's Really Who* by C. Miller (Sphere, 1987)

27. And was still considered sufficiently venal for the substitution of another track on the Spanish pressing.

28. *Daily Star*, 4 July 1983

29. *Scott Walker: A Deep Shade Of Blue* by M. Watkinson and P. Anderson (Virgin, 1994)

30. *Jimi Hendrix* by B. Mann (Orion, 1992)

31. This was the subject of 'Trouble Comin' Every Day' (1966) by Frank Zappa, who was to compose a burlesque of 'Salt Of The Earth' for 1971's *200 Motels* movie.

32. *Inside Classic Rock Tracks* by R. Rooksby (Backbeat, 2001)

EPILOGUE:
AFTERMATH

*'Suddenly, shows were incredibly long, and there would
be no audience reaction until after the number. Then everyone
went mad. It was really a concert.'* Charlie Watts[1]

The more clear-headed reviews of the new album were guardedly glowing. Usable quotes seemed to jump out the page. 'The most sophisticated and meaningful statement we can expect concerning the two themes – violence and politics – that will probably dominate the rock of 1969,' wrote *Rolling Stone*, who previewed it in not so much a review as a long article, noting too that it was 'the formal end of all the pretentious, non-musical, boring, insignificant, self-conscious and worthless stuff that has been tolerated in the past year in the absence of any standards set by the several great figures in rock'n'roll'.[2] Closer to home, *International Times* reckoned that *Beggars Banquet* 'retained the cynicism and drive of earlier albums, but replaced the roughness with intrinsically thematic simplicity.'[3]

According to chart statistics, *Beggars Banquet* was less successful than *Satanic Majesties* – which, while it too peaked at Number Three in Britain, spent more weeks in the Top Forty. In the States, *Satanic Majesties* had come close to the top, but *Beggars Banquet* stalled at Number Five. Unlike its predecessor, it was not to be registered as a vinyl million-seller. Moreover, despite Mick Jagger being 'rather pleased'[4], the exclusion of 'Street Fighting Man' from consternated airwaves hindered its progress as a US single (with a different mix to the album version). Not helping either was the *Sympathy For The Devil* movie being too 'challenging' (i.e. incomprehensible) for Joe Average – if he was ever able to see it.

The title song, however, if broadcast a little late for the target audience, had Mick singing it and the others miming to pre-recorded accompaniment on ITV's *Frost On Sunday*. There were also full-page advertisements for the album in trade journals, and an alarming publicity stunt in a suite at London's Kensington Gore Hotel. Its inspirational source was the album's gatefold inner photograph – of the Stones in approximations of medieval garb, apart from Jagger in top hat and hacked-about modern formal wear, sated, half drunk and lolling round the remains of a sumptuous and candlelit banquet at what might be a table above the salt in some pop Valhalla, where manners have no place.

Costume Party: the Rolling Stones dress the part for promoting the album *Beggars Banquet*, 5 December 1968.

Keith was late as usual when they dressed and conducted themselves in similar fashion at the hotel party for the benefit of the press and supper guests, of whom the most illustrious was Lord Harlech. When British ambassador in Washington, DC, he had hosted a flag-waving reception at the embassy for the Beatles during their first US tour – at which, to his embarrassment, the group had been jostled, politely insulted and hailed like taxis.

He, the Stones and the other diners tucked in to hog roast washed down with mead, served by aproned wenches in mob-caps and low-cut blousons. Voices got louder, jokes coarser, eyes brighter and faces redder. The revellers pushed damp hair aside as they gnawed and scooped, piling and re-piling their plates as the maids cleared up the worst messes and filled and refilled glasses. With the album blasting on automatic replay, the feasting and toasting concluded as planned with the hurling of fake custard pies hither and thither. Exhilarated by alcohol and being thrillingly out of bounds among these long-haired pop stars, Lord Harlech proved a good sport – as did, through gritted teeth, Brian Jones, recipient of more of the sloppy missiles than anyone else.

The riotous meal had the desired effect, and there was coverage in the tabloids and as light relief to gloomy TV news about the latest rearing-up of Arab-Israeli conflict and the stationing of Russian troops in Czechoslovakia. However, what would have been the most far-reaching and accessible plug for *Beggars Banquet* did not encroach upon public consciousness to even the small degree of Jean-Luc Godard's avant-gardening – at least, not until 1996 when *The Rolling Stones Rock And Roll Circus* was deemed to be of interest as a footnote in cultural history, and its associated compact disc sneaked into the lower reaches of the US Hot 100.

The Rolling Stones Rock And Roll Circus had been intended as an hour-long Christmas spectacular on BBC Television, as the Beatles' *Magical Mystery Tour* had been the previous winter. It was shot between the afternoon of 10 December 1968 and the following morning in the same Wembley Studios used for the later editions of *Ready Steady Go!*. The accumulated footage contained spoken links chiefly by members of the group, and a sequential assortment of clowns, gymnasts, fire-eaters and a tiger. Most importantly, there was retake after retake of music that mashed up blues, rock, rock opera and ballads – by artists such as Jethro Tull, the Who, bluesman Taj Mahal and Marianne Faithfull – plus a Beatles number and a piece that beggared precise categorization by the Dirty Mac, an ad hoc group containing John Lennon, Yoko Ono, Eric Clapton, classical violinist Ivry Gitlis, Keith Richards (on bass) and Jimi Hendrix Experience drummer Mitch Mitchell.

The show closed with a performance by the Stones that commenced between midnight and the grey of morning before a crowd that, if star-struck, had exercised patience above and beyond the call of duty. The musicians too were wilting slightly, especially Brian Jones, who had found the entire proceedings as onerous as he had the making of 'Sympathy For The Devil' when it was documented by Godard a few months earlier. With specific reference to Brian, the group's wearied musicianship on the graveyard shift was slammed by Ian Anderson, Jethro Tull's singing flautist. Much of the criticism was well founded – and the Stones were not particularly pleased with their section of the show either, especially in comparison with the Who's show-stealing set: hence *The Rock And Roll Circus* gathering dust for decades.

Following an introduction by John Lennon, the group – augmented by Nicky Hopkins and, sharing Charlie Watts' podium, Rocky Dijon – had warmed up with 'Route 66' and, of like vintage, 'Confessin' The Blues', prior to attempting 'Jumpin' Jack Flash' twice before achieving a passable result. Next up were 'Parachute Woman' and a 'No Expectations' on which Keith Richards strummed an acoustic six-string with negligent ease, and Brian endeavoured to emulate the adroit slide guitar with which he had lacquered the *Beggars Banquet* template.

Then came the maiden public unveiling of 'You Can't Always Get What You Want', the outcome of the first post-*Beggars Banquet* session at Olympic Sound the previous month. If not brilliant in absolute terms, it was probably the best they could have managed at the time – 4 a.m. As milk floats braved a below-zero dawn outside, the very slightly more instant familiarity of the penultimate *Rock And Roll Circus* number – a nigh-on nine-minute 'Sympathy For The Devil' – stirred tired onlookers who, as Middlesex awoke, were to be waved off the premises to the sound of the backing track of the studio version of 'Salt Of The Earth' – with 'live' vocals.

While Keith had combined lead and rhythm guitar, Brian had been reduced to shaking maracas on 'Sympathy For The Devil'. He had also struggled to remember the chords of 'You Can't Always Get What You Want'. He had been present at the recording but, as Bill Wyman was to recall, 'his contribution was to lie on his stomach most of the night, reading an article on botany.' (5) This may have distracted his agonized eyes from the canoodling of

Keith and Anita just within the bounds of acceptable ickiness, still going strong, despite her and Mick reputedly taking the 'love interest' too literally in *Performance*. Yet there was no doubt that Mick Jagger had proved himself as natural a screen actor as Elvis Presley, who had shone from the mire of *Paradise Hawaiian Style*, *Girl Happy* and the rest of the streamlined Hollywood vanities that had occupied him for most of the decade.

That Jagger's abilities had testified to virtues other than mere publicity value meant that there was pressure to agree to more film assignments, forcing some unwise decisions. 'I made dumb movies, and turned down the ones I should have done,'[6] he would admit – and, certainly, he never got round to a flick halfway as appealing as *Performance*. At one point, he reportedly approved a treatment by Nigel Gordon, an associate of the Pink Floyd, about the quest for the Holy Grail – with Marianne earmarked to be the Lady of Shalott. He dithered too over something called *The Maxigasm*, but after it fizzled out, a pen would be thrust into Mick's hand to sign a contract lumbering him with the title role in an update of *Ned Kelly And His Gang*, a silent biopic that had appeared less than three decades after bushranger Kelly, romanticized as a sort of digger Robin Hood, was hanged in Melbourne in 1880. Room was found for Marianne to play Jagger's Maid Marian.

With Mick's impending ascent to movie stardom, on top of his alleged fling with Anita, appearing to annihilate further any cosy pretentions about the Rolling Stones as a five-man brotherhood, Brian Jones's related and, apparently, near-perpetual drug-clouded state was mirrored in lethargic indifference towards other sessions during the realization of *Let It Bleed*. This follow-up to *Beggars Banquet* resulted from hundreds of staggered hours in Olympic Sound, beginning during the rainy weather that had protracted 1968's harvest into November, and ending the following July when a high pollen count aggravated Brian's asthma. During these months too, the writing was scrawled on the wall; if not tangibly like that on the contentious original *Beggars Banquet* sleeve, then clear enough to spell out that the group could not carry its self-styled 'founder' for much longer, and that Brian – now referring to 'they' rather than 'we' – was not envisaging being a Rolling Stone for the rest of his life, and was bracing himself for a leap into the unknown.

One name that was cropping up more and more as the Stones made contingency plans concerning a replacement for Jones was that of twenty-one-year-old Mick Taylor, once fleetingly one of Hatfield's boss group the Gods, but now guitar deity in John Mayall's Bluesbreakers, like Eric 'God' Clapton and Peter Green before him. Taylor imagined that he was simply a session musician rather than what amounted to an audition candidate when summoned to Olympic Sound in May to play on 'Live With Me', a bland Jagger-Richards item that also marked the first – but by no means the last – time the Stones employed personnel from the ranks of Delaney & Bonnie & Friends, the ensemble consisting mostly of Los Angeles session musicians to whom Eric Clapton had rendered practical endorsement with finance for a European tour and a place in their ranks as lead guitarist. For 'Live With Me', their Leon Russell arranged a horn section of Friends who, crowed the saxophonist, 'went on to back all the players who really do have a lot of influence.'[7]

For all the ebullience and aggressive friendliness of these 'supersidemen', the Stones were not to look back on the *Let It Bleed* sessions with much more affection than they had *Beggars Banquet*. Although there was no discernable animosity, 'in the studio, nobody was friendly, and everybody acted funny,' noticed Ry Cooder,[8] another guitarist put forward by this or that bored music journalist hunched over his typewriter as a clear favourite to fill the impending vacancy. As

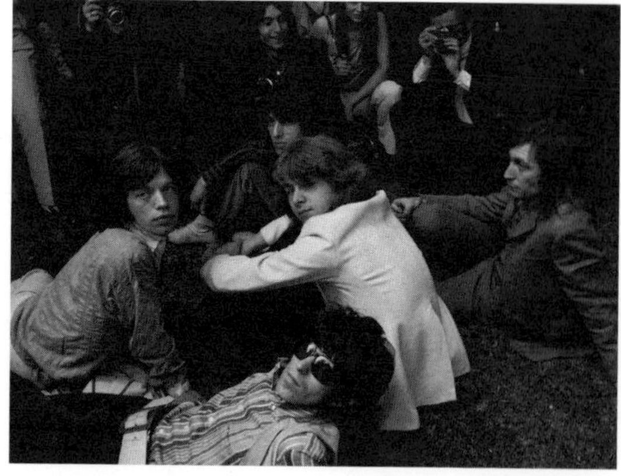

Brian Jones's replacement, Mick Taylor (centre), with the band on a photo call in Hyde Park in 1969.

they had rehearsed with Cooder as early as the previous summer, there was substance in this speculation – though, at the back of Keith Richards' mind was an immovable tenet: 'We had to own up, we were an English band.'[9]

Nevertheless, as well as escorting the man of the moment into Olympic one spring evening in 1969 to shimmer mandolin on a C&W-tinged arrangement of Robert Johnson's 'Love In Vain', Keith Richards was to admit to 'taking Ry Cooder for all I could get'.[8] Reportedly, this went further than merely paying acute attention to the Californian's fretboard dexterity. With some bitterness at the time, Cooder would claim co-authorship of Richards and Jagger's 'Honky Tonk Women' – and its 'Country Honk' derivative – both recorded in the same period. Later, he came to terms with it: 'It's of zero importance. There's nothing I can say about that without looking like a chump. If you want to know, ask Keith. The experience with the Stones showed me one thing – which is that if you don't advance yourself, you'll find yourself left in the dust'.[8]

Keith's nationalism apart, this grievance put the tin lid on any possibility of Cooder, a home-loving sort anyway, superseding Jones, whose tenure as a Rolling Stone would end shortly after his slender and inaudible hand on percussion in 'Midnight Rambler' on 16 May 1969, and finding the emotional detachment to stroke autoharp for 'You Got The Silver', a plea by Keith, its lead vocalist, to Anita, three months earlier. (10) Brian wished he was in hell rather than Olympic Sound for what would be *Let It Bleed*. Well, maybe not hell, but perhaps Morocco for the week-long Rites of Pan festival in Joujouka – or, more conveniently, his newly purchased property in the Sussex Weald.

Near Hartfield, between East Grinstead and Tunbridge Wells, Cotchford Farm stood amid rolling pastures and was half-hidden by woodland. In a dreadful way, Brian Jones's name was to be as synonymous with the place as the most famous of its previous residents, A.A. Milne. Since dwelling there in the 1920s, the late writer's plays, novels and humorous newspaper articles have been forgotten, but his children's books remain popular, especially those with 'Winnie the Pooh', a toy bear, as the hero. Written for Milne's son, Christopher Robin, the second of these, 'The House At Pooh Corner', serialized in the *Sunday Express* in 1928, had been inspired by the ivy-clung mansion from the pages of *Country Life*.

After considering similarly secluded havens in Hertfordshire, Surrey, Essex and even Gloucestershire – with amenities less important than the space between him and the nearest neighbours – Brian had taken up residency at Cotchford Farm just as the *Let It Bleed* sessions got underway. As its exposed oak rafters and stone-flagged floors attested, the house dated back to the Plantagenets – though the aqua-blue, thermostatically heated swimming pool was constructed in 1964. Nevertheless, only the odd aeroplane overhead from Gatwick need remind the new owner of what was over the hills in London.

In the quietude and fresh air, Brian would yawn and stretch, nauseated by the thought of another spell shuttered underground in the clinic-cum-doss-house paradox of the recording studio, where there was no let-up in the underminings, cunning machinations and further tension-charged uglinesses that make pop groups what they are. That flurry of bum notes you just played; they *were* bum notes, weren't they?

Neither did Brian miss yet the limelight of the screaming girls, the interviews and photo shoots, *Top of the Pops* and *The Ed Sullivan Show*, and hanging round with all the other young icons in the clubs. While growing to manhood in the hothouse of the British-beat boom and its endless North American sequel, he had been treated like a food pigeonhole in one of the new motorway service stations in which the Stones had sometimes been refused service. No longer would it necessarily be taken for granted that Brian Jones existed only to vend entertainment with a side-serving of cheap jotted or tape-recorded insight. To watch a rabbit scurry across a meadow or the log fire in the living room subside to glowing embers, was not that entertainment enough?

On the clear nights of early December, the moon in its starry canopy would shine as bright as day over the vastness of storybook meadows and woodlands. Brian would live long enough to see that landscape melt into another summer day – what people who do not suffer from hay fever might call 'glorious'. All the adulation and denigration his life contained – the Number Ones, the court appearances, the limousines, the women, the money down the drain, the booking agents for whom a thousand miles was but a few inches on a map – could be transformed to matters of trifling importance, though it was not as easy to so dismiss the too-real squad of cowboy builders supposedly renovating Cotchford Farm, but behaving as if they did not know the dignity of labour.

Nevertheless, having thus distanced himself geographically from London, Jones was out of earshot of the hastening conspiracy – which now involved Allen Klein too. He was readying himself to pour oil over troubled waters with the hackneyed 'musical differences' as a reason for Brian's departure. After all, about once a month from around the middle of 1966, the music papers had been reporting a split in some group or other. Brian Pendleton's exit from the Pretty Things had coincided with Manfred Mann taking formal leave of Paul Jones at the Marquee in October 1966. By then, Wayne Fontana had cast aside his Mindbenders while Graham Nash had begun talking openly of a solo LP as a prelude to quitting the Hollies to get something going with his new chums, Dave Crosby – lately parted from the Byrds – and Steve Stills from a sundered Buffalo Springfield.

Four years on, whether Brian Jones fell before he was pushed is academic because, at Cotchford Farm early in the evening on the first Sunday in June, it was one of a deputation of Jagger, Richards and Charlie Watts, who marshalled his words and dared the speech everyone knew had to be made. The air was cleared at last, and the prevalent feeling was of release. An unsettled chapter in the respective careers of Brian and the group he had helped form had just ended – though, before Charlie, Keith and Mick drove off into the dusk, not forgetting to pull over at a pre-mobile telephone kiosk somewhere to ring Bill Wyman, the possibility of Jones rejoining one day had been mentioned sham-dispassionately, even if no one present regarded it as likely.

Jones's departure from the group was worthy of an item on BBC Television's *Six O'Clock News* as he pondered whether it was so unreasonable for him to hold in his heart the possibility that the Rolling Stones would be recalled as just the outfit in which he had cut his teeth before going on to bigger and better things. How could poor Brian have known that he had less than six weeks left?

Contrary to Brian's statement that 'We no longer communicate musically. The Stones' music is not to my taste any more' in the shallow press release about the 'amicable split', he had been proud to have played a part in both 'Jumpin' Jack Flash' and *Beggars Banquet*. He was, nevertheless, even more pleased with a promised golden handshake from the Stones of the post-millennium equivalent of just over one million pounds. This compensation for a stolen vocational inheritance would skim the surface of his debts, and hold a decision, that most noxious of human phenomena, of what to do next at arm's length while he continued to take pedantic stock.

If forming another group was not as obvious an option any more, even before Watts, Richards and Jagger's mission to Cotchford Farm, vehicles bearing illustrious callers and their instruments crunched up the gravel drive. Yet, while above having to hire back rooms of pubs and advertise in the music press now, Brian was not to show in John Lennon — though he and Jones spoke often on the telephone — or Noel Redding, very lately parted from the Jimi Hendrix Experience. Each had other agendas, just as Brian had — albeit a much vaguer one — when he did nothing about an apparent offer from Humble Pie, which, following the crass 'supergroup' precedent of Cream and, fresh off the assembly line, Blind Faith, was to amalgamate instead ex-personnel from the Small Faces, the Herd and Spooky Tooth.

In June 1969, Humble Pie booked a studio to make 'Natural Born Bugie', a debut single, that, if nondescript, was at least of more commercial substance than the musical meanderings at Cotchford Farm after Brian had picked the brains of Alexis Korner about anyone available for and interested in playing ... how about back-to-basics, unadulterated blues, maybe — or being just like Creedence Clearwater Revival? Brian had grown fond of this Californian outfit, whose spiritual home seemed to be the Deep South, as instanced by titles such as 'Mardi Gras' and 'Born on the Bayou'. Moreover, without actually looking the part, the Revival was harking back to the energy and standard chord changes of 1950s classic rock'n'roll. Initial domestic chart penetrations had been with an eponymous 1968 LP and its two 45s, but after 'Proud Mary' almost topped the US and British charts the following spring, Creedence had scored again with twelve-bar 'Bad Moon Rising', doing the same in Australasia and Britain, and finding favour with the mainstream pop and heavy rock consumer alike, as well as fellow musicians such as Bob Dylan and John Lennon

Brian listened as keenly to anything by Johnny Winter, a boss-eyed albino Texan who had become a luminary of the late 1960s 'blues boom' after an LP he had recorded for an obscure regional company impressed a *Rolling Stone* magazine journalist. The resulting hagiography in 1968 had catapulted Johnny from parochial renown to headlining at New York's Scene club and the more prestigious Fillmore East. Winter was, nonetheless, annoyed when a compilation of old recordings was issued in the same month as an 'official' second album. Among enthusiastic listeners to both were John Lennon, Keith Richards – and Brian Jones, who went so far as to ring Alexis Korner, put a Winter track on his turntable and hold the receiver next to it.

Drawing on a roll-up and nodding in smiling agreement, Alexis too thought Johnny acquitted himself well, made nice music, but he soothed his friend with the qualification that he was certain that Brian could lead an outfit that was to equal Winter – or Creedence Clearwater for that matter. As the Crazy World of Arthur Brown were fresh from falling apart during a US tour, added Korner, organist Vincent Crane and drummer Carl Palmer had their ears to the ground – and so did Mickey Waller, former sticksman with the Jeff Beck Group. Such was the concord with his old mentor that Brian was emboldened to suggest a link-up with Alexis himself. Maybe Korner's existing outfit,

New Church, could take him on as a guest star for an imminent trek round West Germany.

Via a clumsy sleight of verbal judo, Korner tried to change the subject, pretending not to hear Jones's brittle self-esteem crack into a frown. For a start, Brian's presence onstage with any group then was likely to spark disruption beyond shouted requests for songs such as 'Ruby Tuesday' and 'Jumpin' Jack Flash'. Secondly, despite the country air and assurances that he was off hard drugs, Jones was none too hale, physically or mentally. As well as being pale and noticeably tubbier, he would wake feeling groggy and foul-tempered, and finish the day brimming with the various medications he took compulsively. It was not the firmest foundation for Brian to give the music business another whirl.

Late in June, nevertheless, he managed a trip to London for a tenacious bout of circular and only half-understood discussion with one of Allen Klein's minions about the non-arrival of the pay-off from the Stones. Someone from *Rolling Stone* magazine's UK office – then operating from the same premises – bumped into Brian on the stairs and asked if he fancied a cup of coffee. 'This sweating figure came in and I spent the afternoon talking to him,' recalled advertising manager Alan Marcuson, 'not knowing whether to be nice to him because he was a superstar, but he looked very ill.'[11]

Glassy-eyed musings drew from Jones a sour witticism that the way the Stones felt about him now, he would probably be the only one who would be charged admission after it had been announced earlier that week that the group would be playing a show in London, which – defying belief – would be free of charge! To introduce the new line-up – with Mick Taylor the final choice to supersede Brian – the buckshee bash had been pencilled in by organizers Blackhill Enterprises for Saturday 5 July.

It had been prompted by a similarly altruistic happening a month earlier when Blind Faith, the supergroup spearheaded by Steve Winwood and Eric Clapton – with Ginger Baker on drums and Rick

Grech on bass – were in the Cockpit, the natural amphitheatre beside the Serpentine, the artificial lake in Hyde Park. A calculated risk about the weather meant a stage open to the sky, and there was no obvious security. Shouldering a movie camera, an operator would flit fitfully across the front press enclosure, collating images that would be edited eventually into a one-song snippet in *Cucumber Castle*, a television vehicle for the Bee Gees.

Two of them were among backstage well-wishers to be glimpsed behind performers' heels by those of the common herd in the front rows – and so were Keith Richards and Mick Jagger who, carried away by the occasion, mentioned to someone from Blackhill Enterprises that the Stones might be available if there was another such extravaganza coming up. There was – but it was to be 'tinged with black emotions like everything else about the Stones,' gloomed Keith, 'You were constantly being drawn into the vortex of horrible events.'[12]

Despite his cynicism, the group felt no malice towards Brian Jones, and hoped he would be there on 5 July. Down on the farm, mixed emotions extended beyond inner debate about, say, how he would conduct himself should he feel capable of going to see his old group on that day of days. While she did not quite match the ideal that Brian had won and lost, Anna Wohlin, a Scandinavian dancer, and the latest in a line of long-suffering live-in girlfriends, was more like a hospital orderly than passionate *inamorata* as she let him fulminate and bluster without reproach, and talk him through his two main areas of paranoia: the so-called workmen wasting time and money, and the Stones' apparent procrastination about the pledged cash.

Yet, though the psychological undergrowth was overgrown, the pathway through the forest was becoming less of an impasse as the days dwindled down to a precious few. Moreover, Brian was always capable of getting a grip on himself for the duration of visits from musicians – and for an upbeat telephone chat with Jimmy Miller: 'He said, "I'm clean. I haven't been doing any drugs. I've been down here with these young musicians, who are wonderful. We're going to do an album, and I'd like you to produce it." I said, "Brian, I haven't heard you sound this good since I've known you. I'd love to help out. When can I hear the stuff?" He said, "Why don't you give us another week? Then you can come down, and we'll do a set for you. Bring your family. Maybe stay the weekend. I've got a barbeque and a swimming pool." That was my last conversation with him.'[13]

A similar open invitation was extended to Alexis Korner, whose son Damian would remember 'such a nice man to be around. Brian was kind, considerate and thoughtful. He was a comforting person. If you don't have children [sic], you have to be a nice person in order to comfort children. Staying at the house was a problem for me because it was haunted – but he had the capacity to make a young child who was feeling frightened feel OK.'[14]

During this last month of his life, other intimates left Cotchford Farm or hung up the telephone without formal goodbyes – though wisdom after the event had some claiming that Brian seemed either strangely contemplative or overcome with rose-tinted sentiment. Yet the stirring or otherwise exploits of yore did not impress Ian Stewart, who could not be persuaded to drive down for a 'blow' even for old time's sake, telling Jones: 'I formed one group with you, and that was enough.'[15]

In the wee small hours of Thursday 3 July, Ian was the first Stone to be informed that, just around midnight, an oddly lonely life had ended during a boozy soiree by the Cotchford swimming pool. Brian had washed down his usual bedtime tranquillizer with an injudicious quantity of spirits. He had also been cursing the hay fever that had joined forces with his residual asthma and obliged him to resort to relentless inhalers and antihistamine tablets throughout the previous twenty-four hours. Before dawn, his bronchial tubes had been invaded, and the slow pageant of sunrise was a dishevelled and feverish few hours before an unwholesome weariness overcame the running mucus, the sore nostrils, the croaking, the sniffing and the huffing and puffing.

Though he had swallowed some sort of pick-me-up to see him through daylight hours, the small talk that evening was desultory and petering out when Brian put a full stop to it by proposing a quick dip before retiring. News that the Stones cheque was in the post was resonating still and counteracting the desired effects of the drink and the pills. The floodlit water was as warm as if for a bath, and the exercise might be enough to slip him into a blissful, dreamless and soul-satisfying sleep. However, in the professional opinion of a slightly tipsy off-duty nurse present, it was not especially advisable as Brian was now quite unsteady enough on dry land. Everyone else got out, dried themselves and went indoors until suddenly aware of no sound of aquatic activity from the pool. Death had taken Brian Jones without effort. He had sunk into a blue oblivion at the tiled bottom of the deep end. The heat, the alcohol, the drugs, the oncoming drowsiness had combined to bring about his body's final rebellion after a lifetime of violation.

They dragged him out, and the nurse applied panicked artificial respiration, cardio-pulmonary resuscitation and other ministrations before the paramedics did the same. It was to no avail, and the corpse of Lewis Brian Hopkin-Jones was borne by ambulance to the morgue in the Royal Victoria Hospital in East Grinstead.

While the rest of London slumbered, the other Stones – minus Bill Wyman who had gone home – were told about Brian during a mixing session at Olympic Studios. Not long afterwards, an electric thrill banished sleep for obituary writers who hammered something together for the later editions of the morning newspapers and fuller stories for Sunday – such as the one entitled 'The Wicked Life of Brian Jones' ('strangely old at twenty-five [*sic*]' in *The People*)[16]. The last big show-business death had been almost exactly a year earlier when TV comedian Tony Hancock had overdosed in Australia.

Before twilight thickened, the black carnival was well underway. Pete Townshend – who recommended emulation of the Stones as a recipe for any new pop group's success – was already completing a musical tribute to Jones, entitled 'A Normal Day For Brian, A Man Who Died Every Day',[17] and the Jimi Hendrix Experience had dedicated a number to him during an appearance on US television. *Beat Club*, a German pop series as vital in its way as *Ready Steady Go!*, were preparing an edition devoted to him, and Jim Morrison's 'Ode To L.A. While Thinking Of Brian Jones, Deceased' was to be published in the next week's *Disc And Music Echo*.

Over at the Stones' office, a press release had been duplicated, assuring press and public that, for the time being, the free concert on Saturday was to go ahead as planned – and with an added attraction. Alexis Korner insisted that his New Church be among the preceding acts when the Stones presided over the largest assembly for any cultural event hitherto accommodated by the capital. Certainly, with their potted palm trees, huge backdrop of *Beggars Banquet*'s sepia inner sleeve, six film crews, sky-clawing scaffolding and Cecil B. de Mille-sized crowd, the Stones made Blind Faith's debut seem rather rustic. Twenty feet above them, the PA speakers were loud enough for their chaotic sorcery to impinge upon ears in Putney.

Depending on what Sunday newspaper landed on your doormat, audience estimates would range from two hundred thousand to three-quarters of a million. 'I can't stop dreaming about it,' gasped Keith Richards a month later in the *New Musical Express*, 'It has to be the biggest crowd I've ever seen. They were the stars of the show – like some massive religious gathering on the shores of the Ganges.'[18]

There was, indeed, an element of ritual to an occasion derided by arch-feminist Germaine Greer as 'a kind of self-conscious slumming'[19]. Only a day before there had been talk of cancellation out of respect for the drowned Brian. Bill, Charlie, Mick and Keith's feelings about him ran too deep for simple analysis, but it was decided after much debate to use the event as an open send-off for Jones: 'Brian would have wanted it to go on,' as Mick Jagger permitted himself to be quoted, 'We will do the concert for Brian. I hope people will understand that it is because of our love for him that we are still doing it.'[15]

Thus the Stones' performance before the buzzing tribes began with an oration from Jagger, which had him reading an excerpt from 'Adonais',

Mick Jagger strikes his iconic pose during the show in Hyde Park held in memory of guitarist Brian Jones.

Shelley's elegy for Keats, whose time on this planet had been as brief as Brian's.

With the last syllable still hanging in the air, the founders of the feast dispelled the collective grief with a two-hour set that kicked off with a Johnny Winter number and, in the teeth of Greer's sardonic comments, rode roughshod over drug-bust martyrdom, acid visions, secret doctrines, devilish sympathies and other distant worlds that the-man-in-the-street imagined were known only to the Stones and the Beatles and their circle. Among the ignorant hordes in the heat of the late afternoon, I could not recall much about individual numbers, only – and paradoxically – the claustrophobic, midnight atmosphere that pervaded any given moment. The only remembered flash of levity was when someone shouted, 'Oi, Mick ... do "Mona"!' 'Yeah, we'll try and get to that one,' replied Jagger, knowing that they never would. The buggers at the back couldn't see, but who cared about them? One determined soul clung to the top of a lamppost for the duration.

You had to have been there – because the overall effect was better then than the way it sounded on the *Stones In The Park* video fourteen years on, which appalled me with its careless tonality – though my teenage self hadn't been aware that anything was wrong when the notes were first hung in the air – and Keith was to admit, 'I was shaky at first, but then I started enjoying myself.'[20]

After a fashion, so did I when joining in the booing of the Battered Ornaments who, as compere Sam Cutler boomed when introducing them, had the irksome task of preceding the Stones on to the boards. The Ornaments' avant-garde jazz, like the better-received King Crimson's earlier slot, demonstrated a more commanding instrumental precision than anything the bill-toppers could produce. Next, while the Stones kept everyone waiting in the heat, some halfwit near the guest enclosure begged a newly famous Edgar Broughton to get up on stage and give 'em his celebrated audience participation number, 'Out Demons Out'. 'We don't mind if the Stones do one less number,' the supplicant generalized airily, indicating the perspiring multitudes behind him. He wasn't very popular. Any other artiste's most rabble-rousing show stopper could not be allowed to subtract a split-second from even the most hit-or-miss Stones presentation.

During their 'Sympathy For The Devil' play-out – with a battery of supplementary hand-drummers from Brixton rather than Joujouka – and Jagger's departure by motorboat across the Serpentine, everybody near me was up, shoving, kicking, many of them trying to dance to the noise. Limping to the London Underground afterwards, I noticed two contradictory ideologies: a bootlegger checking his tape, and some environmentalists clearing up litter – for which they were rewarded with virtue and an advance copy each of the Stones' new single.

It had been with uncalculated guile that Decca had shipped out 'Honky Tonk Women' as scheduled during the following week, just as Brian's funeral was taking place in Cheltenham in the rain – while master tapes for *Through The Past Darkly* (1969), a 'greatest hits' compilation for release in September, were signed for at the factory. Correctly anticipating a worldwide smash, this collection included 'Honky Tonk Women', Mick Taylor's disc debut as a Rolling Stone. It was remarkable too for Jimmy Miller tapping a cowbell in slightly awry counterpoint to a stomping and not-quite-medium tempo Watts introduction. If as technically wrong as the guitar interlude in 'Jumpin' Jack Flash' had been – plus a rhythm that had all but doubled in speed by the final chorus – 'Honky Tonk Women' had gone unchanged to the pressing plant for much the same reasons as the Dave Clark Five's percussion-driven 'Bits And Pieces' in 1964. 'Sometimes you make mistakes,' confessed Clark, 'and out of them, good things happen.'[1] Indeed, they did – for 'Honky Tonk Women' was to be another Rolling Stones 'Best Single of the Year' – in 1969's *New Musical Express* poll. It was also opportune that, on top of this accolade, the single was at Number One in the US, and still in the Hot 100 when the Stones were about to hit the road as a working band once again with a major coast-to-coast assault – their sixth – on North America.

Before they played so much as a quaver, blizzards of dollar bills had subsided into wads to pay for luxury suites, chauffeurs, private jets and sufficient days off for Mick to gather the energy for what amounted to a nightly equivalent of the London marathon. Already, he was in training to sweat away pounds, goading himself, the group and, vicariously, the ticket-holders to near collapse. He also polished up an array of facial expressions, flickering hand-ballets and more exertive antics through which to bombard audiences with the characters and scenarios of the selected songs.

Keith Richards, however, was not quite ready to tear himself away from his new London abode – 3, Cheyne Walk on the opposite side of the road to Mick. It was to this eighteenth-century town house that Keith had brought his and Anita's first child after delivery on 10 August 1969 at King's College Hospital. Named Marlon – after Brando – the boy had survived a pregnancy blighted by a road accident, the second of many involving his father. The outcome of a misjudged exit from a Sussex roundabout in a vintage Mercedes was treatment for shock and a fractured collarbone for Anita.

For a while after the birth, sedate domesticity was the order of the day, expressed by Keith in the beginnings of a countrified ballad entitled 'Wild Horses' – that 'couldn't drag me away' from this protective bubble as he stole nervous glances at the increasing depth into which the Stones would plunge if they failed to live up to a selfish public's expectations now that five weeks of confirmed dates in the USA, starting in Colorado on 1 November, had sold out within hours.

With Brian out of the way, and Mick Taylor seemingly as meek as a lamb, Richards, onstage with one of these newfangled transparent Plexiglas guitars, was to be regarded as more than just one of the four human walls of quicksilver Mick-as-Jumpin'-Jack-Flash's padded cell. Previously, many onlookers had not given him much notice, but, while Jagger was not yet to wave him in to hog the central microphone, he was switching to acoustic and seating himself on one of two stools carried on to enable him and Mick to duet folk-club style on 'Prodigal Son', while the other three took a breather.

During more typical Stones fare, the interaction between Richards and Taylor revealed a stronger differentiation between lead and rhythm guitars than there had been under the old regime of Brian and Keith's fretboard counterpoint – so much so that critics were lauding Keith's chord-flaying as much as they were his and Taylor's most dazzling solos. Suddenly, a rhythm guitarist no longer skulked in grey mediocrity beyond the main spotlight while the other fellow enraptured listeners with his note-bending cleverness. 'Without Keith's rhythm guitar, there would be no Rolling Stones,' declared Jack Nitzsche, 'What Keith does is play guitar without trying to be flash. It's all taste. Keith doesn't make a lot of faces.'[21]

Unheeded was the lad himself's cry, 'I didn't say I was a rhythm guitarist. Other people made my reputation for me.'[21] He was, nevertheless, the unintended hero of the hour – as far as there was one – when the tour culminated in an attempt on Saturday 6 December to recapture that Serpentine magic with a free concert at Altamont, a race track under more usual circumstances, near Livermore, California.

It had been prompted when the Stones had been accused – unfairly – of arrogance and parsimony in *The San Francisco Chronicle*. Swooping on a general price of admission – designated, incidentally, by venue management rather than the artists – that was fractionally higher than that for Blind Faith, the editorial argument was that, however demonstrative the Stones' giving on that summer's day in Hyde Park, the purpose of their sold-out concerts in the States was the same as that of any other 'breadhead' rock act – to make a monetary killing.

Aggrieved, the group responded with another free open-air concert. With the benefit of hindsight, the first time in England should have been the only time because, while the Stones delivered more routinely solid goods than at Hyde Park, Altamont would be remembered by Charlie Watts as 'badly organized. You couldn't see the audience. All you could see was the Hell's Angels, who were near us. The thing that stuck in my mind was somebody being hit on the head with a billiard cue, and seeing a motorbike fall over in front of the stage, and the guy whose motorbike it was complaining.' (22)

The so-called 'West Coast Woodstock' had been turned into 'a horrible experience,' glared the singer in the middle of it all, 'not so much for me as for the people that suffered.'[23] The twenty-mile traffic jams fanning out in all directions were the least of it. It was not the paucity of portable toilets, washing facilities and vendors of over-priced food and tepid soft drinks either. The most brutal punch-ups had been within the range of vision of the acts that preceded the Stones – and violence had actually infiltrated the low stage when one of Jefferson Airplane was knocked out cold by some leather-jacketed lout able to venture with ease into the compound at its rim. Most serious of all were the injuries inflicted on Meredith Hunter, the eighteen-year-old black youth spotted by Charlie, who, to amused jeers, squirmed and screamed with pain and panic in the thick of kicking motorbike boots and sawn-off pool cues. With multiple knife wounds and profound bruising, he slid into a coma and died in the ambulance provided originally to whisk the Stones away afterwards.

The central figures of this and other of the more dangerous commotions at Altamont were held to be members of local chapters of the Hell's Angels. The collision of anti-heroes – the Stones and the Angels, the Union's resident bad boys, employed as security – had seemed a sound notion on paper. It would also look impressive if a cavalcade of motorbikes flanked the Stones in quasi-royal procession through the Altamont crowds: satanic majesties, indeed – although they may have been endeavouring to shake off this particular mantle. In 'Monkey Man', another track from the only just issued *Let It Bleed*, impish and self-referential lyrics trivialized the diabolism that the general public may have insisted it could sense emanating from the Stones, who projected themselves instead as nice-lads-when-you-get-to-know-them who only 'love to play the blues'.

In the face of contradictory observations, it was reckoned too that, for all its Nazi regalia, the invidious motorcycle brotherhood asked to assist at Altamont had a special rapport with equally non-conformist hippies. All that love-and-peace nonsense in 1967 might have grasped the wrong end of the stick, but the stick still existed.

That's as maybe, but the Angels declined to provide any perceivable escort or protection for the festival's main attraction, and a growing cluster of them came to be under the impression that they had been granted licence to simply mill around on the boards, close enough to touch the official entertainment, project psychopathic thousand-yard stares into the crowd and exact bloody reprisals against anyone who dared do as little as stare back. Hemmed in by their so-called bodyguards, the Stones resolved tacitly to quit the stage, the site and the district as swiftly as possible. Perhaps unsurprisingly, their performance of 'Sympathy for the Devil' only seemed to further fuel the unrest and aggression in the audience, causing Mick to declare that 'something very funny happens when we start that number.'

Altamont would be remembered by Keith Richards as 'chaos. I wouldn't say frightening, but definitely high in adrenaline. I was wondering who the hell was running the joint. Five hundred thousand people, and the Hell's Angels out of it on acid and Thunderbird wine. The only way you could cool it was by facing them down. The one thing you can't do is give way to fear or intimidation.'[12] At one point during the nerve-wracking set, Richards was distracted by fans who were being subjected to arbitrary manhandling so exultant that, boldly, he rebuked the attackers from the footlights. His precise words were 'If those cats don't stop fighting, we're going to split' – and there would be a spreading tale that Sonny Barger, an Angel of high office, levelled a pistol at him and barked, 'Start playing or you're dead!'[22]

While this may have been merely one of the self-created myths that adhered to the fearsome Barger, Keith again retained clearer pictures of 'the actual getaway: everyone running up this hill to a hovering helicopter. It was like Vietnam. You had to jump and climb up this rope-ladder, trying to make sure you got the women on there first.'[11]

With another lesson learned – 'not to try and do anything like that again'[23] – Keith confirmed with the other Stones that any proceeds from television and film coverage of Altamont should go to an orphanage for Vietnamese children. It was the least they could do in the light of an additional three more dead – via accidents not murder, mind – and the understandably negative portrayal of Altamont in the US tabloids and broadsheets.

Throughout this US visit, the Stones' most trying public journey, the recording studio was an infinitely more agreeable location to contemplate than ordeals like Altamont. Yet, even then, everyone was firing on all cylinders on the boards. Never had they been more effective as a team after they had become accustomed to the lengthier gatherings that were post-psychedelic rock extravaganzas, especially in Uncle Sam's concrete coliseums, designed for championship sport and 'festival seating' (i.e. 'no seating'). 'Rock bands' – not pop groups – no longer thought that a ten-minute slot on something-for-everybody scream-circuit packages was sufficient. Moreover, onstage silences and pianissimos were undercut by a ceaseless barrage of not the indiscriminate shrieking and squealing of teenage girls, but more grown-up stamping, whistling, discomforted snarls and, worst of all, bawled requests for the good old good ones like 'Satisfaction', '19th Nervous Breakdown', anything loud in a corner of a foreign field that will be for ever 1960s.

Such occupational irritations were not peculiar to the Stones. In a travesty of legitimate admiration, homely, receding Ginger Baker, Blind Faith's newly sanctified 'high priest of percussion'[24], was once scragged behind his kit by maverick souvenir hunters, who fled with his sticks as the cops eventually waded in.

It might not have been the case at Altamont, but elsewhere on the Stones' US tour, security had been too tight for Charlie Watts to be a potential victim of such undignified mauling as he assimilated the virtues of new onstage technology: 'when they miked drums up, it became a whole other world – but they can't take away the character you develop in your relationship between the cymbal and the snare drum. Great players have that, but when you get somebody else's version, when you get a guy mixing you, it's very loud but flat.'[25]

Occurring as it did in the final weeks of the Swinging Sixties, indolent historians were to view the Stones' trek across North America and its grim close from a distance of years not as the start of a new phase of modernism and breakthrough, but as the end of an era, a final nail in the coffin of the Swinging Sixties. 'It's all so wonderfully convenient,' scoffed Mick Jagger, a living relic of the age gone by, 'Things aren't quite as simple as that.'[26] In truth, pop's turbulent adolescence had been over long before 1 January 1970 – or, for that matter, the previous month's disastrous Altamont, the darker of the twin climaxes of hippy culture. The other had been in August when half a million drenched North Americans had endured the equally large assembly at Woodstock in upstate New York.

Crucially, nearly all the old idols had gone down. The Yardbirds, the Small Faces, the Animals, the Byrds, Jefferson Airplane, the Spencer Davis Group, the Dave Clark Five, Manfred Mann, the Zombies and, of course, the Beatles had all either disintegrated or were about to disintegrate, leaving a residue of splinter groups, supergroups and solo performers to add to a growing pile. The Yardbirds, for instance, had split into two contrasting factions: Led Zeppelin, soon to be stereotyped as the ultimate heavy metal outfit, and Renaissance, whose maiden album embraced folk, *musique concrète* and the post-Serialist tonalities of Ligeti and Penderecki. Many 1960s acts were to reform, but such a possibility was denied the Jimi Hendrix Experience after the death in 1970 of its leader – though the Doors struggled on for a while without their focal point, Jim Morrison, found dead in a bath two years to the day after Brian Jones was found dead in his swimming pool. Finally, Bill Wyman turned twenty-eight as far as the Stones fan club was concerned, and thirty-five to his immediate family as the bland 'Woodstock Generation' began the 1970s as a rerun of 1967 without colour, daring, humour – or, arguably, originality. Indeed, while the Beach Boys and the Crosby, Stills, Nash and Young 'supergroup' made homespun attempts to address contemporary issues à la 'Street Fighting Man' in, respectively, 'Student Demonstration Time' and 'Ohio', *the* hit song of 1970 was Free's 'All Right Now', which had appropriated the salient points of 'Honky Tonk Women'.

As well as giving 'em 'Honky Tonk Women', and 'Jumpin' Jack Flash', the Rolling Stones on tour had alternated tracks from *Beggars Banquet* with a slew of golden oldies, and premiered items from the album yet to come, *Let It Bleed* ('out in about ten years time', Mick had chaffed at Hyde Park) – notably blood-and-thunder 'Gimmie Shelter' and 'Midnight Rambler', an episodic stop-start melodrama into which had been incorporated quoted dialogue from the police-station confessions of Albert de Salvo, the knife-wielding Boston Strangler.

More outrageous musically was a third highlight of *Let It Bleed*, 'You Can't Always Get What You Want'. Its entire first verse was carried by a bona fide choir under the baton of Jack Nitzsche, before acoustic guitar strumming and French horn heralded Jagger's lyrical wanderings, flitting fitfully – in similar manner to 'Jigsaw Puzzle' – from some posh do to a militant protest demonstration via an eschatological conversation with a junkie acquaintance at a local chemist.

If they did not chance 'You Can't Always Get What You Want' in the States, the Stones had reproduced it as accurately as they could with conventional beat group instrumentation for the *Rock And Roll Circus*. Less risky were 'Prodigal Son' and its closest *Let It Bleed* relation, 'Love In Vain' (which, by coincidence, also bore an erroneous 'Jagger-Richards' composing credit). Both were performed on US stages, but only 'Love In Vain' was selected for *Get Yer Ya-Yas Out* (1970), a vinyl souvenir and the first Stones album with Brian's replacement firmly in harness. The album's near-fifty minutes needle-time, including continuity and audience response, was the result of the pruning down, if you believed the sleeve notes, from two nights – 27 and 28 November 1969 – at New York's Madison Square Garden, though 'Jumpin' Jack Flash' and 'Love In Vain' actually came from a previous evening at Baltimore Civic Center, also with the Stones spending almost three hours on the boards.

A cacophony of very London-inflected dialogue by Jagger and, retained from Hyde Park, Sam Cutler was the frontispiece to the 'Jumpin' Jack Flash' opener, a hard yardstick for any group to follow – but, with an unseen Ian Stewart vamping Chicago-style piano, the Stones tried hard with an affectionate trawl through 'Carol', the Chuck Berry item that had been a fixture in the stage repertoire from the beginning until circa 1965. Most relevant to this discussion, however, are the *Beggars Banquet* revisits – a brisk 'Stray Cat Blues' in which Jagger subtracts two years from the fifteen-year-old groupie's age on the studio blueprint; 'Sympathy For The Devil', prefaced by some female cawing for 'Paint It Black! Paint It Black!' and showcasing a Richards solo that, if lacking the pin-sharpness of the studio version, is in keeping with the emergency of the in-concert situation, almost as if he was playing it whilst parachuting from a high altitude; and 'Street Fighting Man' with amplifiers flat out on what just managed to steer a few degrees clear of a sound-picture of Genghis Khan carnage.

The converse of Hyde Park, these came to actually sound better on vinyl than they had when they were vibrations in the air in Baltimore and New York. This was down to careful mixing back in Olympic Sound by Glyn Johns, elevated from engineer to co-producer for the only time on a Rolling Stones LP, though he was to continue to work with the outfit, and be regarded as a friend as much as a professional colleague. Much of his fine-tuning concerned lead vocals, owing to Jagger's instances of near-breathlessness during his energetic performances. *Get Yer Ya-Yas Out* had been subject to so much ironing out of further faults that the group calculated that as much time was spent on it as on some of the studio albums.

A lot of attention was paid to the packaging too. Though it was not as onerous a public office on his group's behalf as vocalist Roger Daltrey's self-immersion into a bath of baked beans for the cover of *The Who Sell Out* (1967), Charlie Watts permitted himself to be photographed for the front cover, prancing gleefully before a backdrop of a flat countryside landscape, wearing a top hat and with an electric guitar in either hand. Bearing Bill Wyman's four-string, a bass drum and a floor tom-tom, a donkey peers indifferently at him. While only the most hooked Stones devotee might have bothered trying to decipher this symbolism – if that's what it was – *Get Yer Ya-Yas Out* topped the domestic chart and hung around for weeks in the US Top Ten that autumn.

In this respect, it represented a victory over the recent practice of bootlegging stage performances and other recordings that leading rock artists might have preferred to remain unheard by the man-in-the-street. Such merchandise had been common in jazz circles for years, but had come into pop prominence in 1969 when *Great White Wonder,* an illicit Bob Dylan double album, opened the floodgates for countless more enterprises of this type, so much so that *Rolling Stone* took to reviewing some as seriously as if they were legitimate releases.

At the beginning of 1970, *Live R Than You'll Ever Be*, taped at Oakland Coliseum, the third stop on the US trek, was the first such Stones album to defy every known copyright law. It sold in sufficient quantities to qualify technically for a *Billboard* gold disc. I bought a *Live R Than You'll Ever Be* from the suitcase of a pavement trader on London's Oxford Street. On thrusting it on to my Dansette, I was astonished by the high fidelity – especially when set against the questionable clarity of similar product. It compared so favourably with even official *Get Yer Ya-Yas Out* that it fuelled a rumour that the Stones themselves had been responsible for their own bootleg.

This had been in the air when, before the Altamont month was out, artificial snow had cascaded on to entering ticket-holders at the Strand Lyceum when the Stones played their first 'home games' – a matinee and a soiree here and a week earlier at the Saville Theatre – since Hyde Park. There was also a tinge of a prodigal's return. Though the corrupted endeavour that was Altamont had been represented as an overall success in most of Britain's national newspapers, a harsher truth had resonated from an edition of *Rolling Stone* magazine, devoted almost entirely to the event. Not a page went by without some vestige of blame sticking to the Stones.

This report, however, had only just leaked into London, and the full bitterness of what had occurred had not been understood by the majority of the Saville and Lyceum crowds. Therefore, if there was any rancorous puzzlement, the Stones were still able to exact their customary submission from whoever had not wanted to like them amongst the post-Woodstock flurry of long print dresses, pre-faded Levis embroidered with butterfly or mushroom motifs, clogs, bell-bottomed loon pants, cloche hats, grandad vests, air force greatcoats and, even in the winter chill, stars-and-stripes singlets revealing underarm hair. If they were 'totally lacking in energy'[27] – as Jagger growled backstage in a troposphere of perspiration and tinted smoke – waiting for him out there had been condolence for the horror at the end of the trail in North America: the acclamation of the Great British Public.

Into the bargain, *Sticky Fingers*, the Stones' first album since transferring from Decca to Atlantic, was to sell millions the following spring – though there had been familiar concern about the packaging in a provocative sleeve designed by Andy Warhol. Like a protruding square of plastic on the cover of *Satanic Majesties*, a real zip on the fly of the denim-clad – and very obviously male – loins that graced the front obstructed the snug insertion into a wire record rack of what many fans still feel was the last truly great Stones LP.

Looking for a new record company had been as chancy as looking for a new girlfriend. On the other side of the same coin, ridding yourself of a manager could be as fraught and as delicate as proceeding with a divorce. A pressing matter for the Stones in the mid-1970s was the seemingly insurmountable task of establishing an administrative concordat with Allen Klein, once a hero, but now a villain of the darkest hue. Auditors appointed by the Stones had uncovered enough apparent proof of 'mismanagement of funds' from his mazy balance sheets to justify a multi-million dollar lawsuit. Counter-suits and further mud-slinging were to ensure that it would take years for the blizzards of writs to subside into complicated but fixed channels whereby the assorted and incoming monies could be divided and sent to the frequently disgruntled parties, a process summarized by Keith Richards as 'the price of an education'.[28]

'Klein would probably sue if I told you my opinion of him,' snarled a less phlegmatic Mick Jagger, 'He's a person to be avoided as far as I'm concerned.'[29] Jagger was grim-faced too about a general reek of corruption more pungent than usual that was so pervading the entire industry then that a North American television news channel commissioned a one-hour special, *The Trouble With Rock*, that placed dirty dealings in the music business on a par with the winkling out of guilty secrets that had just led to US President Nixon's resignation.

A talking head on the programme, Mick was 'sure there's other industries in America that are far dirtier than the record industry'[30], but associated allegations, however unfounded, by other of Allen Klein's charges, his increasing unavailability, and headlines such as *Rolling Stone*'s 'Did Allen Klein Take The Bangladesh Money?' had renewed the Stones' protracted determination to curtail the fellow's handling of their affairs both during and after his official tenure as manager. He remained, for instance, de facto controller of all recordings from the Decca era. Since 1971, some had been prised already from the label's stockroom for issue in various formats – as exemplified by 1975's *Metamorphosis* ragbag.

To many, the Stones too had never been or would be as great as they had been when with Decca in the 1960s. Yet there were fiscal advantages in this. As commodity began to assume more absolute sway over creativity, the history of pop was seized upon more avariciously than ever as an avenue for shifting records – as demonstrated by the market performances of the likes of *Metamorphosis* (1975) and the earlier *No Stone Unturned* (1973) collection of mostly B-sides. While fizzling out at a lowly Number 45 at home, *Metamorphosis* rose to Number Eight in the USA. Moreover, most of the out-takes, alternative versions and hitherto unissued tracks (including 'Downhome Suzie') that filled the album were as entertaining as they were documentary – after a qualified fashion anyway – because, haphazardly programmed, this motley array of tracks was a corruption of an original intention for Bill Wyman, the group's most meticulous archivist, to prepare an authorized audio anthology. It had even been given a provisional title, *The Black Box*. Nevertheless, pragmatism ruled, and Allen Klein rode roughshod over the idea, favouring a rushed compilation with a preponderance of royalty-earning group originals.

Often by leasing ancient tracks to K-Tel and similar conglomerates specializing in re-issues, repackaging of the likes of the Beach Boys, Glen Campbell, the Dave Clark Five and even Perry Como had been or were to be chartbusters too. That *Metamorphosis* was also a profitable exercise was but one symptom of a Swinging Sixties hangover. Another was the multitudes scouring bargain bins, junk shops and jumble sales for overlooked artefacts from earlier musical eras, breaking into an anticipatory sweat whilst hurrying towards a pile of scratched 45s. It kept at bay a ghastly present, unpalatable for not only its supergroups, gruff heavy metal, pretentious pomp-rock and precious singer-songwriters, but its rash of schoolgirl heart-throbs like David Cassidy, the Osmonds, the Jackson Five with their precocious youngest member Michael, Andy Gibb, younger brother of the Bee Gees – and the Bay City Rollers, who, in outsized bow ties and half-mast tartan trousers were hyped as the 'New Beatles'. None of them shaped up remotely as either new Beatles or new Elvi any more than the more independently talented Free had been, according to *Record Mirror* in 1970, 'the new Stones'.[31]

The compounding, especially in North America, of one of pop's slowest moments came to a head circa 1974, when the title of a new Stones single, 'It's Only Rock 'n' Roll' became a global catch phrase. There was nothing hysterical or outrageous going on unless you dug deep. Whether teenagers or post-psychedelic casualties, all had to make their own amusements – and they were uniformly dire. Cheap spirits, Mandrax, headbanging and streaking were among desperate diversions that caught on in the States – and, by implication, everywhere else – during this apocryphal year. At approximately the same mental level were stadium-fillers such as Rush, the Climax Blues Band, Supertramp and Bachman-Turner Overdrive as well as the better-known 'dinosaur bands' lampooned in the most radical quarters of the music press as either over-the-hill like the Grateful Dead or wholesomely Americanized like Fleetwood Mac, who were far removed from the rough-and-ready blues quartet they once were. Still, at least they were an excuse for buddies to get stoned together on the drugs on offer in the toilets, and hurl urine-filled beer cans towards the stage if the band didn't boogie or play the good old good ones in the good old way. Few of these odious projectiles landed within the spotlight's glare, where matchstick figures with V-shaped guitars and double drum kits threw their stringy hair back with eyes screwed shut, oblivious to the squalor in front of them.

Until the punk thunderclap resounded, North America's 'progressive' FM radio would remain amenable to such practitioners – as it would towards the Stones, whose third in-concert album – a double – clambered to Number Five in the US list. Though taken from shows taped up to two years before, it did not appear until late in 1977. Its title, *Love You Live* was at deliberate doe-eyed odds with punk – for, as well as marking the twenty-fifth anniversary of Elizabeth II's accession, 1977 was as much of a pop watershed year as 1963 and 1967 had been. Reacting against the distancing of the humble pop group from its essentially teenage audience, a fair-weather music media was denouncing the Stones as moneyed megastars, for ever in America and throwing a wobbler in the green room at the Los

Angeles Forum because of a misconstruing of a dressing-room amenities stipulation about *apricot* rather than *cherry* brandy.

Musically, too, they and their kind were out of synch with the inspired amateurism of rising acts such as Television, the Ramones, the Sex Pistols, the Stranglers, Patti Smith, Wreckless Eric, the UK Subs, Squeeze, the Police, the Clash and Adam & the Ants. 'We're another generation,' scowled Joey of the Ramones, 'They're rich and living in another world altogether.'[32]

There was, however, a certain déjà vu about aspects of the trendsetting Sex Pistols' career path. As many degrees beyond the Stones in outrageousness as the Stones had been beyond Elvis Presley, the Pistols became notorious for performances accompanied by violence. Like Andrew Loog Oldham had, Malcolm McLaren welcomed headline-hogging boorishness from his charges. Following a small Top Thirty beginning, their second single 'God Save The Queen' almost topped the UK charts. Yet, after two more hits in 1977, the public seemed to have got over the initial shock of the Sex Pistols, even when – surely paralleling the *Beggars Banquet* toilet sleeve – they titled their debut album *Never Mind The Bollocks* (1977), and their Sid Vicious was arrested in New York for the murder of his girlfriend. A morning-after comment from ex-New York Doll Johnny Thunders surfaced in *Rolling Stone*: 'Well, he beat Keith Richards for the story of the year'. (33)

Keith still made the front page late in February 1977, not long after an idea of taping a Stones performance for possible inclusion on *Love You Live* before a small audience

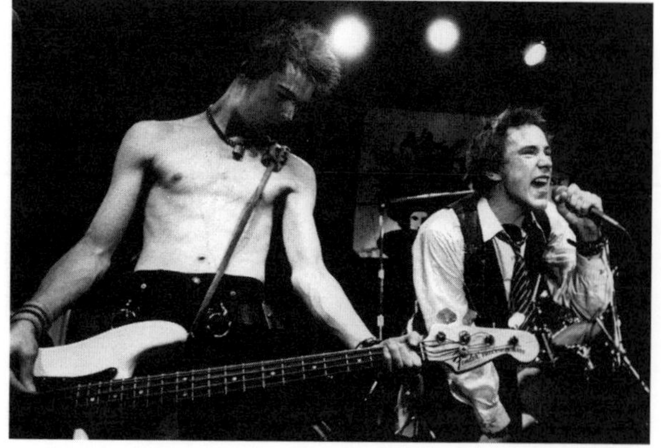

Sid Vicious and fellow Sex Pistol Johnny Rotten performing in 1970.

went past discussion. The four-hundred-capacity El Mocambo club in Toronto was the chosen venue, and Keith was expected to drag himself from his moated farmhouse to cross the Atlantic for rehearsals. Yet plane after British plane landed, and Richards would still be shuttered away in Sussex. Then, on 24 February, just over a week before the reckoning, he shuffled through customs. The next day, a squeak of feedback from Keith's amplifier launched an unproblematic run through a mooted selection that delved as far back as their earliest Craw Daddy stumblings. Conducted by Richards' tempo announcements, nods and eye contact, the Stones started to relax.

A general mood of quiet confidence was, however, to be disrupted when, armed with a search warrant, a squad of Royal Canadian Mounted Police invaded Keith's – purportedly bugged – hotel suite as he lay in bed. It was so heart-sinkingly familiar to one harassed over and over again in like fashion since that most famous bust in 1967: the voices at the door, the uniforms, the execution of duty, the ransacking, the emptying of ashtrays into polyethylene bags, the uncovering of the dope (principally heroin), the monotone caution. This time, Keith dozed through most of it before, with a pincer-like squeeze on both arms, he was hastened outside.

Then there was the back-seat ride to the station; sitting sullen and white-faced on a wall bench; the mounting anxiety, and the illuminated desk on a raised platform where the sergeant filled in the booking slip. Under 'Charge', he wrote 'Possession of controlled drugs with intent to re-sell'. Canadian drug laws were stringent, harsh and effective. Richards could be facing decades in jail, reckoned the duty solicitor – although he was eventually reprieved.

Just the ticket for the accused were the endless centuries of daily scrutiny of tapes of the two El Mocambo concerts undertaken during the 1977 week of the latest trouble – as well as ones in the States, Europe and elsewhere in Canada. Tellingly, among the most glowingly received selections were the twin peaks of the post-psychedelic rallying. By now, 'Jumpin' Jack Flash', if the first or second number in from Hyde Park to *Get Yer Ya-Yas Out*, had become the traditional finale, and stretched out like toffee to last at least twice its studio length. In the late 1970s too – but not for always – 'Sympathy For The Devil' was a frequent choice of encore, even when Jagger's voice had grown limp and tattered. 'The important thing about singing is to get the personality across,' he advised, 'Forget the notes.'[34]

'Sympathy For The Devil' had come from a performance at the LA Forum in July 1975, but the source of most of *Love You Live* was concerts on 5 and 6 June 1976 at Les Abattoirs in Paris. Playbacks of these were especially trying for Keith Richards, a trouper of 'the show must go on' stamp, who demanded that the first of two hours or so of songs about devils, street fighting and Jumpin' Jack Flash being a gas-gas-gas, went ahead despite the telephoned bombshell that very afternoon that his son, Tara, less than three months old, was dying of influenza. Understandably, he left the exploitation of *Love You Live* to Mick, who gave his blessing to a press kit containing a pair of rubber lips, visualizing perhaps office jokers putting them on and doing a Jagger impression. Condoning such mockery of yourself was a cheap shot, but necessary.

Pop music, eh? Who needed it? It was becoming like a dull but remunerative job that Mick Jagger, had he completed his degree course at the London School of Economics in 1963, might have ended up doing until he retired. For every creative act, there was an infinite number of tedious mechanical processes. Sometimes, Mick couldn't wait for knocking-off time. 'My whole life isn't rock'n'roll,' he shrugged while weathering the punk storm, 'It's an absurd idea that it should be – but it's no more than anybody's whole life should revolve around working in Woolworth's'.[35]

Principally because increasingly longer periods between tours had loosened professional bonds, the individuals in the Rolling Stones were no longer as inseparable as they once were, very much the opposite sometimes. A growing schism – personal as much as artistic – between Mick and Keith, now self-appointed co-producers of the records, did not lift the depressed forbearance, the 'atmospheres', the sotto-voce rancour and the odd overt ruction that informed the overall spirit of 1986's *Dirty Work*. Furthermore, of late, Bill Wyman had been talking with increasing frequency of his long-mooted plan to quit the group, and was surrendering more and more of the bass playing chores to Keith – and Ronnie Wood from the Faces, who had replaced Mick Taylor in 1974.

Even when the group brought in a third producer – Steve Lillywhite, whose previous clients included Ultravox, Steel Pulse (whose biggest-selling single was a reggae revival of 'Prodigal Son') and U2 – the

Rolling Stones member Ronnie Wood at the American Music Awards in 1977.

underlying tension could not be directed towards a healthy commercial end either. 'One Hit (To The Body)' was the first Stones single to miss the domestic Top Fifty completely. It foundered in the US Top Forty too. The way had been paved by an exhumation of 'Harlem Shuffle', a turntable hit on pirate radio in the mid-1960s for soul duo Bob & Earl. This turned out to be the last unarguable smash on both sides of the ocean for a near future invested with a suspicion that the Stones were in a slow but sure decline.

The scum of internal disharmony that had risen to the surface of the seemingly unsolvable problem boiled down inevitably to Mick and Keith. Even on the most superficial level, the guitarist's constant retakes and overdubbing of minor fills were starting to pall, and the singer's fastidiousness in other creative areas was just as irritating. 'If we're doing a video, it's never right,' complained Charlie Watts, 'He can never just leave it alone. He has to go and spend another four thousand pounds.'[36] Yet Watts had sympathized with Jagger when

Richards chose to go on a holiday in Jamaica in the middle of mixing sessions for *Undercover*.

Nonetheless, Keith was to steer the Stones towards a relatively uncluttered follow-up album, but brisker finesse could not dispel what he saw as Mick's malcontent shiftlessness, and the general muttering about the sessions' similarity to those for *Beggars Banquet* with Brian. 'Mick was there so infrequently for *Dirty Work*,' he would sigh in retrospect. 'It was just Charlie, Ronnie and me trying to make a Stones record. It was very unprofessional of Mick'.[37]

Jagger, who had just issued his first solo album, was coming to understand perfectly why old Bill Wyman did not want to be a Rolling Stone unto the grave, and the mist of closure shrouding the Stones thickened. Over the next two years, there were periods when only the rare postcard filtered between Jagger and Richards. Other than these, they knew each other only by what was in the newspapers, the same as everybody else. As 1987 got underway, Mick made a second album without the others – and Keith his first, *Talk Is Cheap*, which, like *Dirty Work*, was designed to be reproduced on the boards without difficulty. Meanwhile, *Dirty Work* had earned another platinum disc for the Rolling Stones, albeit a Rolling Stones who couldn't care less any more – or so it appeared for more or less the rest of the decade.

During these years, Jagger's non-Stones ventures proved the most financially viable – though sales figures for *Talk Is Cheap* were healthy enough for moderate placings in Top Forties around the globe. Nevertheless, after their longest period apart artistically, both of the estranged boyhood chums had experienced different revelations that had arrived at the same conclusion: that there was to be no more circling round the issue with solo albums. They anchored themselves to the notion that they were going to be Rolling Stones once more, and would have to put up with constantly being told that their best work was behind them. They may or may not have been aware, for example, of the Counterfeit Stones, a 'tribute band' then undertaking its first bookings with a repertoire containing little, if anything, beyond the mid-1970s.

It would be easier, so Mick and Keith had each thought independently, for the genuine articles to let go, stop trying to prove themselves, get out of step with the strident march of computer-proficient hip hop, techno, acid house et al., and go back to making music that felt as if it was hanging on a thread.

The Stones would be back in business in 1989 with *Steel Wheels*, an album notable for its accomplishing more in one evening than in the weeks of remakes and scrapped tracks that had had to be endured for *Dirty Work* and certain of its predecessors. The unadorned production criteria and sparser ensemble work in the *Beggars Banquet* tradition coincided with a worldwide resurgence of 'garage bands', who recorded in defiantly anachronistic mono if possible, and performed with a thrillingly retrogressive and riff-based verve that married rockabilly and punk thrash to veneration for the form's elder statesmen.It took just three months in total – from first plug-in to final mix – between 1989's early spring and midsummer to record *Steel Wheels*: fast work by the blinded-by-science standards of millionaire rock stars as the turn of the millennium loomed.

Yet, as it had been with *Beggars Banquet*, form did not overrule content, and the aim was not necessarily to make every track grippingly slipshod. While booking time at Olympic Sound of cherished memory as well as George Martin's Air Studios in Monserrat, the Stones also managed a side trip to Morocco in May for the backing track of the outstanding 'Continental Drift', dipping into the geographical casket of non-Western culture as freely as Malcolm McLaren, Adam & the Ants and Peter Gabriel had over the previous ten years. Thus, at Palais Ben Abbou in the Casbah just beyond Tangier, the *Steel Wheels* sound crew taped a twinning of the Stones and the Master Musicians Of Joujouka, the tribal ensemble discovered by Brian Jones. 'Continental Drift' was the most quoted title during the critical weighing of *Steel Wheels*'s faults and merits. As it span its little vinyl life away, the rhetorical question on most lips was along the lines of 'Who'd have thought that the old boys still had it in them?'

This was reflected in the album all but topping the charts in Britain and the States – which boded well for the world tour that tied in with its release.

This expedition was to spawn *Flashpoint* (1991), the first in-concert offering since *Love You Live* – and Bill Wyman's final release as a Rolling Stone after three decades since that try-out at the Wetherby Arms in 1962. Its selections were born of stops in North America, Japan and Europe, and supplemented by a twelve-page booklet and two studio tracks of which 'Highwire' was a CD single, sneaked into the British and US Top Forties, despite unease within certain media factions about the political opinions it expressed – as inflammable in their way as those in 'Street Fighting Man' – over similarly plain yet intense accompaniment.

The essence of *Flashpoint*, however, was reprises of many old favourites – though the group explored a few remote pathways too, chief among them 'Factory Girl', a resurrection of fourth track, side two of *Beggars Banquet*. This was a surprising selection, but an absorbing one, judging by the silence you could almost hear from the tens of thousands in one of three concerts at Wembley Stadium – where the local-boys-made-good's time on the boards flew by as quickly as the reading of the most page-turning thriller, and they pulled a far bigger audience than Frank Sinatra crooning to seven thousand on plastic seats at the London Arena that same night. Moreover, the Stones were to finish the year voted the Greatest Rockers of All Time in a poll by US periodical *Entertainment Weekly*, with Bob Dylan and the Beatles in second and third place.

The following April, *Flashpoint* reached Number 16 in the States, Six in Britain, sent on its way by glowing reviews, even though it had been once more with feeling for such as 'Sympathy For The Devil' – beginning with what seems like an explosion – from Tokyo's Korakuen Dome, and 'Jumpin' Jack Flash' from the same venue – though a 'Street Fighting Man' (which had been enhanced visually by an inflatable Rottweiler that swallowed Jagger) fluttered on to the cutting room floor.

Something less ordinary lay in wait for 'Street Fighting Man' as the first of fourteen mostly invigorating reinvestigations utilized time intriguingly on 1995's *Stripped*, a quainter audio postscript of a Stones round-the-world jaunt – in that it was the furthest the Stones ever went towards boarding the 'unplugged' bandwagon. Relaxed and primarily acoustic ambles down memory lane were what everyone-who-was-anyone was doing then.

Eric Clapton, the Kinks and Paul McCartney were but three big names who had either released something like *Stripped* or were preparing to do so. McCartney's had been manufactured on the hoof from pre-concert run-throughs and soundchecking – and only the previous May, Rod Stewart – with accompaniment from old Faces sparring partner, Ronnie Wood – had put out an album entitled *Unplugged ...and Seated* (1993). Moreover, from the now-defunct Led Zeppelin, Jimmy Page and Robert Plant had renewed their creative partnership via a project with the working title of *Unledded*, which was about to culminate in a best-selling album, *No Quarter* (1994), which comprised principally Zeppelin favourites scored for exotic instrumentation that evoked visions of both Arabia and the ancient Celts.

Jagger, Richards et al. had not the inclination to be as adventurous. Nevertheless, during rehearsals in the assembly hall of a school – bare of pupils during the 1994 summer recess – in Toronto, some exploratory numbers were taped as an audible gauge of progress. Thus an idea blossomed for recording items for what would become *Stripped* along the way, as the fancy took them. It did in various locations in England, Portugal, France, Holland and Japan, both in convenient studios and on the boards, particularly in the smaller venues that punctuated the itinerary.

'We're as accustomed to playing acoustic as we are electric,' Keith was to inform the *St. Louis Post-Dispatch*, 'It's not just learning the songs or deciding which ones to play. It's the process of welding together. There's no pressure on you. It's all, "Play this. Try this. Try that" – like brainstorming sessions. That's the kind of feeling I wanted.'[38]

While it was by no means completely acoustic, there was an almost down-home feel about the overhauls of blues throwbacks, near-forgotten B-sides and fourth-track-side-one of vinyl LPs, not to mention those of

'Street Fighting Man' and nothing else that could be dated past the early 1970s, apart from a minor *Steel Wheels* item – and who could not derive vicarious pleasure from the Stones piling into Bob Dylan's 'Like A Rolling Stone' when the entourage hit England?

Whether looking forward to the past is a healthy situation for any artist is open to conjecture, but the record-buying public were as delighted as the group with the results – as exemplified by *Stripped* touching an apogee of Number Nine in the States – and it was 'Street Fighting Man' that was lauded by most as the standout track. This, the only item germane to the year after the flowers wilted, was unrevised in essence as an encore at Amsterdam's Paradiso, once as famous a European 'underground' venue as Middle Earth in London.

When the Stones appeared there just shy of thirty years of technological and sociological advancement later in mid-May 1995, they were seen both by the capacity crowd of seven hundred and via satellite on a giant video screen set up outside for the benefit of a vast multitude, most of them envious of the surviving street fighting men's unquiet journey to the gateway of the new century, bedevilled no longer, and with more money than sense.

Twelve years later, I saw the Stones in person for probably the last time when, out of the blue, a press pass had arrived days before their bill-topping appearance at summer 2007's Isle of Wight Festival. You don't need me to tell you they were wild. Certainly, they brushed aside all that had preceded them like matchsticks, especially one keenly fashionable combo whose chubby lead singer I found truly offensive for incessant and patronizing milking of us 'beautiful people' in an undisguisably posh accent.

Sir Mick Jagger's still no workin' class 'ero either, despite his on-mic insistence that he'd camped out among the ordinary folk the previous night. Yet, while everyone else had been half killing themselves to work up the mob, his Stones were sensational as a matter of course – while delivering a spectacular with prideful thought for the paying customer that extended to a hydraulically-operated platform that bore Charlie, Keith and Mick plus Ron Wood and the bass and keybaord players into the very centre of the arena and full all-round view. Thus, for around 20 minutes, the tiny figures beneath the proscenium became flesh-and-blood mortals within reach yet completely untouchable like deified Caesars in the midst of the conquered Gallic peasantry – but, hey, lighten up, man. It's only rock'n'roll. Well, they didn't do that particular hit during a necessary streamlining of their usual stadium show. Nonetheless, room was found for the most recent single – 'Rough Justice' – a just sufficiently ramshackle 'You Got Me Rockin'' off 1994's *Voodoo Lounge*, an obligatory lull for two lead vocals from Keith, and retrospective duets with Jagger by Paolo Nutini and trendier Amy Winehouse. Yet it was far from jovial old timers making way for up-and-coming young stars – for 'Satisfaction', an inspired 'Sympathy for the Devil', 'Brown Sugar', the fixed 'Jumpin' Jack Flash' encore and the other ancient fireworks will be in the air long after the music of both these trendy exquisites and that of the rest of the also-rans that weekend has faded away.

NOTES

1. *The Big Beat* by M. Weinberg (Billboard, 1991)

2. *Rolling Stone*, 10 August 1968

3. *International Times*, 9 December 1968

4. *Daily Express*, 8 January 1969

5. *Record Collector*, April 2001

6. *Who's Really Who* by C. Miller (Sphere, 1987)

7. *Melody Maker*, 16 May 1970

8. *The Sunday Times*, 17 August 2003

9. *The Rolling Stones In Their Own Words* eds. D. Dalton and M. Farren (Omnibus, 1985)

10. It was to be used on the soundtrack to *Zabriskie Point*, one of the big rock movies of the turning decade.

11. *Days In The Life; Voices From The English Underground 1961–1971* ed. J. Green (Heinemann, 1988)

12. *Q*, October 1987

13. *Record Collector*, November 1993

14. *Alexis Korner* by H. Shapiro (Bloomsbury, 1996)

15. Translation from *Con Le Mie Lacrime* (Italian fanzine), November 1986

16. *The People*, 6 July 1969

17. *Rolling Stones '76* ed. M. Farren (Cumbergrove, 1976)

18. *New Musical Express*, 9 August 1969

19. *Hippie Hippie Shake* by R. Neville (Bloomsbury, 1995)

20. *Keith Richards In His Own Words* ed. M. St Michael (Omnibus, 1994)

21. *Mojo*, September 2003

22. *Rolling Stone*, 5 November 1987

23. *Shattered*, Issue 19, 20 June 2000

24. *Zigzag*, volume 4, issue 3 (undated)

25. *Rhythm*, June 2001

26. *Faithfull* by M. Faithfull and D. Dalton (Penguin, 1994)

27. *Melody Maker*, 20 December 1969

28. *Arena*, BBC2, 27 November 1989

29. *The Rolling Stones Chronicle* by M. Bonanno (Plexus, 1995)

30. *The Trouble With Rock*, CBS News, 11 August 1974

31. *Record Mirror*, 27 June 1970

32. *Rock Quotes* ed. J. Green (Omnibus, 1977)

33. *Loose Talk* ed. L. Botts (Rolling Stone Press, 1980)

34. Translated from *Con Le Mie Lacrime* (Italian fanzine), August 1982

35. *Daily Express*, 14 September 1977

36. *Howling At The Moon* by W. Yetnikoff and D. Ritz (Abacus, 2004)

37. *Q*, May 1995

38. *The Guardian*, 27 February 1989

CHRONOLOGY

1963

7 June: the Rolling Stones' first single, 'Come On'/'I Want To Be Loved', released by Decca Records

1965

26 February (UK)/13 March (US): 'The Last Time' released, the first of an unbroken run of almost ten years of Jagger-Richards A-sides
5 June (US)/20 August (UK): '(I Can't Get No) Satisfaction' released, the first Rolling Stones single to top charts in both the USA and Britain
14 September: Brian Jones meets Anita Pallenberg backstage at a Stones concert at Munich's Cirkus Krone

1966

15 April (UK)/2 July (US): *Aftermath* released, the first Rolling Stones album consisting entirely of Jagger-Richards compositions
5–9 September: Brian Jones supervises sessions at IPC Studios, London of his soundtrack to *Mord Und Totschlag*

1967

12 February: Mick Jagger and Keith Richards charged with drugs offences following police raid on Richards' home in Sussex
25 February–16 March: Brian Jones, Mick Jagger, Keith Richards and Anita Pallenberg holiday in Morocco

24 March–17 April: Rolling Stones' tour of Europe
5 May: Brian Jones, Anita Pallenberg and Keith Richards attend the premiere of *Mort Und Totschlag* in Cannes, France
10 May: Brian Jones charged with drugs offences
13–18 June: Brian Jones attends Monterey International Pop Festival
29 June: Mick Jagger and Keith Richards sentenced, respectively, to three months' and one year's imprisonment for drugs offences
30 June: Mick Jagger and Keith Richards bailed
31 July: Mick Jagger's sentence reduced to three months conditional discharge, and Keith Richards' sentence quashed
18 August: release of 'We Love You'/'Dandelion'
29 September: official announcement that original co-manager Andrew Loog Oldham no longer represents the group
30 October: Brian Jones sentenced to nine months imprisonment for drugs offences
31 October: Brian Jones bailed
8 December (UK)/9 December (US): *Their Satanic Majesties Request* released
12 December: Brian Jones's sentence reduced to probation

1968

17 February–31 March: sessions for *Beggars Banquet* at Redlands (West

Wittering, Sussex), RG Jones Studios (Morden, Surrey) and Olympic Sound (Barnes, South West London)

17 March: Mick Jagger joins anti-Vietnam war demonstrators outside the US Embassy, London

Early April: Brian Jones visits Morocco to record native music

9–10 May, 13–18 May: sessions for *Beggars Banquet* at Olympic Sound

12 May: the Rolling Stones appear at the *New Musical Express* Poll Winners Concert at the Empire Pool, Wembley

13–18 May: sessions for *Beggars Banquet* at Olympic Sound

21 May: Brian Jones charged with drugs offences

23 May (UK)/24 May (US): 'Jumpin' Jack Flash'/'Child Of The Moon' released

4–11 June: director Jean-Luc Godard films the Stones recording 'Sympathy For The Devil' at Olympic Sound

19 June: 'Jumpin' Jack Flash' tops UK chart

28 June: 'Jumpin' Jack Flash' reaches Number 3 in US Hot 100

Early July: sessions for *Beggars Banquet* at Sunset Sound Studios (Los Angeles, California)

26 July: release of *Beggars Banquet* cancelled

2–23 August: Brian Jones in Morocco to record native music

2 September–1 November: Mick Jagger filmed on set in Knightsbridge, London for *Performance*

26 September: Brian Jones fined for drugs offences

November: sessions for *Let It Bleed* and 'Memo From Turner' at Olympic Sound

5 December: *Beggars Banquet* launch party at Kensington Gore Hotel, London

6 December (UK)/7 December (US): *Beggars Banquet* released

11 December: *Beggars Banquet* reaches Number 3 in British album chart

12–13 December: *The Rolling Stones Rock And Roll Circus* filmed at the Intertel Studios, Wembley

21 December: *Beggars Banquet* reaches Number 5 in US album chart

1969

22 February: release of 'Sister Morphine' by Marianne Faithfull

9 February–15 March: sessions for *Let It Bleed* at Olympic Sound

8 June: Brian Jones leaves the Rolling Stones

3 July: death of Brian Jones by drowning

5 July: Rolling Stones concert in Hyde Park, London with new member, Mick Taylor

4 July (UK)/11 July (US): 'Honky Tonk Women'/'You Can't Always Get What You Want' released

17–27 October: sessions for *Let It Bleed* at Elektra Studios (Hollywood) and Sunset Sound Studios (Los Angeles)

7–30 November: the Rolling Stones tour North America and record in-concert album, *Get Yer Ya-Yas Out*

28 November (US)/5 December (UK): *Let It Bleed* released

6 December: concert by the Rolling Stones at Altamont Speedway, Livermore, California

14 December: two concerts by the Stones at the Saville Theatre, London

21 December: two concerts by the Stones at the Lyceum ballroom, London

SESSION DETAILS

NON-ALBUM TRACKS

'JUMPIN' JACK FLASH' (Jagger-Richards) 3.40

Mick Jagger, lead vocals; Keith Richards, bass guitar; Brian Jones and Keith Richards, guitars; Charlie Watts, drums; Bill Wyman and Ian Stewart, keyboards

'CHILD OF THE MOON' (Jagger-Richards) 3.12

Mick Jagger, lead vocals; Bill Wyman, bass guitar; Brian Jones and Keith Richards, guitars; Charlie Watts, drums; Brian Jones, saxophone; Nicky Hopkins, organ; Mick Jagger, Keith Richards and Jimmy Miller, backing vocals

BEGGARS BANQUET ALBUM

Producer: Jimmy Miller; Running Time: 39:49

'SYMPATHY FOR THE DEVIL' (Jagger-Richards) 6.18

Mick Jagger, lead vocals; Charlie Watts, drums; Keith Richards and Brian Jones, guitars; Bill Wyman and Rocky Dijon, percussion; Keith Richards, bass guitar; Nicky Hopkins, piano; Mick Jagger, Keith Richards, Brian Jones, Bill Wyman, Marianne Faithfull, Anita Pallenberg, Nicky Hopkins and Jimmy Miller, backing vocals

'NO EXPECTATIONS' (Jagger-Richards) 3.56

Mick Jagger, lead vocals; Keith Richards, guitar; Bill Wyman, bass guitar; Charlie Watts, drums; Brian Jones, slide guitar; Nicky Hopkins, piano

'DEAR DOCTOR' (Jagger-Richards) 3.21

Mick Jagger, lead vocals; Brian Jones, harmonica; Keith Richards and Dave Mason, guitars; Bill Wyman, bass guitar; Charlie Watts, drums; Nicky Hopkins, piano; Mick Jagger and Keith Richards, backing vocals

'PARACHUTE WOMAN' (Jagger-Richards) 2.20

Mick Jagger, lead vocals, harmonica; Keith Richards, slide guitar; Brian Jones, guitar; Bill Wyman, bass guitar; Charlie Watts, drums; Nicky Hopkins, piano

'JIGSAW PUZZLE' (Jagger-Richards) 6.05

Mick Jagger, lead vocals; Keith Richards, bass guitar; Keith Richards and Brian Jones, slide guitars; Bill Wyman and Brian Jones, keyboards; Charlie Watts, drums; Nicky Hopkins, piano

'STREET FIGHTING MAN' (Jagger-Richards) 3.15

Mick Jagger, lead vocals; Charlie Watts, drums; Keith Richards, guitar, bass guitar; Brian Jones, sitar, tamboura; Nicky Hopkins, piano; Dave Mason, percussion

'PRODIGAL SON' (Wilkins) 2.51

Mick Jagger, lead vocals; Keith Richards, guitar; Bill Wyman, bass guitar; Charlie Watts, drums; Brian Jones, harmonica; Nicky Hopkins, piano

'STRAY CAT BLUES' (Jagger-Richards) 4.37

Mick Jagger, lead vocals; Keith Richards, guitar; Bill Wyman, bass guitar; Charlie Watts, drums; Brian Jones, mellotron; Nicky Hopkins, piano; Rocky Dijon, percussion

'FACTORY GIRL' (Jagger-Richards) 2.08

Mick Jagger, lead vocals; Keith Richards, guitar; Bill Wyman, bass guitar; Charlie Watts, tabla; Nicky Hopkins, piano; Dave Mason, mandolin; Rick Grech, violin; Rocky Dijon, congas

'SALT OF THE EARTH' (Jagger-Richards) 4.47

Mick Jagger and Keith Richards, lead vocals; Keith Richards, guitar, slide guitar; Bill Wyman, bass guitar; Charlie Watts: drums; Nicky Hopkins, piano

DISCOGRAPHY

Decca: *
Rolling Stones Records: §
London: #

UK RELEASES

SINGLES

F 12782* 'Jumpin' Jack Flash'/
'Child Of The Moon' (23 May 1968)

F 13195* 'Street Fighting Man'/two
non-*Beggars Banquet* tracks

F 13203* 'Street Fighting Man'/non-
Beggars Banquet track (20 July 1971)

FX 102* 'Jumpin' Jack Flash'/
'Child Of The Moon' (25 May 1987)

FX 102* 'Jumpin' Jack Flash'/
'Child Of The Moon'/'Sympathy
For The Devil' (25 May 1987)

TWELVE-INCH SINGLES

Sony RSR 656756.6§ 'Sympathy
For The Devil' (live)/three non-
Beggars Banquet tracks
(21 March 1991)

CBS RSR 656756.2§ 'Sympathy For
The Devil' (live)/three non-*Beggars
Banquet* tracks

CBS RSR 656756.5§ 'Factory Girl'
(live)/three non-*Beggars Banquet*
tracks (21 March 1991)

US RELEASES

SINGLES

908# 'Jumpin' Jack Flash'/'Child
Of The Moon' (24 May 1968)

909§ 'Street Fighting Man'/'No
Expectations' (19 August 1968)

TWELVE-INCH SINGLES

LONX 264# 'Sympathy For
The Devil' (live)/two non-*Beggars
Banquet* tracks (11 June 1990)

UK AND US RELEASES

ALBUMS

UK: LK/SKL 4955*/US: LL
3539/PS 539# *Beggars Banquet*
Side 1: 'Sympathy For The Devil';
'No Expectations'; 'Dear Doctor';
'Parachute Woman'; 'Jigsaw Puzzle'
Side 2: 'Street Fighting Man'; 'Prodigal
Son'; 'Stray Cat Blues'; 'Factory
Girl'; 'Salt Of The Earth' (1968,
UK: 6 December/US: 7 December)

UK: SKL 5065*/US: NPS 5#
Get Yer Ya-Yas Out
Side 1: 'Jumpin' Jack Flash' (live);
'Stray Cat Blues' (live); three
non-*Beggars Banquet* tracks.
Side 2: 'Sympathy For The Devil'
(live); 'Street Fighting Man' (live);
three non-*Beggars Banquet* tracks.
(UK: 4 September 1970/US:
4 September 1970)

UK: COC 89101§/US: COC 79104§
Love You Live
Side 4: 'Jumpin' Jack Flash' (live);
'Sympathy For The Devil' (live);
three non-*Beggars Banquet* tracks.
(23 September 1977)

UK AND US CD LONG PLAY NON-COMPILATION

(April 1986–April 2006)

UK: Virgin CDV 2801/V2801/US:
Virgin 7243.8.41040-2-3 *Stripped*
'Street Fighting Man' (version);
thirteen non-*Beggars Banquet* tracks
(13 November 1995)

ABKCO 1268.2 *Rock And Roll
Circus*
'Jumpin' Jack Flash' (live); 'Parachute
Woman' (live); 'No Expectations'
(live); 'Sympathy For The Devil'
(live); 'Salt Of The Earth' (live);
one non-*Beggars Banquet* track;
tracks by other artists.
(15 October 1996)

UK: Virgin/EMI CDVDX3000/US:
Virgin/EMI CDV2880 *Live Licks*
Disc One: 'Street Fighting Man'
(live); nine non-*Beggars Banquet*
tracks (2 November 2004)

UK COMPILATION LONG PLAY

SKL 5019* *Through The Past
Darkly (Big Hits Vol. 2)*
Side 1: 'Jumpin' Jack Flash';
'Mother's Little Helper'; four
non-*Beggars Banquet* tracks
Side 2: 'Street Fighting Man'; five
non-*Beggars Banquet* tracks
(12 September 1969)

SKL 5101* *Gimmie Shelter*
Side 1: 'Jumpin' Jack Flash'
(live); 'Street Fighting Man' (live);
'Sympathy For The Devil' (live);
three non-*Beggars Banquet* tracks

SKL 5173* *No Stone Unturned*
Side 1: 'Child Of The Moon';
five non-*Beggars Banquet* tracks (5
October 1973)

ROST 1/2* *Rolled Gold*
Side 4: 'Jumpin' Jack Flash';
'Sympathy For The Devil'; 'Street
Fighting Man'; five non-*Beggars
Banquet* tracks (14 November 1975)

Arcade ADEP 32 *Get Stoned: 30
Greatest Hits 30 Original Tracks*
Side 4: 'Jumpin' Jack Flash';
'Street Fighting Man';

'Sympathy For The Devil';
four non-*Beggars Banquet* tracks
(21 October 1977)

US COMPILATION LONG PLAY

NPS-3# *Through The Past Darkly*
(Big Hits Vol. 2)
Side 1: 'Jumpin' Jack Flash';
four non-*Beggars Banquet* tracks
Side 2: 'Street Fighting Man'; five
non-*Beggars Banquet* tracks
(12 September 1969)

2PS 606/607# *Hot Rocks 1964–1971*
Side 3: 'Jumpin' Jack Flash'; 'Street
Fighting Man'; 'Sympathy For The
Devil'; two non-*Beggars Banquet*
tracks (11 January 1972)

2PS 626/627# *More Hot Rocks*
(Big Hits And Fazed Cookies)
Side 3: 'Child Of The Moon'; 'No
Expectations'; four non-*Beggars
Banquet* tracks
(1 December 1972)

UK AND US COMPILATION LONG PLAY

UK: TAB 30*/US: 820 455-1#
Slow Rollers
Side 1: 'Dear Doctor'; six
non-*Beggars Banquet* tracks
(UK: 19 August 1981/US: 21
August 1981)

UK: ABKCO 92312/US: ABKCO
1218-1 *The Rolling Stones Singles
Collection: The London Years*
Side 7: 'Jumpin' Jack Flash'; 'Child
Of The Moon'; 'Street Fighting
Man'; 'No Expectations'; three non-
Beggars Banquet tracks
Side 8: 'Sympathy For The Devil';
six non-*Beggars Banquet* tracks (15
August 1989)

UK AND US CD LONG PLAY

UK: Columbia RS 47456§/US:
Sony 468135.2 *Flashpoint*
'Factory Girl' (live); 'Sympathy
For The Devil' (live); 'Jumpin'
Jack Flash' (live); fourteen non-
Beggars Banquet tracks (UK: 2
April 1991/US: 8 April 1991)
This was also issued in vinyl format
in the UK (Sony 468135.1) minus
two non-*Beggars Banquet* tracks.

Virgin 13325.1.1/13378.2.0 *Forty Licks*
Disc 2: 'Street Fighting Man';
'Jumpin' Jack Flash'; 'Sympathy For
The Devil'; fourteen non-*Beggars
Banquet* tracks (UK: 30 September
2002/US: 1 October 2002)

Beggars Banquet is also available
on digitally re-mastered cassette
(Decca KSKCD 4955) and CD
(ABKCO 95392).

FURTHER READING

Armstrong, Garner Ted, *Modern Dating,* Ambassador (US), 1969

Bergman, B. & R. Horn, *Experimental Pop*, Blandford (UK), 1985

Bonanno, Massimo, *The Rolling Stones Chronicle*, Plexus (UK), 1990; Henry Holt and Co. (US)

Botts, L. (ed.), *Loose Talk*, Rolling Stone Press (US), 1980

Brown, J. & B. Tucker, *James Brown,* Sidgwick & Jackson (UK), 1987; Thunder's Mouth Press (US), 1990

Brunning, B., *Blues In Britain*, Blandford (UK), 1995

Buckle, R. (ed.), *Self-Portrait With Friends; The Selected Diaries Of Cecil Beaton 1926–1974*, Book Club Associates (UK), 1980; Times Books (US), 1979

Burdon, E. & J. Marshall Craig, *Don't Let Me Be Misunderstood*, Thunder's Mouth Press (US), 2001

Carr, Roy, *The Rolling Stones: An Illustrated Record*, New English Library (UK), 1976; Harmony (US)

Carson, A., *Jeff Beck: Crazy Fingers*, Carson, 1998; Backbeat (US), 2001

Charone, Barbara, *Keith Richards*, Futura Publications (UK), 1979

Clayson, Alan, *Beat Merchants*, Blandford (UK), 1995

Clayson, Alan, *Brian Jones*, Sanctuary (UK), 2003

Clayson, Alan, *Charlie Watts*, Sanctuary (UK), 2004

Clayson, Alan, *Keith Richards*, Sanctuary (UK), 2004

Clayson, Alan, *Mick Jagger*, Sanctuary (UK), 2005

Clayson, Alan, *The Rolling Stones Album File*, Cassell (UK), 2006

Clayson, Alan, *The Rolling Stones: The Origin Of The Species*, Chrome Dreams (UK), 2007

Dalton, David (ed.), *The Rolling Stones In Their Own Words*, Omnibus (UK), 1980; Putnam Publishing Group (US), 1983

Dalton, David, *The Rolling Stones: The First Twenty Years*, Thames & Hudson (US & UK), 1981

Davies, D., *Kink*, Boxtree (UK), 1996; Hyperion (US), 1997

Davis, Stephen, *Old Gods Almost Dead*, Aurum (UK), 2002; Broadway (US), 2001

Egan, Sean, *The Rough Guide To The Rolling Stones*, Rough Guides (UK), 2006

Elliott, Martin, *The Rolling Stones: Complete Recording Sessions 1963–1989*, Blandford (UK), 1990

Faithfull, M. & D. Dalton, *Faithfull*, Penguin (UK), 1995

Farren, M. (ed.), *Rolling Stones '76*, Second Foundation, 1976

Green, J. (ed.), *Days In The Life; Voices From The English Underground 1961–1971*, Heinemann (UK), 1988

Green, J. (ed.), *Rock Quotes*, Omnibus (London, UK), 1977; Delilah/Putnam (US), 1982

Hand, A. (ed.), *Pop Weekly Annual*, World Distributors (UK), 1965

Further Reading

Harry, B., *The John Lennon Encyclopedia*, Virgin (UK), 2000

Heatley, M. & S. Leigh, *Behind The Songs*, Blandford, (UK), 1998

Hockenhull, C., *Streets Of London: The Official Biography Of Ralph McTell*, Northdown, (UK) 1997

Jagger, Mick, Keith Richards, Charlie Watts & Ronnie Wood, *According To The Rolling Stones*, Weidenfeld & Nicolson (UK), 2003; Chronicle (US)

MacDonald, I., *Revolution In The Head*, Pimlico (UK), 1995; Henry Holt and Co. (US), 1994

Mann, B., *Jimi Hendrix*, Orion (UK), 1992

Miller, C., *Who's Really Who*, Sphere (UK), 1987

Miles, B., *Paul McCartney; Many Years From Now*, Vintage (UK), 1998; Henry Holt and Co. (US), 1997

Motion, A., *The Lamberts*, Chatto and Windus (UK), 1986; Farrar, Straus and Giroux (US)

Napier-Bell, S., *You Don't Have To Say You Love Me*, New English Library (UK), 1982

Neville, R., *Hippie Hippie Shake*, Bloomsbury (UK), 1995

Neville, R., *Playpower*, Jonathan Cape (UK), 1970

Norman, Philip, *The Stones*, Elm Tree (UK), 1984

Oldham, Andrew Loog, *Stoned*, Secker & Warberg (UK), 2000; St Martin's Press (US)

Oldham, Andrew Loog, *Stoned II*, Secker & Warberg (UK), 2002

Oliver, P., *Blues Fell This Morning*, Cassell (UK), 1960; Collier (US) 1963

Oliver, P., *The Story Of The Blues*, Penguin (UK), 1969; Chilton (US)

Rawlings, Terry & Keith Badman, *Good Times Bad Times: The Definitive Diary Of The Rolling Stones 1960–1969*, Complete Music (UK), 1997

Ride, Graham, *Foundation Stone*, Broad Brush (UK), 2001

Rooksby, R., *Inside Classic Rock Tracks*, Backbeat (US), 2001

Shapiro, H., *Alexis Korner*, Bloomsbury (UK), 1996

Sounes, H., *Down The Highway*, Doubleday (UK), 2001; Grove (US)

Spector, R., & V. Waldro, *Be My Baby*, Pan (UK), 1991; Harmony (US) 1990

St Michael, M. (ed.), *Keith Richards In His Own Words*, Omnibus (UK), 1994

Tobler, J. & S. Grundy, *The Record Producers*, BBC (UK), 1982; St Martin's Press (US)

Underwood, L., *Blue Melody: Tim Buckley Remembered*, Backbeat (US), 2002

Watkinson, M. & P. Anderson, *Scott Walker: A Deep Shade Of Blue*, Virgin (UK), 1994

Weinberg, M., *The Big Beat*, Billboard (US), 1991

Weiner, S. & L. Howard, *Rolling Stones A–Z*, Grove (US), 1983

Wenner, J. (ed.), *The Rolling Stone Interviews Volume One*, Straight Arrow (US), 1971

Wilson, B. & T. Gold, *Wouldn't It Be Nice*, Bloomsbury (UK), 1991; HarperCollins (US)

Wyman, Bill & Ray Coleman, *Stone Alone,* Viking (US) 1990

Yetnikoff, W. & D. Ritz, *Howling At The Moon*, Abacus (UK), 2004; Broadway (US)